GW01339250

ASHURST MORRIS CRISP
A RADICAL FIRM

ASHURST MORRIS CRISP
A RADICAL FIRM

JUDY SLINN

GRANTA EDITIONS

© Ashurst Morris Crisp, 1997
Broadwalk House, 5 Appold Street, London EC2A 2HA, United Kingdom

First published in 1997 by Granta Editions
25–27 High Street, Chesterton, Cambridge CB4 1ND,
United Kingdom.

*Granta Editions is a wholly owned imprint
of Book Production Consultants plc*

All rights reserved. No part of this publication may be
reproduced, stored in any retrieval system or transmitted in any form
or by any means, electronic, mechanical, photocopying, recording or otherwise,
without prior written permission of the copyright holder for which application should
be addressed in the first instance to the publishers. No liability shall be attached to the
author, the copyright holder or the publishers for loss or damage of any nature
suffered as a result of reliance on the reproduction of any of the contents
of this publication or any errors or omissions in its contents.

A CIP catalogue record for this book is available from the British Library.

ISBN 1 85757 054 5

Designed by Peter Dolton
Design, editorial and production in association with
Book Production Consultants plc, 25–27 High Street, Chesterton,
Cambridge CB4 1ND, United Kingdom
Reproduction by Jade Reprographics, Braintree, Essex CM7 2RF, United Kingdom
Printed and bound by Butler & Tanner Ltd, Frome and London, United Kingdom

Contents

List of illustrations — vi
Acknowledgements — ix
Foreword — x
Author's note — xii

CHAPTER 1
The radical founder and the early years — 1

CHAPTER 2
Ashurst & Son — 23

CHAPTER 3
Exit Ashurst: enter Morris, Crisp & Morris — 47

CHAPTER 4
The firm and the Morrises in the 1880s — 69

CHAPTER 5
'The Lord High Accoucheur of joint stock companies' — 95

CHAPTER 6
The Edwardian Era and beyond — 117

CHAPTER 7
The doldrums: 1919–46 — 135

CHAPTER 8
From crisis to success: the firm from 1947 until 1974 — 157

CHAPTER 9
'Truly modern' radicalism? — 187

Partners' list: 1822–1997 — 205
Appendix 1: Ashurst, Morris, Crisp & Co. Profits and Costs, 1883–1927 — 208
Appendix 2: Cost of living comparison table — 210
Sources and bibliography — 212
Notes and references — 216
Index — 223

Ashurst
Morris
Crisp

List of illustrations

Illustration	Page number
Andrew Soundy	x
Sir William Henry Ashurst, judge	3
Ashurst family tree	5
William Henry Ashurst	6
St Mary Magdalene, Bermondsey	8
Sculpture of James Morrison	11
Cheapside in the 1830s	16
Sir William Molesworth	19
Penny Black stamp	25
Emilie Ashurst	26
Caroline Ashurst	27
Robert Owen	29
Giuseppe Mazzini	31
6 Old Jewry	34
Reform Club	37
Clerks' wages book	39
Page of William Henry Ashurst's diary	41
Firm's wages book, 1855	43
John Morris	49
John Morris's wallet	50
Garibaldi fund notebook, 1860	51
Building the District Line in 1871	53
Liverpool Street Station, newly opened for the Great Eastern Railway	54
Petter & Galpin's 'Belle Sauvage' printing machine	58
1860s wages book	60
Frank Crisp's school bill	63
Morris family tree	64
Early horse tram, 1870	65

List of illustrations

Page from William Morris's office diary, 1876	67
Early telephone	71
First London telephone directory	72
Electric light patent, 1849	75
Florence Terry's last stage performance, 1882	77
Edward Ashurst Morris	84
Agreement between John Morris and William Slaughter	87
Late nineteenth-century annual staff outing	88
Table: Ashurst, Morris, Crisp & Co.: Net profit, 1881–85	89
Table: Partners' shares of the profit plus interest, 1885	90
Laying the foundation stone of the Garden House	91
Garden House, 1890	92–93
Vanity Fair cartoon of Frank Crisp	97
Nobel–Dynamite Trust diagram	99
City clerks at lunch in the late nineteenth century	101
Sir Charles Tennant	107
Battleship built for the Japanese navy	109
Firm's salary book, 1887	110
Plan of Friar Park gardens	112–113
Collage 'Honouring Sir Frank Crisp'	114
Bank station	119
Golden Wedding testimonial to John Morris and his wife, 1904	122
Sir John Crisp	124
Sir Frank Crisp and a gardener at Friar Park	125
Separate stones of the Cullinan diamond	126
Sir Frank Crisp's melted down inkstand	127
Anglo-Persian Oil Company prospectus, 1909	128
Asquith Cup	131
Ashurst Morris Crisp Roll of Honour, 1914–19	132
American Viscose Company's factory at Marcus Hook	133
Ingot presented to Thomas Outen by the British Aluminium Company	137
William Morris	138
Letter from Sir John Gielgud describing his godfather William Morris, 1995	139
Bill Rowe's certificate of war service	141
Ashmor Sports Club dinner, 1937	145

vii

Ashmor Football Club badge	145
Address prepared for presentation to Ernest Stallwood	148
Arthur Gilbert	149
Dinner for the partners and staff, 1938	150
'Mac' Macaree	151
Original signatures supporting the formation of a table tennis section at the Ashmor Sports Club, 1936	153
British Celanese advertisement	155
Destruction of the Fore Street Warehouse in the Second World War	156
Roland Outen	160
Heath Row airport in the early days	161
Michael Richards	164
G C D'Arcy Biss	166
Chair kept at Ashurst Morris Crisp made from wooden panelling of 6 Old Jewry	168
IBM typewriter	169
Martin Lampard and John Goble	171
Martin Lampard at a Pergamon Press AGM	177
Sir Philip Shelbourne	180
Babycham glasses	181
Dinner celebrating the firm's 150th anniversary	182–183
Martin Bell	188
Correspondence between Martin Bell and an uncomfortable theatre-goer	189
Partners' race horses, *Corrupt Committee* and *Crooked Counsel*	190
Dinner to mark Martin Bell's retirement, 1993	192–193
Broadwalk House	194
Queen Elizabeth II Bridge, opened in 1991	197
Linda Walker	198
Canary Wharf, 1995	199
Lake Magadi, Kenya	200
Linda Humphreys-Evans and John May	201
Annie Keener, still serving tea	201
Guide dogs sponsored by the firm	202

Acknowledgements

The author and publishers are grateful to the following for their kind permission to reproduce illustrations on the pages indicated:

Adrian Meredith Photography/British Airways Archives: p.161; Mrs Jean Biss: p.166; British Museum: p.3; The British Petroleum Company p.l.c.: p.128; BT Archives: p.72; Courtaulds plc: pp.133 and 155; Dartford River Crossing: p.197; Her Majesty's Stationery Office © Crown copyright and de Beers: p.126; Sir Peter Crisp: p.63; Peter Froste: p.138; Sir John Gielgud: p.139; John Goble: p.171; Allan Gordon: p.199; Guildhall Library, Corporation of London: pp.8, 16, 54, 101 and 156; IBM (UK) Ltd: p.169; ICI PLC: pp.99 and 107; Richard James: p.25; London Transport Museum Film and Photo Library: pp.53, 65 and 119; Mr S R Macaree: p.151; Lord Margadale and Mrs Pamela Gatty: p.11; National Maritime Museum, London: p.109; National Portrait Gallery, London: pp.19 and 29; RCHME © Crown copyright: p.37; J Stansfeld: pp.26 and 27; St Bride Printing Library: p.58; Theatre Museum, V & A: p.77; Peter Welford: pp.1, 23, 47, 69, 95, 117, 135, 157 and 187.

All other pictures are the copyright of Ashurst Morris Crisp.

Crown copyright material is reproduced by permission of Her Majesty's Stationery Office.

Every effort has been made to obtain permission for the reproduction of the illustrations and photographs in this book; apologies are offered to anyone whom it has not been possible to contact.

A Vision of Britain, an extract from which appears on p.194, is published by Transworld Publishers.

Foreword

SINCE NO SERIOUS attempt has previously been made to record the firm's history in the form comprised within this book, I neither have a precedent (to which all lawyers seek first to turn!) for this introduction nor an inspirational source. So I must rely on my own muse.

We have been most fortunate in the preparation of this work to have had two such enthusiastic individuals as our author and publisher. To them the writing and presentation of the firm's history to coincide with our 175th anniversary have been a labour of love and fun. That has infected all of us who have participated in the project; and I hope that much of that spirit, which is such a trademark feature of the firm, will be apparent to the reader from the text and supporting pictures. We are most grateful to them both.

Any firm which has survived for 175 years will have been through a myriad of changes; confirmed in the case of Ashursts from the history chronicled in the chapters which follow, from its beginnings in the sole hands of our 'radical founder' to the present-day partnership comprising 74 individuals and more than 800 staff. That it still remains a true partnership, notwithstanding a size outside the contemplation of those who originally framed the law for partnerships, is a reflection of the goodwill which binds us together within that culture.

It is also with some sense of relief that I now see the firm's history at last properly recorded. We are all aware, upon becoming partners in Ashursts, of something of that past and take pride in it. But to date it has been fragmented and unstructured; a series of separate events passed on to the next succeeding generation as if by folklore. And

Foreword

subject accordingly to the fallabilities of memory and the distortions of the next teller of those past stories. Here we now have it in 'black and white': albeit, of course, reflecting, especially in regard to the more recent past, the perspectives of those who have contributed to the work and the interpretation put upon them by our author.

And yet in narrating that history it has also brought home most forcibly the responsibility which each partner individually bears in continually shaping the firm presently and for the future. I trust that those who look back on my own generation of partners will conclude that we recognised the legacy which had been passed on to us and that, as in the parable, we applied our talents to nourish and strengthen that inheritance.

January 1997

Andrew Soundy
Senior Partner

Author's note

A CITY FIRM of solicitors in the 1990s is a very different animal from the firm founded by William Henry Ashurst in 1822 but there are strands of continuity to be seen through the firm's 175 years in the City. In the nineteenth century three men successively dominated the firm and ensured its commercial success; they were its founder, William Henry Ashurst, followed by John Morris and Sir Frank Crisp. In this century, too, there have been significant individual partners, whose personality and professional strength rescued the firm from the doldrums, enhancing and recreating its reputation and position in the City.

In researching and writing the history of Ashurst Morris Crisp I am most grateful to the senior partner, Andrew Soundy, for his time, interest and hospitality and to his secretary, Kim Chantry. Special thanks to Richard James, whose close involvement in the history, both before and since his retirement, has been enthusiastic. The firm's retired partners, particularly Martin Bell, Michael Legge and Sir Peter Crisp have been most helpful, as have the present partners. Ian Doolittle had already done sterling work on the nineteenth century and commented on the first draft. Jim Stansfeld kindly lent me his family papers which added much to the early chapters. Miss Ruth Ashurst Coles gave me the benefit of her researches on the Ashurst family.

The discovery of sets of the firm's ledgers and other papers dating back to the 1830s was an unanticipated joy, offering a wealth of detailed information.

I am also grateful to retired members of Ashursts' staff, Fred Brock and 'Mac' Macaree and to former partners' widows, Jean Biss and Winnie Heilbut, for their help. I should also thank present staff members for their help and interest in the project.

Joanne Potier and Beth Wood were excellent researchers and my thanks, as ever, to Stephanie Zarach and Book Production Consultants. Any mistakes, of course, are mine.

Judy Slinn

CHAPTER 1
The radical founder and the early years

WILLIAM HENRY ASHURST, the founder of the firm was born in London on 11th February 1791. He was the second son of Brazil and Mary Ashurst (née Hook) who had married in 1785 at the church of St Giles, Cripplegate in Fore Street. William had an older brother called Drury and at least one younger sister, Elizabeth, born in 1799; they were all baptised in St Giles or its sister church, St Luke's, Old Street, which suggests that the family lived in that area of London. Brazil Ashurst was himself the illegitimate son of Sir William Henry Ashurst (1725–1807; his name and that of the family is sometimes spelled Ashhurst), a member of the Inner Temple who was appointed a judge in the Court of the King's Bench and knighted in 1770.[1]

It seems most likely that Brazil was born between 1750 and 1760; it has not been possible to establish the precise date, but it was before his father achieved such eminence and became the heir to the Ashurst family estates in Lancashire and Oxfordshire. Sir William was the third son of Thomas Henry Ashurst, vice-chancellor of the Duchy of Lancaster and Recorder of Liverpool and Wigan. Brazil's unusual Christian name, family records suggest, is that of his mother's family, the Brazils, a well-established if less grand family than the Ashursts. They (the name is variously spelled as Brazil, Brazel, Brassel) flourished in the eighteenth and nineteenth centuries as farmers, dairymen, carpenters and bakers in several Buckinghamshire parishes, including Quainton, Hogshaw, Grendon Underwood, Shabbington and Wing. These were all close to the eastern border of Oxfordshire and the Waterstock estate, home of the Ashurst family who also owned land and had connections in Buckinghamshire.

Judge Ashurst has been described as:

an impartial administrator of justice, and a careful expounder of the law, united with a benevolent heart and polished manners. His countenance was expressive of the kindness and amiability of his disposition; but being rather lank, was often made a subject for the barristers' jokes. Mr (afterwards Lord) Erskine is said to have indited this complimentary couplet on him:

> *'Judge Ashurst, with his* lanthorn *jaws,*
> *Throws* light *upon our English laws.'*[2]

Whether Brazil was the outcome of youthful wild oats or of a longer-term relationship between his father and a common law wife is not known, but it seems that Ashurst acknowledged his paternity, allowing his illegitimate son to bear his name and made provision for him in his early years: he was 'placed at nurse … [supplied with fine] linen … marked Brazil Ashurst and … [provided for] his education, apprenticeship and establishment in business'.[3] There, however, the help ended. In 1772, Sir William married and fathered a legitimate family, including a son and heir, also named William Henry Ashurst, who inherited Waterstock in 1807 and later became MP for Oxford.

In the nineteenth century illegitimacy came to carry a greater social stigma than it had in the previous century and it was 'our' Ashurst's grandchildren, in the early years of this century, who were more open about the connection. 'Our descent from Sir William Henry Ashurst … is unquestioned – I mean is admitted by the Waterstock people,' wrote a granddaughter of 'our' William Henry around the turn of this century.[4] The founder's children, however, more particularly his youngest daughter, Emilie, who wrote a memoir of him, dismissed the relationship as a fiction, developed on the basis only of circumstantial evidence by a grandfather she characterised as 'aimless and thriftless'.

Emilie's life and that of her brother and sisters, as well as that of their father provide another and powerful reason for not seeking to claim or acknowledge descent from Judge Ashurst. They were, as we shall see,

Sir William Henry Ashurst (or Ashhurst), 1725–1807, judge in the Court of the King's Bench, knighted in 1770, was the grandfather of the founder of the firm.

political radicals. It was 'our' Ashurst's belief that 'Aristocracy is but another name for inequality, as inequality is but another name for injustice ... Government in this country has grown up *over* the people, not *from* the people.' Contrast this with Judge Ashurst's Charge to the Grand Jury of Middlesex, an address delivered on the subject of 'seditious meetings and corresponding societies consequent on the French Revolution' on 19 November 1792 (when his grandson, the future radical, was 18 months old):

... there is no Nation in the world that can boast a better System of Government than that under which we have the happiness to live. Here no man is so high as to be above the reach of the Law, and no man so low as not to be within the protection of it. ... There is no Country where the Law is more uprightly or more impartially administered. For this blessing we are indebted to the wise and prudent form of our Constitution, and to that security which naturally results from it.[5]

To claim as an ancestor one who had put forward such views might well have been embarrassing for the Ashurst radical credibility.

The Ashurst family, however, had not all or always been pillars of the establishment; in the late seventeenth century the Henry Ashurst who bought the Waterstock estate, a City merchant in the West Indies trade, was a prominent Nonconformist, a puritan and politically a Whig. His brother, William (knighted in 1687), was also a merchant and a financier, a Director of the Bank of England in its infancy and MP for London, while their father, another Henry and also a City man, had been a leading Nonconformist.[6] These were ancestors more to the taste of 'our' William Henry and their involvement in the City's politics we shall see echoed in his own life (see page 15).

Whatever the business in which Brazil Ashurst had been established by his father, he does not seem to have been able to provide much of a start in life for his own son. Armed only with the rudiments of an education gathered at dame school, William Ashurst, 'when barely more than a boy', entered the office of a City attorney, Thomas Tilson, in Coleman Street. His ability and his industry impressed his principals and, after some ten years with the firm and at the age of 25, he was given his articles to Tilson's partner, John Preston. Giving Ashurst his articles meant that the firm waived the payment of the lump sum known as a premium which articled clerks or their parents usually paid for the

The radical founder

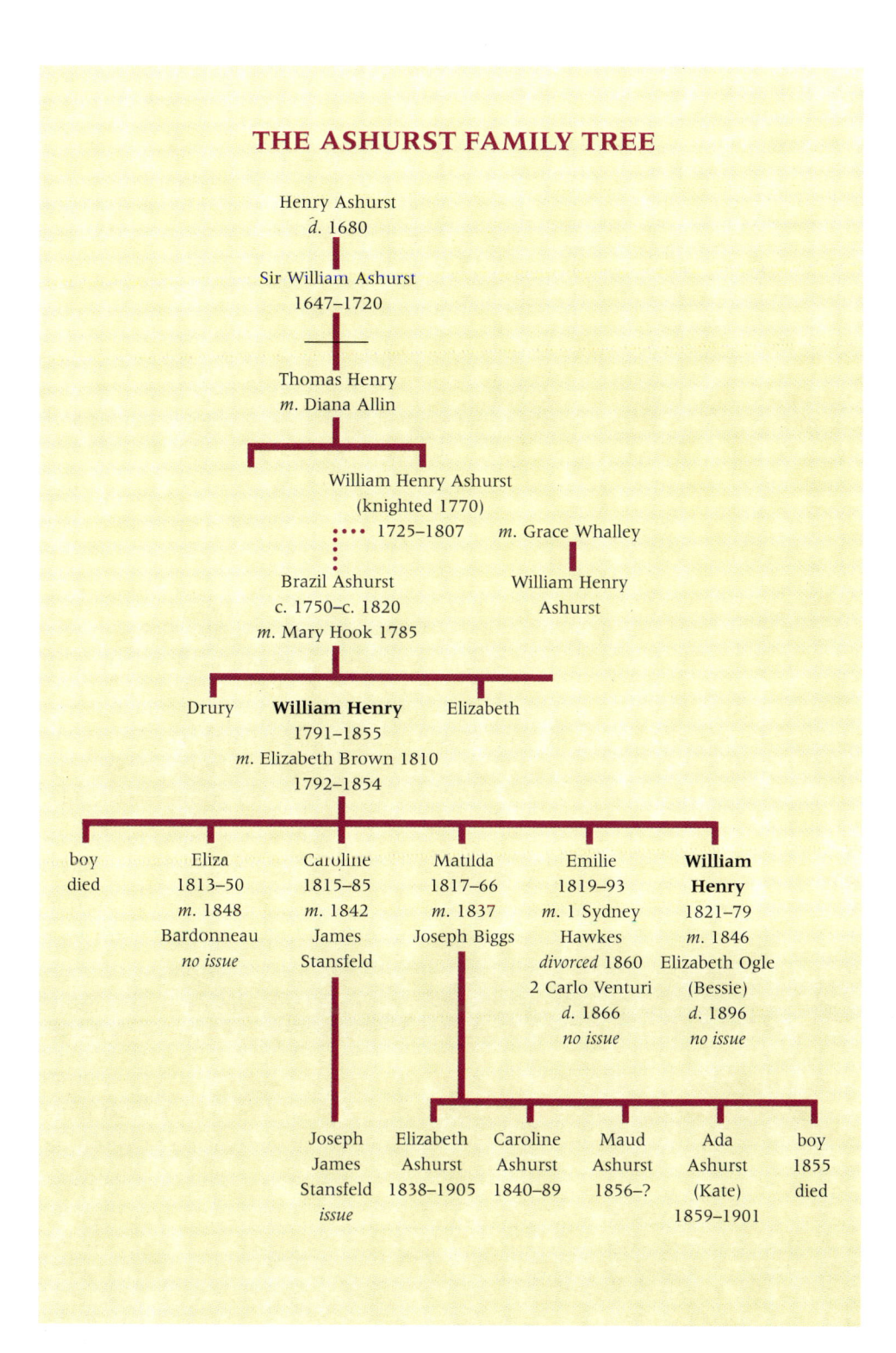

THE ASHURST FAMILY TREE

Henry Ashurst
d. 1680

Sir William Ashurst
1647–1720

Thomas Henry
m. Diana Allin

William Henry Ashurst
(knighted 1770)
•••• 1725–1807   *m.* Grace Whalley

Brazil Ashurst   William Henry
c. 1750–c. 1820   Ashurst
m. Mary Hook 1785

Drury   **William Henry**   Elizabeth
         1791–1855
         m. Elizabeth Brown 1810
         1792–1854

| boy died | Eliza 1813–50 *m.* 1848 Bardonneau *no issue* | Caroline 1815–85 *m.* 1842 James Stansfeld | Matilda 1817–66 *m.* 1837 Joseph Biggs | Emilie 1819–93 *m.* 1 Sydney Hawkes *divorced* 1860 2 Carlo Venturi *d.* 1866 *no issue* | **William Henry** 1821–79 *m.* 1846 Elizabeth Ogle (Bessie) *d.* 1896 *no issue* |

Joseph James Stansfeld *issue* | Elizabeth Ashurst 1838–1905 | Caroline Ashurst 1840–89 | Maud Ashurst 1856–? | Ada Ashurst (Kate) 1859–1901 | boy 1855 died

William Henry Ashurst, 1791–1855; his portrait, from which this engraving derived, was painted by his youngest daughter, Emilie.

privilege; in London at that time, then as always, more expensive than the provinces, the sum ranged from 100 guineas upwards to 400 or even 500 guineas, the amount depending on the standing and reputation of the firm and its clients. Benjamin Disraeli's father paid a premium of 400 guineas in 1821, when he articled his son to City solicitors, Messrs Swain, Stevens, Maples, Pearce & Hunt of Frederick's Place, Old Jewry. Some 20 years later Ashurst's own firm was able to charge 300 guineas as a premium for an articled clerk.[7]

Tilson's clients included the London Corn Exchange, housed then in the building erected for it in Mark Lane in 1749, the Lead Company and Sion College, a society of Anglican clergy with an almshouse and a distinguished library, endowed in the seventeenth century; these were not inconsiderable clients and suggest that Tilson's firm had some standing in the City.[8] Even without a premium to pay, however, entry to the profession was expensive. A tax in the shape of stamp duty on articles had first been imposed in 1794 at £100. Many members of the profession complained but successive governments, seeing the tax as a useful source of revenue to set against the expenses of the long war against France (1793–1815), raised it to £110 in 1804 and to £120 in 1815. Stamp duty was usually paid in instalments over the five-year clerkship, but it had to be paid in full before an attorney could be admitted. An annual instalment of £24 represented probably at least 20 per cent of the clerk's annual salary.

For Ashurst it was an added strain on slender resources at a time when he had a wife and a young family to support. On 30 October 1810, when he was 19, William married Elizabeth Ann Brown at St Mary Magdalene, the parish church of Bermondsey. Their first child, a son, died when still a baby but the successive births of four daughters – Eliza in 1813, Caroline in 1815, Matilda in 1817 and Emilie in 1819 – were followed in 1821 by the birth of a son, who completed the family and who was also, and confusingly, named William Henry.[9]

It is not surprising that in these early years Ashurst, his daughter Emilie recorded, 'was for some time compelled to increase his income by writing for the press and even by passing several hours of each night in copying and engrossing legal documents'. Ashurst was a writer of political documents all his life. In the first half of the nineteenth century young would-be lawyers in both branches of the profession often wrote

William Henry Ashurst and Elizabeth Ann Brown married at the church of St Mary Magdalene, Bermondsey on 30 October 1810.

for the press. The greater rewards offered by professional success usually forced them to give up journalism. Copying there was to do in quantity, for all documents had to be prepared by hand in an attorney's office. Until the arrival of the typewriter towards the end of the nineteenth century, copying and engrossing (i.e. producing a fair copy of a document) provided overtime work for clerks even after specialist agencies were set up to which work could be sent out, often to be completed overnight.

Despite the extra work and his reading – Ashurst was a 'voracious reader' – he found time to attend the meetings of a small and radical Protestant sect known as the Free-thinking Christians. Founded in 1798 by Samuel Thompson, a wine merchant and City radical, the sect attracted Nonconformist rebels mainly from the Baptist and Unitarian churches. It was regarded by the authorities with some suspicion for free-thinking was sometimes a disguise for 'infidelism' (i.e. atheism) and, in the official view, also for political ultra-radicalist and revolutionary discussions, particularly at the City locations where the Free-thinking Christians met. Ashurst acted for a time as a deacon in the sect and he was a regular contributor to the sect's *Free-thinking Christian Magazine*, which was first published in 1811 and lasted until 1814.[10]

Ashurst spent his formative years as a young man in the City at a time when it was the centre of political protest and popular demand for reform. Like many other radicals he was, and remained throughout his life, an admirer of Thomas Paine's writings. *Common Sense* (1776), the *Rights of Man* (1791) and the *Age of Reason* (1794) became 'the three most-widely read political tracts of the eighteenth century' and underpinned the ideology of the nineteenth-century demand for reform. Paine's writing was deliberately phrased in plain language and, in his own words, avoided 'every literary ornament' in order to reach the widest number of readers; his major works expressed a hearty 'contempt for monarchical and hereditary principles ... an unbounded faith in representative institutions and the power of reason' and provided 'a sustained invective against State religion and every form of priestcraft'.[11]

The publications were regarded by the authorities as seditious literature. To a government composed of members of the aristocratic landowning class, who had only recently seen their counterparts in France violently deprived of their lands, their political power and their lives, such books spelled danger. Fearing what it considered to be the contagion of the French Revolution spreading across England, the government prohibited meetings, large and small, and relied on a network of spies and informers to infiltrate radical movements. Even so, in the City there were many respectable businessmen who were active in the radical and reform movements, without being revolutionaries; men such as Robert Waitham (1764–1833), whose emporium at Blackfriars successfully funded his radical activities, became MP for the City 1818–20 and served as Lord Mayor 1823–4.[12]

The Free-thinking Christians eventually disintegrated, largely through the disputes occurring between the sect's members, but several of the young men attracted to it in its heyday in the first 15 years or so of the nineteenth century found their religious and political views converged; they remained linked in dissent, radicalism and business for the rest of their lives. It was at the meetings of the Free-thinking Christians that Ashurst met James Morrison, who was to become both a friend and the firm's first and most significant client.

Born in Somerset in 1789, James Morrison arrived in London in the early years of the century. In 1809 he was employed as a shopman (£40 a year salary, plus board and lodging) by Messrs Todd & Co whose already prosperous haberdashery business in Fore Street in the City was expanding rapidly. Morrison's aptitude and enthusiasm for business soon advanced his career and his salary and, in 1814, he became a partner and married Mary Ann Todd, daughter of his employer, now partner, Joseph Todd. The City was at that time more of a place for shopping than the West End; Richard Rush, the US minister in London who arrived in 1817 wrote after a visit to the City:

The shops stand, side by side, for entire miles. The accumulation of things is amazing; it would seem impossible that there can be purchasers for them all, until you consider what multitudes there are to buy; then you are disposed to ask how the buyers can all be supplied.[13]

As his business continued to grow, Morrison persuaded John Dillon, whom he had also met at the Free-thinking Christians to join him. Dillon became a partner in 1828 but well before that the friendship between Morrison and Ashurst had also led to a fruitful professional relationship.

In November 1821 Ashurst completed his articles and was admitted to the Court of the King's Bench. Attorneys then still had to seek admission to each court separately and it was not until the end of January 1822 that Ashurst was admitted to the Court of Common Pleas. Early in 1822 he left the Tilson firm and set up on his own at 2 Sambrook Court in Basinghall Street. Several reasons for his doing so suggest themselves. Thomas Tilson had a son (Thomas Tilson Junior) who was at this time serving his articles. He became his father's partner in 1826, an outcome which could almost certainly be envisaged in 1821. In other words, it was no doubt clear to Ashurst that there was no prospect of a partnership in Coleman Street. Indeed, his own former principal and Tilson's partner for some years, John Preston, left Coleman Street in 1826 and set up on his own in Tokenhouse Yard, Lothbury.[14]

There was no shortage of qualified members of the profession; between 1816 and 1822 the total number taking out practising certificates increased by an average of almost 3 per cent a year and many admitted men who worked as managing clerks (assistant solicitors today) did not take out practising certificates.

London's gutters, garrets and pot-houses were crammed with over-educated and under-employed solicitors and attorneys whose lives were barely distinguishable from those of their struggling clerks. When they lacked capital or influence, solicitors ... occupied a position of social and economic marginality similar to artisan intellectuals.[15]

If to 'capital and influence', to neither of which, as far as we can tell, Ashurst had access, we add 'connection', we can come much nearer to the reason for his confidence in establishing his own practice. By 1822 James Morrison was senior managing partner of the Todd textile business which, in that year had a turnover of £1.5m and was still growing. It is possible that Ashurst was already doing work for Morrison before he qualified and while still at Coleman Street, or there may well have been an understanding between the two men that Morrison would bring his business to Ashurst as soon as the latter was admitted and able to set up on his own. What is certain is that in 1822 Ashurst was acting for Morrison and the business. Some 80 years later, one of Morrison's sons, Walter recalled:

My father … wanted to find a clever young solicitor to do the work of the firm. Like a good businessman, he was a keen judge of character. He selected Mr Ashurst, who from that day did the whole of the business of the firm, and he not only acted as the Solicitor of Morrison, Dillon & Co, but my father and he became great friends.

The success of the Fore Street business was based on the application of a policy closely allied to the twentieth-century's 'pile 'em high, sell 'em cheap', described by Morrison himself rather more lengthily as:

… the real art of mercantile traffic was to find sellers rather than buyers: that if you bought cheap, and satisfied yourself with only a fair profit, buyers – the best sort of buyers, those who have money to buy – would come of themselves … uniting this theory with another, that small profits and quick returns are more profitable in the long run than long credits with great gains.[16]

Morrison's business was, like most trade at the time, domestic and export, largely financed by bills of exchange which were used, passing from hand to hand and endorsed by each acceptor, as a means of settling debts. The process was described thus, by a London banker:

Let us imagine a farmer in the country to discharge a debt of £10 to his neighbouring grocer, by giving him a bill for that sum, drawn on his corn factor in London, for grain sold in the metropolis; and the grocer to transmit the bill, he having previously endorsed it, to a neighbouring sugar baker, in discharge of a like debt, and the sugar baker to send it, when again endorsed, to a West India merchant in an out-port, and the West India merchant to deliver it to his country banker, who also endorses it and sends it further into circulation. The bill, in this case, will have effected five payments, exactly as if it were a £10 note payable on demand to bearer. It will, however, have circulated chiefly in consequence of the confidence placed by each receiver of it in the last endorser, his own correspondent in trade.[17]

James Morrison was Ashurst's first client; this bust of Morrison was sculpted by Sir Francis Chantrey (1781–1841), whose success had been achieved from humble origins, very similar to those of Morrison himself.

Confidence could, however, be misplaced, and the bills required careful scrutiny to see that they were presented at the right date and paid up; it seems that from 1822 on this task was delegated by Morrison to Ashurst. Not untypical among the surviving documents is a 12-month bill dated 25 November 1822 for £44 6s due to Todd & Morrison. A note on it to Ashurst says, 'We are rather at a loss how to act with this' and Ashurst's reply written on it is, 'If you refer you will find you have received a composition hereon but may prove the balance in due course.' There is another bundle of bills dating from later in the 1820s in Ashursts' archives, with a note from Morrison attached which says that 'Messrs Ashurst & Green are requested to write to both parties'; this suggests that these are bills where the endorsers had failed to pay up in time.

Morrison's income from the business had reached a four-figure sum by 1822 and he had bought a small estate in Balham (five acres, a house and a cottage). As his business ventures became more profitable, he bought more land and in all such transactions, Ashurst acted for him. Walter Morrison recalled, 'My father, in fact, had such confidence in the firm that he used to sign papers put before him without reading them through.' In 1823 a difficult family dispute arose between Morrison and his father-in-law Joseph Todd and his brother-in-law John Todd, who were, by an arrangement made in 1818, due to retire from the business in 1822 and 1826 respectively. No doubt they both wished to ensure that they did so on the best terms possible from such a thriving business. In John Todd's case, there was also resentment at being outshone and, in effect, ousted by an outsider even, or perhaps especially, one who had married his sister. The disagreement got as far as some proceedings in the Court of Chancery before, in 1824, the Todds resolved that settlement of the quarrel, on generous terms offered by Morrison (advised by Ashurst), was preferable to lengthy and expensive litigation.[18]

With such a significant City businessman as Morrison as a client, others followed the path to Sambrook Court, taking their legal work to Ashurst. There were more than 8,000 small and medium-sized businesses in the City of London in 1815 and, following the end of the long war with France, we can safely assume that there were more, rather than less, in the early 1820s. The City's role as a world financial centre had expanded and continued to do so; between 1822 and 1825 some 20 loans for foreign states totalling £40m, were issued in London. Trade and mercantile enterprise flourished as an economic recovery began in 1821, signalled by the return to the gold standard in that year.

London was also the country's largest industrial centre for ship-building and engineering and, more significantly, for the manufacture of consumer goods 'fitting and finishing all the commodities requisite for the consumption and vast commerce of the metropolis'. Many of these were to be found in and around the City, with, for example, furniture-makers and printers in Holborn, Finsbury and Southwark, hat-makers and leather manufacturers in Bermondsey, clothing manufacturers in the City and to the east of it, while brewers, distillers, vinegar-makers, food-processors, soap and candle-makers and pottery manufacturers clustered on the banks of the river. They all as well as many others served the increasing population of London, by 1800 'the grandest city in the West' with a population of 1m, still growing.[19]

Professional success came quickly to Ashurst, according to his daughter Emilie and, since barely two years after he had established himself in practice he took a partner, there seems no reason to doubt her account. William Henry Green had been articled in Leicester but, as was then customary, travelled to London to complete his articles. He gave his address, when he was admitted in 1818, as Angel Court, Throgmorton Street.[20] The firm became Ashurst & Green, a partnership that lasted some five years.

Disputes of the kind that had arisen between James Morrison and the Todd family were not uncommon. When members of a family were in business together, ownership and profit-sharing provided plentiful grounds for squabbling; and at that time most British businesses were family-owned. Most of them were partnerships for it was difficult legally then to adopt any other form. Since the passing of the legislation which became known as the Bubble Act in 1720, a company could only be incorporated by Royal Charter, by the grant of letters patent or by private Act of Parliament, all lengthy and costly processes. Only large undertakings which required the kind of capital that it was impossible to obtain in any way other than by inviting public subscription, such as canals, docks, roads and waterworks, sought incorporation. Small and medium-sized businesses did not think of incorporation, not least because:

Respectable business men then [1825] and for many years afterwards were inclined with some reason, to regard company promotion as the work, if not of the Devil, then of financiers and stockbrokers quite closely related to him, and limited liability as a method of cheating one's creditors.[21]

The financial crisis of 1825–6 offered ample evidence, if needed, to 'respectable' businessmen of the evils of incorporation and company promotion. In 1825 the Bubble Act was repealed. Prospectuses for more than 600 companies were issued and the speculation that followed in their shares was not far short of that which had led to the downfall of the South Sea Company and the passing of the Bubble Act a century before. Many of the proposed incorporations were for grandiose schemes in remote parts of the world, ranging from the merely dubious to the downright dishonest; few of them got beyond a prospectus. The speculation sparked credit restriction and that led in turn to the collapse of some 50 banks and, in their wake, a large number of small businesses. The general mayhem created a good deal of work for City solicitors in 1826 and 1827, including no doubt for Ashurst & Green.

At the same time James Morrison was developing his business interests in different directions and seeking a place in politics, both of which involved Ashurst, as his solicitor, in different areas of work. In 1826 Morrison was persuaded to stand as a parliamentary candidate in Marlow, in Buckinghamshire. The seat was traditionally in the hands of a local land-owning family, the Williams, and despite Morrison's enthusiastic canvassing, Owen Williams and his son Thomas were elected. Angered at Morrison's attempt to break their influence in the town, the Williams gave notice, after the election, to a number of their tenants who had voted for Morrison. Ashurst was brought into the matter to advise and help the tenants under notice, using 'every step that his ingenious legal mind could devise to obstruct Williams' action'.[22]

Undeterred by his failure in Marlow, Morrison determined on entering the House of Commons. It was not, however, until 1830 that he was successful in being returned for the seat of St Ives in Cornwall. His election there was made possible by a complex financial transaction, not untypical of the way in which seats changed hands in the unreformed Parliament. During the 1820s Morrison lent large sums of money to a number of landowners and members of the aristocracy; their need for funding offered a useful and more secure investment opportunity and one where the Bank of England itself had led the way. The transactions were all supervised by Ashurst, providing yet more work for his office. It was through a loan to William Long-Wellesley (later the fourth Lord Mornington) to purchase the St Ives estate that Morrison, as a *quid pro quo*, secured the constituency and Wellesley's agreement to back him.[23]

In 1828 the partnership between Ashurst and Green was dissolved. Unusually, Ashurst, the senior partner, was the one who moved, taking his practice and his family to 84 Newgate Street. It seems that the reason was a family, rather than a professional matter. Mrs Ashurst had always disliked the house in Sambrook Court; situated in the right-hand corner of the Court, the house was probably tall and narrow, with the practice occupying, as was common, the ground floor and the Ashurst family living above. There was a large hall on the first floor with a door hidden in its panelling concealing the entry to a spiral staircase which led down to the clerks' offices. The reason why Mrs Ashurst disliked the house is not known; it may have been gloomy – there is, in the surviving description of it, mention of a long unlighted passage – but apparently her feelings were the decisive factor. William Green continued to practise in the City – for some years at Sambrook Court – until 1872, for most of the time on his own.[24]

Ashurst's new office and home was at the Cheapside end of Newgate Street. At the other end, where the Old Bailey now stands, was Newgate Prison, outside which public executions had taken place since 1783, when the gallows at Tyburn had been demolished. Large crowds regularly attended the spectacle: when Henry Fauntleroy was hanged for forgery in 1824, it was estimated that 100,000 people turned out to watch. The proximity of his home and office to the place of execution probably strengthened what his daughter described as the 'abhorrence' that Ashurst felt for capital punishment. Between 1826 and 1830, 89 people were executed outside the prison.[25]

For the next seven years Ashurst practised alone. Despite his busy practice, his interest in and enthusiasm for radical political causes were undiminished. He was active in the City's corporate and political life in these years. He became a freeman in 1830, as a liveryman of the Lorimers' Company, and he was a member of one of the City's governing bodies, the Court of Common Council, from 1832 until 1847, representing the ward of Farringdon Within. He served as Under-Sheriff for one year. Consistently advocating reform, particularly of the Court

Ashurst Morris Crisp

In 1836 Ashurst moved the firm's offices to 137 Cheapside where he practised until 1847. Cheapside was at the heart of the City and by 1847 its shops rivalled and sometimes surpassed those of the West End.

of Aldermen, Ashurst published in 1832 *The Corporation Register*, setting out his ideas.

He was also an ardent supporter of Parliamentary reform, expressing his views forcefully thus: 'If the House of Peers may be called the house of incurables, the House of Commons may be called the house of wordy twaddlers – spouters of dead verbiage – men who meet to bury the nation's business under a mass of words.' When it seemed, in 1832, that the Reform Bill would not be passed, he was one of the first to display on the front of his house the announcement. 'This house pays no taxes until the Reform Bill becomes law', the action agreed upon by the Bill's supporters. In the event the Bill was passed.

During the struggle for the Reform Bill James Morrison had been in the House of Commons as MP for Ipswich, the constituency where he stood and was elected in 1831. In the 1832 election he was returned at the top of the poll but in the election of 1834 he was defeated. It was immediately apparent that not only had the Tories threatened local businessmen with the loss of business should they vote for Morrison and his fellow candidate but also that they had bribed a number of voters with cash payments. There was sufficient evidence for a petition against the election result to be made and a committee of the House of Commons started to look into the matter in March 1835. However, the key witnesses had, to a man, disappeared and by May in the light of their absence, the committee was about to give up when the witnesses returned home. They were briskly served with notice to appear by Ashurst who was acting for the petitioners. One witness, Pilgrim, managing clerk to a Norwich firm of solicitors, did not return home until 25 May. But Ashurst's intelligence network was able to cope with this, according to Morrison's biographer: 'The night mail-coach from London arrived punctually next morning in Norwich about half past seven. Off it here stepped a Mr Waller, an enterprising and trusted clerk of William Ashurst's. He made straight for Pilgrim's house.' Although Pilgrim prevaricated, he agreed eventually to go with Waller, but a last-ditch attempt to prevent his giving evidence was made by local Tories, who had him arrested and remanded in custody on a spurious charge of embezzling £6 from his employers. It took Ashurst several days to extricate Pilgrim from this but on 1 June he finally appeared before the House of Commons committee. Shortly afterwards the committee declared the election invalid and ordered a fresh election to be held. At that James Morrison was comfortably elected.[26]

Morrison continued to represent Ipswich until 1837 and then he spent some three years out of the House. This may well have been in part because he had a new business venture, taking up more of his time as well as that of his solicitor, Ashurst. Since the 1820s Morrison had been running a separate merchanting business from a small office in Kings Arms Yard, importing such varied goods as leathers for glove-making and olive oil and exporting hosiery to Australia. The business was financed by bills of exchange, discounted originally by commission merchants but increasingly in the early nineteenth century by the recently established merchant banks.

Morrison's keen business sense and nose for a profit led him to establish, with an American partner, John Cryder, his own merchant bank. On 1 January 1836 Morrison, Cryder & Co. opened for business in Broad Street. It became rapidly one of the leading Anglo-American merchant banks, with its capital, according to contemporary estimates, second only to that of Brown, Shipley & Co. and larger than that of Barings. The strength of Morrison, Cryder & Co. enabled it to weather, with the help of a loan from the Bank of England, the storm of the 1836–7 financial crisis while others fell. In 1839 Cryder retired from the business, leaving it in the hands of Morrison and his sons.[27]

There is no doubt that Morrison's retailing, trading and merchant banking businesses and the country estates he bought provided a good deal of work for Ashurst; equally, however, the surviving ledgers of the firm (from the 1830s) indicate that this was by no means a one-client firm. There are many other City businesses appearing as regular clients, including White and Greenwells, Caldicott & Co. (retailers), Bradbury & Greatorex (which did a large wholesale trade in sheets, towels and other textiles at its premises in Aldermanbury), Cordingley & Co., Capper & Co., all of whose names appear in the ledgers throughout the decade. There were others with only one or two transactions recorded; in 1831 Ashurst acted for Burton Ale Brewers in a libel action, the costs of which stood in the ledger in June that year at £175 10s 4d, while Smith & Osman came to the firm in 1836 for their partnership to be dissolved; they were charged £9 8s 6d for this in October that year.

The radical founder

In July 1835 Ashurst took a partner for the second time. The practice was continuing to grow as the surviving ledgers indicate and as well as the commercial work, he was acting in two other election petition cases that year, Yarmouth and Bridgnorth, in addition to the Morrison case at Ipswich. Edward Barnevelt Elliott Gainsford joined the firm as a junior partner, putting in £250 capital to Ashurst's £750 which entitled Gainsford to a quarter of the profits and Ashurst to three-quarters. The firm's work by then was covering a wide range of subjects. There was probate and other work for private clients and property work, both commercial and private, which included purchases and mortgages as well as drawing up leases; there was financial work, the drawing up of partnership agreements and dissolutions and litigation. There was agency work too; country solicitors were often obliged to use London solicitors as agents to attend to matters in the courts or parliamentary matters. In 1836 the firm's ledgers show that Ashurst was acting as agent for Wells & Son in the matter of the Chester and Crewe Railway Company.

Increasingly, too, it is clear that Ashurst and the firm had become the natural choice of solicitor for radical clients and their business. He was already acting for a number of groups campaigning against church rates (see Chapter 2) and for several radical newspapers and journals. In April 1836 the ledger shows costs of £152 14s 6d to be charged to the proprietors of the *Morning Chronicle;* later that year Sir William Molesworth became a client. Molesworth (1810–55) came from an old Cornish family whose estate was at Pencarrow near Bodmin. He had studied at Edinburgh, Cambridge and in Germany before he declared himself for

Sir William Molesworth (1810–55) was a very rich radical MP whose purchase, in the 1830s, of the *Westminster Review* brought him to the firm as a client.

the reform movement in 1831. He was returned as member for East Cornwall in the first reformed Parliament. 'Young, very rich and a bit of a dandy', Molesworth soon made his mark in London radical society and in 1835 he financed the publication of the *London Review*, supported by the philosophical radicals. In 1836 he purchased the *Westminster Review* and soon after merged the two journals.[28] The indications are that Ashurst acted for him on these transactions, for although the ledger is not specific, in August 1836 charges of £360 2s 8d were debited to Molesworth and, in November that year a further sum of costs amounting to £270 was charged.

Through the 1830s the firm's office expenses and salaries rose steadily, as the practice expanded. In 1831 office expenses were just over £1,200; in 1836, a particularly busy year, they rose to nearly £1,900 and in the following three years they ran at between £1,400 and £1,500. The major part of this sum went on salaries and the figures suggest an establishment of a size comparable with the mid-1850s (see Chapter 3) with some 12 clerks employed. In 1824 William Vizard, a solicitor with an extensive practice (he had acted for Queen Caroline during her trial) gave evidence to the Commission investigating the Court of Chancery that his annual office expenses were between £800 and £1,000 a year for rent, taxes and clerks' salaries. He had heard, he said, of solicitors with office expenses of £2,000 a year. When Ashurst's rent and taxes are added to the costs of salaries, stationery, coals and candles, the expense of running his office came to over £2,000 a year. This suggests a large and profitable practice, and profits ran at between £2,000 and £3,000 a year in the 1830s.

Shortly before Gainsford became a partner Ashurst had moved to new offices at 13 New Bridge Sreet, Blackfriars and in 1836 the partnership moved again to 137 Cheapside. Ashurst's own house and family expenses are detailed in some of the surviving ledgers and a note of rent and taxes paid in Holloway in 1832 suggests that he had by then moved his family out of the City. If so, he was well ahead of a trend that became marked in the 1830s and the 1840s. By the late 1830s it was becoming unfashionable to live in the City 'over the shop'. Marianne Freshfield, whose family lived over Freshfield & Sons' offices at New Bank Buildings until 1840 noted that there were then few families living in the City. There was living accommodation at the offices of Ashurst &

Gainsford at 137 Cheapside and a housekeeper and her family were installed there. The firm's accounts include regular payments to Mrs Leahy and the 1841 Census shows that her husband John Leahy was working for the firm as a clerk.[29]

In December 1836 the Ashurst family moved to a new home in Muswell Hill; the rent was – and remained for the 18 years the family lived there – just over £100 a year. A contemporary writer, Morier Evans, noted in the 1840s that City men moved out to the suburbs for fresh air and economy, and rents in the City were certainly higher; in 1830 Ashurst was paying £155 a year in rent for the New Bridge Street premises. A good deal was spent by the Ashursts late in 1836 in equipping the new house. The items listed included £121 14s to Messrs Broadwood & Sons for a piano, some £4 on lamps, £20 to the carpenter and another £8 on decorating, carving and gilding. New furniture and china were also bought, all suggesting a comfortable standard of living which the profits from the practice enabled its senior partner to afford and enjoy.

Muswell Hill was a pleasant suburb but it was singularly inaccessible when the Ashursts moved there and remained so for most of the time the family lived there: 'It was customary for the friends who had enjoyed Mr Ashurst's hospitality to assemble in the porch at about half past ten and journey together on foot as far as the Angel, Islington, where cabs and omnibuses were available.'[30]

Ashurst's partnership with Gainsford lasted, as had that with Green, for five years and was dissolved in July 1840. In the Law Lists from 1840 onwards there is no entry for Gainsford, so we can only guess that he retired or took up some other occupation; his partnership may have been deliberately intended as a stop-gap measure. Ashurst did not take another partner at this time, probably because in January 1837 his only son, William, had been articled to him.[31] Ashurst had sent his son to the school founded by Thomas Wright Hill, father of Rowland Hill (see Chapter 2) who, with his brothers, took over its management in the early 1820s.

The school became famous in the mid-1820s, winning the approval of Jeremy Bentham and other leading radicals who sent their sons to it. Its appeal lay in its system of self-government by the boys, the abolition of corporal punishment and a disciplined and rigid punctuality. Rowland Hill, who taught there until the late 1820s when he left it to three of his brothers, was a close friend of James Morrison, two of whose sons had been educated at the school. Originally in Birmingham, first at Hill Top and then at the purpose-built Hazel-wood House, the school moved to Bruce Castle in Tottenham in 1827 where the young William Ashurst attended it.[32] In December 1836 Ashurst paid what was presumably the last school bill to Messrs Hill, totalling £62 6s 5d. With his son in articles, Ashurst was waiting for his admission to the profession to ensure that the fruits of his professional success, so hard won over the last 20 years, would remain in the family.

CHAPTER 2
Ashurst & Son

ON 12 JULY 1840 the House of Commons passed, with a majority of just over 100, a clause in the budget establishing the penny post. It was a signal victory for those who had been campaigning, for more than two years, for the introduction of a cheap and uniform rate of postage, among them William Ashurst. Credit for the invention of the idea of the penny post has long been given to Rowland Hill, who suggested it, unsuccessfully, to the government in 1837. When a parliamentary committee was appointed in November 1837 to examine Hill's scheme, 'the necessity of leading the public to support the Uniform Penny Post became evident and especially so to Mr George Moffat, a large tea merchant in the City'.[1]

Eager to ensure that the case for a uniform and cheap postage rate was made, Moffat (who was James Morrison's son-in-law) was instrumental in the City's decision to establish its own committee to make representations. With Joshua Bates, a partner in Barings, as chairman and Moffat himself as treasurer, the Committee of Merchants in Aid of the Parliamentary Committee (often referred to as the Mercantile Committee) came into being in the spring of 1838. John Dillon, partner of James Morrison, was a member of the committee and William Ashurst was asked to act as its solicitor. According to Rowland Hill's own account, Ashurst 'went promptly to work; and though by choice he acted gratuitously, he laboured with as much ardour as if important personal interests were involved in the issue'.[2] Ashurst, his daughter Emilie recorded, 'undertook, at great personal and pecuniary sacrifice, the labour and responsibility'. Not only did he conduct the parliamentary enquiry (it sat for three days a week for more than four months), he also wrote and had published, in 1838, a 130-page pamphlet entitled *Facts and Reasons in Support of Mr Rowland Hill's Plan for a Universal Penny Postage*. Ashurst argued the case cogently and persuasively, embodying his own views on the improvements that would result for society at large from the introduction of the uniform penny post. They give a distinctive flavour of the man and his philosophy:

The strength, the power, and the prosperity of this country, is mainly dependent upon her commerce. Commerce has arisen, subdued and humanized, under institutions and restrictions, all tending to check its peaceful progress and benign influence. It is the peaceful and effective means by which God spread the fruits of the earth over the face of the earth, and realizes his blessings to all.

These blessings are dependent on the power of men to communicate with each other; and it is the business as well as the duty of legislators to facilitate it.

He concluded:

There need be no apprehension of any injurious results, either in business or in science, from extending the utmost possible knowledge to all. There are some that feel an apprehension that the circulation of business knowledge, and the increase of business activity, will discover too soon all that is to be known; and by exhausting the field of business activity, leave men without anything new to discover; so some men thought when fly waggons took the lead of broad wheels, and coaches accomplished what was then thought the wonderful effort of travelling from York to London in three days…

Improvement and the world will expire together; and until the final end of all things, we may diffuse knowledge without fear of exhausting it. We need not be apprehensive of becoming infinite or perfect.[3]

In 1840 Ashurst was 49 years old. His professional practice was, as we have seen, well established and sufficiently remunerative for him to be able to devote more of his time – and sometimes without payment – to the causes in which he believed. His personality impressed itself favourably on those he met, as the description of him given (some eight years later) by the American anti-slavery activist, William Lloyd Garrison, shows:

I cherish for Mr Ashurst a profound regard, as a rare man on earth. His ability is unquestionable and great, his philanthropy expansive, his spirit catholic, his practical knowledge of men and things uncommon, his philosophy serene and comprehensive, and his perception of truth quick and steady.[4]

Ashurst first met Garrison, editor of the American anti-slavery newspaper *The Liberator*, and a man 14 years his junior, in June 1840, when the first World Anti-Slavery Convention assembled in London. At the opening session there was a day-long debate on the question of whether the eight women delegates from the USA should be permitted to take their seats.

The Penny Black was Britain's first adhesive postage stamp. It was issued in 1840 when the penny post, for which Ashurst and others campaigned so vigorously, was introduced.

Ashurst Morris Crisp

Emilie Ashurst (1819–93) was the youngest of the four daughters of William and Elizabeth Ashurst. Emilie was one of, if not the, most devoted and faithful followers of Mazzini; she was a talented artist and writer whose life was given up to radical causes.

Arguing forcefully in their favour, Ashurst demanded of the Convention delegates whether it was their intention 'to employ your efforts to annihilate slavery throughout the world, are you to commence by saying you will take away the rights of one half of creation?' Despite his eloquence, however, and the support of Garrison, the women were excluded from the floor of the Convention. Ashurst's presence at the Convention and his spirited defence of the women delegates reflected two of the many causes he publicly espoused at this time. Afterwards he wrote to Garrison, asking for copies of *The Liberator* to be sent to him as they were published (he soon became, under the pseudonym of Edward Search, a frequent and, according to the journal's editor, much valued contributor). He also requested articles and papers, 'upon the woman question. Their emancipation from serfdom is next in importance to the slavery question'.[5]

Ashurst's views on the 'woman question' had been formed, he told his family as a young man:

'When I was but a lad, I attended the trial of a girl under sixteen for child murder. That girl had been first seduced and then forsaken by a man; she was tried and found guilty by twelve men; condemned to death by a man and hung by a man. It set me thinking.'

They had also been translated into action in the rearing of his own children, his son William and, more particularly, his four daughters, Eliza, Matilda, Caroline and Emilie. They had been brought up 'to the habit of independent thought and action',[6] encouraged to speak their minds and educated to play a part in the world beyond the mere domestic sphere generally allowed to women at that time. It was this that, together with their radical politics, earned them, with their brother and his friends, the collective description by which they were known – the Muswell Hill Brigade.

Ashurst 'believed in bringing up his girls to callings which would render them independent should fortune ever play them an evil trick'. This was not easy at a time when employment opportunities for middle-class women were so limited as to be virtually non-existent. The girls all spoke and wrote French well and Eliza, the eldest daughter, was occupied with translating the works of George Sand in the early 1840s (her translations were later published). The youngest daughter, Emilie, who displayed a talent for drawing and painting, was 'apprenticed' to the painter, Frank Stone; she 'developed considerable powers in portraiture'. She also 'plunged in an informal way, into legal studies besides making herself a first-rate hand at engrossing'.[7]

Entry to the profession was not, of course, open to women and the training that her brother, William, was then undergoing was not accessible to Emilie, should she or her father have wished it for her. William junior had been, as we have seen, articled to his father in January 1837. The education and training of articled clerks was grounded at that time in copying and learning precedents, a process described by the *Law Journal* as 'five years of office education without even the tincture of scholarship and liberal arts…'. Some three years later the House of Commons Select Committee on Legal Education was even more dismissive of the value of clerkship; it concluded tersely: 'No legal education worthy of the name is at this moment to be had in England.'[8]

Articled clerks were mainly occupied in copying lengthy documents, intended both to help their principals and to instil into them the customary practices of drafting. Legal textbooks were few but in 1833 the newly established Law Society, the founders of which were conscious of the shortcomings of legal education, had begun offering courses of lectures to articled clerks; by Ashurst junior's time a course of 12 lectures was given each year on each of five topics – common law, conveyancing, equity, bankruptcy and criminal law. Two of these – common law and equity – were compulsory subjects in the formal written examination instituted in 1836 and an articled clerk had to choose one further subject from the other three on which he would answer questions. Contemporary opinion did not consider

Caroline Ashurst (1815–85) married James Stansfeld, barrister, brewer and politician. They were both great friends and admirers of Mazzini after whom their only child, Joseph, was named.

that the examination (which took some three hours to complete) was particularly exacting and more than 90 per cent of those taking it passed.[9] Following his admission as a solicitor in 1843, Ashurst junior became his father's partner and the firm took the name Ashurst & Son.

In 1843 Ashurst senior took a new articled clerk. William Shaen (1821–87), was the youngest son of Samuel Shaen of Hatfield Peveril in Essex, one of the first Nonconformists to be appointed a country magistrate after the repeal of the Test and Corporation Acts in 1828. William Shaen had been educated at Hove House School, a Nonconformist academy of good reputation in Brighton, and then he spent some three years (1833–6) at the newly established University College School in London.[10] He took his degree at University College, London in 1840.

In the 1820s there were only two English universities, Oxford and Cambridge: membership of the Church of England was a prerequisite for admission to the one and graduation from the other, so that Nonconformists, Jews and Roman Catholics were effectively excluded from university education. Representatives of these three groups, together with a number of liberals who, like Jeremy Bentham regarded Oxford and Cambridge as 'public nuisances ... storehouses and nurseries of public corruption', were the prime movers in the establishment of University College in 1826. It was not, however, until 1836 that the college was granted its Charter by Parliament and empowered to grant degrees. University College School was established in 1830 in a house in Gower Street.[11]

At University College, referred to by the Tory press variously as the 'Cockney College', 'Stinkomalee' and the 'godless institution of Gower Street', William Shaen was a member of a group of 'young men of ample promise, which in after-life they have fully redeemed. Their presence in Gower Street was to a certain extent a pledge of their Liberal opinions and of the conscientiousness with which these opinions were entertained.'

Shaen then read law at Edinburgh University and began to read for the Bar at the Middle Temple before deciding instead to become a solicitor. In Ashurst, Shaen found a principal whom he could admire and with whose principles he was in complete agreement. Shaen, with his 'well-knit frame ... broad brow, frank eyes, delicate features and firm, resolute mouth, attracted at first sight ... a man to be relied upon in trouble'. He was for the whole of his life, 'a strenuous supporter of female education and female suffrage' and he soon became a friend of the young Ashursts. To them he introduced one of his closest friends from his days at University College, James Stansfeld, who was then reading for the Bar.[12]

Stansfeld came of a family similar in many ways to the Ashursts. His father, born in 1792, had also started his working life as a clerk in a solicitor's office in Halifax and 'made his way rapidly in his profession'; he was appointed a judge of the Court of Requests in 1841 and later a County Court judge.[13] The Stansfelds, however, were an old established Nonconformist family – the father was a trustee of the Halifax chapel – while the Ashursts considered themselves to be 'irreligious' (although, it may be noted, the family's links with the Unitarian establishment remained strong and Ashurst's accounts include a regular subscription to St John's Chapel in Clerkenwell). The Ashurst girls were 'independent and bold' and they all smoked, behaviour which was regarded as unconventionally bohemian at best, but beyond the pale by most of polite society.

Sunday, for the Ashurst family, was not a day for church-going but for entertaining their friends at home at Muswell Hill, the house and gardens described by Garrison as 'a perfect gem of a place, quite equal to Paradise before the Fall'. Friends and like-minded radicals gathered to eat and drink – although Ashurst himself was converted to total abstinence from alcohol by Garrison on one visit – to talk and to play bowls. One long-standing friend and client was Robert Owen (1771–1858); although Ashurst had not agreed with his attempts to foster trade unionism and socialism in the 1830s, 'certain of a welcome Mr Owen would present himself, bag in hand, not unfrequently with the announcement: "Now Ashurst, I'm come to quarrel with you," knowing well that no man was less likely to quarrel about difference of opinion'.[14]

Best known for his social and business experiments with the New Lanark Mills in the 1840s, Owen, in his seventies, was dedicating his efforts to the creation of cooperative communities, mainly in the United

Robert Owen (1771–1858), socialist and philanthropist best known for his social experiments with the New Lanark Mills and the Equitable Labour Exchange, as well as the attempt to create communistic settlements in America, was a friend and client of Ashurst.

States. He was also increasingly attracted by sects which strained the credulity although it was not until 1853, when he was 82, that he became a convert of spiritualism. In the early 1840s he was, briefly, an adherent – as were others, including the Unitarian reformer Harriet Martineau – of mesmerism, a form of hypnosis named after an Austrian physician, F A Mesmer. On a memorable Good Friday at Muswell Hill Owen attempted, without success, to mesmerise James Stansfeld.[15]

Stansfeld, however, had by then other reasons for his attendance at Muswell Hill, and in 1842 he married Caroline Ashurst. At around the same time her younger sister, Emilie, married Sydney Hawkes, also a former fellow student of Shaen and Stansfeld at University College and now, with Shaen, serving his articles in Ashurst's office. After their marriage James and Caroline Stansfeld lived in chambers at Lancaster Place. Sydney and Emilie Hawkes went to live at Tavistock House in Bloomsbury, formerly the home of James Perry, editor of the *Morning Chronicle*, and later to be the home of Charles Dickens.[16]

The first of the Ashurst daughters to leave home had been Matilda, who in 1837 married Joseph Biggs, a leading radical from Leicester. Joseph was the youngest of three brothers who had, in 1827, inherited their father's hosiery factory and business in Leicester; Joseph managed the glove-making branch of the business. Under the direction of the brothers it had become one of the largest businesses in Leicester, and was much admired for the enlightened lines on which it was run. The Biggs brothers paid good wages, were sympathetic to demands for shorter hours and offered better working conditions than other similar factories. The brothers were also politically active, both locally and nationally, and the two elder ones, John and William, both served terms as mayor of Leicester and sat with the radical group in the House of Commons.[17] In the early 1850s Matilda and Joseph Biggs moved from Leicester to live in Tunbridge Wells.

Although the sisters and their families visited Muswell Hill regularly and often participated in the Sunday gatherings, only the eldest daughter, Eliza, remained unmarried and living at home, along with her brother William. It was Eliza and William who, in July 1844, visited Giuseppe Mazzini, the Italian nationalist and ardent advocate of Italian independence and unity, who had been living in exile in London since 1840. They called on Mazzini at the request of their father, to express his sympathy and outrage at the discovery, recently made public, that the English government had been opening Mazzini's letters. Mazzini visited Muswell Hill and soon became a close friend of all the family. He had never, he wrote, met such sympathetic people.[18]

His intimate involvement with the Ashursts, who invited him to live at Muswell Hill in 1846, an offer he declined, upset some who had befriended him earlier. Thomas Carlyle's wife, Jane, not always easy to please, wrote:

Mazzini is pretty well – very busy as usual with his benevolent schemes – not so solitary as he used to be – having got up to the ear in a good *twadly family of the name of Ashurst – who have plenty of money – and help 'his things' and* toady *him till I think it has rather gone to his head. A Miss Eliza Ashurst – who does strange things – made his acquaintance first by going to his house to drink tea with him all alone, eh, eh !! and when she had got him to* her *home she introduced him into innumerable other houses of her kindred – and the women of them paint his picture – and send him flowers, and* work *for his bazaar, and make verses about him, and heaven knows what all-while the men give him* capital *towards his* Institutions *and adopt the 'new ideas' at his bidding.*[19]

In fact, the friendship of the Ashursts and Stansfeld and Shaen with Mazzini lasted until his death in 1872 and their support for Italian unity and independence continued after that. When the People's International League was launched at a public meeting, held at the Crown and Anchor tavern in the Strand on 25 April 1847, William Ashurst senior was appointed one of its trustees and his son and sons-in-law, Hawkes and Stansfeld as well as his clerk, Shaen, all became members of the League's Council.[20]

Giuseppe Mazzini (1805–72) the Italian patriot and architect of the Risorgimento, lived in exile for many years in London. He was a close friend of the Ashurst family.

Mazzini was a regular visitor to the Ashurst Sundays at Muswell Hill, as were other radicals and reformers. Among the 'large social gathering' that Garrison recorded meeting at Muswell Hill on 'a very delightful Sunday' in September 1846 he noted 'the celebrated and eloquent Unitarian preacher, William Johnson Fox, who, after preaching his forenoon sermon … came and spent the remainder of the day with us, engaging in sport after dinner in rolling balls on the green sward'. William Fox (1786–1864) was not only a preacher but also a powerful public orator and campaigner for such causes as the Anti-Corn Law League. He had, in 1824, taken on the ministry at the South Place Chapel. Situated between Finsbury Square and Finsbury Circus, the great hall of this 'large building of Ionic design' held 800 people. Fox was a close political associate of the Peter Taylors, father and son, both radicals and the father was the brother-in-law and business partner of Samuel Courtauld – the textile business they were developing in Essex became, later in the century, the company Courtaulds.[21]

It may have been through Fox and his connections that Ashurst acted for Samuel Courtauld in what became known as the Braintree Rate Case, a *cause célèbre* and ultimately a decisive case in the fight against church rates. In any case, Ashurst was the obvious choice as solicitor in such an action, given both his own sympathy for the cause and the fact that he was already acting for several other groups of anti-rate campaigners. For some years Nonconformists had been aggrieved at the obligation to pay rates levied by local vestries for the upkeep of Anglican churches. In the 1830s local protests started to coalesce into a national movement calling for the abolition of church rates, a movement with which Ashurst had a great deal of sympathy. He had already been campaigning for some years against church rates; he 'set the example by systematically refusing to pay the Church rate in every parish in which he happened to reside', his daughter Emilie recorded. It was Ashurst's view that 'A meeting to make a Church Rate is a meeting to make legal an exaction from *all* men to pay the expenses of a *few* in worshipping God … There is no more reason why one man should pay another man's teacher than another man's doctor.'

In 1835 he acted for the printer, John Childs, of Bungay in Suffolk who had been imprisoned in Ipswich Jail for non-payment of church rates and he brought the case to public attention by writing and issuing two pamphlets on it. In 1837 and in 1839 he had issued further pamphlets in the form of letters to the parishioners of St Saviour's, Southwark and Chelmsford in Essex, where agitation against the rates had also started.

The Braintree case first came to court in 1837 in the shape of *Veley v. Burder*, the former a churchwarden and the latter a Nonconformist refusing to pay the rate. Samuel Courtauld, who had led the fight against the rate being levied in the first place, organised a Committee of Management to fund Burder's defence, so that Ashurst's work in conducting the litigation was not, in this instance or in most of the other anti-church rate cases he undertook, unpaid. In the Consistory Court, the judge, Dr Lushington, found in favour of Veley, relying on the authority of an obscure judgement in the Court of the Arches in 1791. Ashurst then took Burder's case to the Court of the Queen's Bench, where, after some years' delay, condemned in the contemporary legal press as possibly a deliberate manoeuvre to allow time for the agitation to die down, in 1840 Lord Denman overturned Lushington's judgement. Denman was upheld in the Court of the Exchequer the following year.

This was not, however, the end of the affair. In 1841 the churchwardens of Braintree, advised that there might be a loophole in the Court of the Exchequer's judgement, again levied a rate. A second test-case, *Veley v. Gosling*, began and 'was trundled slowly through various relevant courts'. It was not until 1853 when the case finally reached the House of Lords, that it was settled, with a decision that a rate must be made by a majority and no other rate was valid. The Braintree Case, according to *The Times*, 'practically gave the law of Church rates in every shape its *coup de grace*'.[22] From then on in parishes where Nonconformists were in the majority church rates could not be set. In other parishes, however, Nonconformists still found themselves obliged to pay until, in 1868, Gladstone secured the passage of legislation abolishing church rates.

In 1847 Ashurst & Son moved from 137 Cheapside to new offices at 6 Old Jewry. It was a significant move for Ashurst himself had leased the land from Lord Dartmouth and commissioned the construction of the building. It is an indication both of the success and the prosperity of the practice and may well have been unusual at that time. The new house was sited in the street running between Cheapside and Gresham Street which took its name from the Jews who had inhabited it in the twelfth and thirteenth centuries and again in the eighteenth century.[23]

The firm moved into new offices at 6 Old Jewry in 1847 and stayed there until 1890. Ashurst had the house built on land he leased from Lord Dartmouth.

There was sufficient space in the new building for the firm and for some other offices which were rented out. Candles no longer featured in the list of office expenses for gas lighting had arrived in the City and 6 Old Jewry had the benefit of it.

By the mid-1840s a new area of work was opening up in the City. In 1844 legislation (the Joint Stock Companies Act) introduced by Gladstone, then President of the Board of Trade, made incorporation available by a simple process of registration, as opposed to the lengthy, difficult and costly process of obtaining an Act of Parliament, previously necessary. It was not until 1855 that the Limited Liability Act was passed, allowing companies (except in banking and insurance) to obtain limited liability also by registration and, in the following year, limited liability was incorporated into the Joint Stock Companies Act. In 1862 the legislation of 1844 and 1856 was consolidated and codified in a new Companies Act which was not changed substantively until 1908 and, in some respects, not until 1948. By the abolition in the 1856 Act of some of the provisions intended to protect investors, including the two-stage registration which had been embodied in the earlier legislation, a more liberal system of commercial law was created in England than then existed anywhere else in Europe.[24]

The easy accessibility of incorporation after 1844, even without limited liability, led to the formation of an increasing number of companies and their flotation on the London Stock Exchange. Projects for all kinds of activity, many of them in strange and unknown places both at home and abroad were launched and speculation, as in 1825, ran riot, coinciding also with the formation of a very large number of railway companies. Ashurst & Son acted (jointly with another old-established City firm, Sudlow & Sons & Torr) on the flotation of one railway company in 1845.[25] The Direct London and Manchester Railway Company had a capital of £5m; its chairman was John Dillon of Morrisons and its directors included such Manchester worthies as two aldermen. Its prospectus assured those thinking of investing in the company that 'the interests of the Public and the interests of the Proprietors are identical', a necessary assurance at a time of feverish 'railway mania'.

Not surprisingly the bubble burst; from late in 1845 there emerged increasing evidence of 'the fertility of invention among the promoters of joint-stock companies', or as the *Morning Chronicle* graphically put it in April 1846:

This mirror of national hallucination when every bubble was invested with a value as the true offspring of English joint-stock genius, shows the progress of the evil of a plethoric speculation, without at all unveiling the disastrous and uncalculated consequences of the period – consequences, which can only be thoroughly arrived at by visiting Whitecross-street and other debtors jails, half-peopled with projectors and speculators, who have sported in the late railway game.

Some idea of the dimensions of the 'railway mania' of the 1840s may be gleaned from the fact that, of the 9,000 miles of railway sanctioned by Parliament between 1844 and 1848, less than a quarter was actually built and opened for use. Although the firm began some company work in the 1840s, it was not until the 1860s and the 1870s that it became a large part of the practice. In 1850 Ashurst & Son acted on the flotation of the Financial Union Bank of Paris; a quarter of its capital of £800,000 was to be raised in England.[26]

The surviving journals and accounts of the firm in the 1840s, although incomplete, are sufficient to indicate that the practice was thriving with many of the clients already mentioned still active and new clients such as the mustard manufacturers of Norwich, J & J Colman appearing. Ashurst's radical contacts continued to provide work; the Reform Club, established in 1836 (Sir William Molesworth was one of its most enthusiastic founders), was a client and Ashurst himself was a member. The Club opened at 104 Pall Mall but a year later was able to lease the site of 101–3 Pall Mall and commission the building it has occupied ever since, designed by Sir Charles Barry. Here the members enjoyed a 'palatial luxury', not apparently intended by the hard core Radicals when the Club was established.[27] The annual subscription was then eight guineas, an amount that Ashurst could well afford given that his income from the profits of the practice was running, in the second half of the 1840s, at £2,000 a year. William junior was allowed £600 a year from the profits, an amount that was not increased after he married in 1846. He and his wife Elizabeth (née Ogle), known in the family always as Bessie, went to live at Park Village West, Regents Park, where the 'pretty but sophisticated cottages' had been planned by Nash.[28]

At the end of the decade there were changes in the office. William Shaen left early in 1849 to establish his own practice and Ashurst's son-

**Ashurst
& Son**

The Reform Club was established by and for the radicals in 1836. Ashurst acted for the Club and he, and later his son, William, were members. This photograph of the interior of the club was taken in the 1990s; it has not changed since it was built.

in-law, Sydney Hawkes also left to go into partnership in business – the Swan Brewery in Fulham – with his brother-in-law, James Stansfeld. Both had, apparently, found the law (Stansfeld had been called to the Bar in 1849) unprofitable. 'Both had to earn a livelihood and both wished to have time and opportunity for taking part in public affairs.' Ashurst helped them to establish themselves in the brewing business with a loan of £2,300 each. In the office Ashurst had the assistance of the 'faithful' Mr Waller (see page 17) and of another articled clerk, John Morris, 'industrious, punctual, intelligent and determined to get on'.[29]

Morris was born at South Molton, a small town in North Devon on

12 December 1823, the grandson of a successful builder in the town, after whom he was named. John Morris the elder had built a new market in South Molton in 1806 and, in the following year, had hung a new peal of bells in the parish church. He married twice and had seven children. George Morris, his third and youngest son was a wool-stapler and he was the father of John Morris, the solicitor with whom we are concerned.[30] South Molton was, by Morris's own account 'a very sleepy place and it was said that you might fire a gun in the principal street in the afternoon without risk of hurting anybody'. It seems that the grandfather's wealth had been dissipated by the family by the time John Morris came of an age to embark on a career, for, as he recalled:

What chance I should have had with the small patrimony my grandfather left me if I had, in accordance with his wishes followed his business, I don't know, but his old Solicitor, Mr Gilberd Pearce, a worthy gentleman well known in our parts as an honest lawyer, offered me a seat in his office.

Morris spent three years in Pearce's office, becoming 'well-grounded in the practice of a Country Solicitor', and then, in 1841 he came to London and joined Ashurst as an office clerk.

He went on to record: 'In 1845 Mr Ashurst offered me my Articles on condition of my serving for ten instead of the usual period of five years, to which I agreed. Mr Ashurst said that at the end of that time he hoped to be able to do something more for me.' In the event Morris was admitted as a solicitor in 1851 and he was then employed by the Ashursts as a senior managing clerk, earning weekly £3 9s, then the highest salary paid. This rose to a more princely four guineas a week at the beginning of 1854, five shillings more than the weekly salary of his fellow and longer-serving senior managing clerk, Waller.

By 1854 Ashurst senior – who was 63 – was seeking to reduce his commitments. In April that year he and his son came to an agreement with William Rutter, a solicitor practising at 5 Hare Court, Temple. The Ashursts had been appointed as solicitors to the Commercial Credit Mutual Assurance Society when it was established in 1852. Part of their work was the recovery of debts owing to the Society and it was this that they had apparently found onerous. The agreement with Rutter provided that he should act as their agent for this work, in return for an annual fee of £50 plus a third of the profit on all legal business transacted for the Society.

Further evidence of Ashurst's desire to cut back his professional commitments is to be found in the new partnership agreement of June 1854, admitting John Morris as a partner. The agreement set out that the firm's capital, £1,000, was to be supplied by Ashurst and it was to practise under the name of Ashurst, Son & Morris; Morris was to be entitled to one-sixth of the profits of the business, the remainder to be shared by the Ashursts in proportions to be determined between them. The agreement was to run for 14 years but only a month after it was signed it was superseded by another agreement.

This admitted Waller as a partner on the same terms as Morris, entitled to one-sixth of the profits. It is tempting to speculate, given the closeness of the two agreements that Waller, who had been with the firm for much longer than Morris, had been angered at the latter's partnership and had in some way forced the Ashursts to make him a partner too. The agreement stipulated that during the first three years of the partnership Morris and Waller were limited to drawing an income of £250 from the business, to be increased thereafter to £300. There was an additional clause giving the Ashursts the right, in the first 10 years of its 14-year term, to terminate the partnership by giving three months' notice to Morris or Waller. Barely four months after the signing of the agreement, in November 1854, Ashurst gave notice to Waller of the dissolution of the

The firm's clerks were paid weekly and listed in the wages book by seniority.

partnership. It seems that the long connection with Waller had ended with a quarrel for Ashurst noted in his diary in November 1854 that, when he visited the office, Waller had been 'impudent'.[31]

This sequence of events suggests that all was not well at 6 Old Jewry in 1854. There are some signs in the firm's accounts and ledgers that the volume of work had fallen off in 1852 and 1853; the firm's profits for those years were not as high as they had been in 1848, although the difference was only about £1,000 (some £5,000 instead of £6,000). Individual client accounts are hard to identify but it does look as though there was less work, temporarily, for the Morrison businesses. The number of clerks employed in the office had also fallen (see below). Ashurst himself was, by his own account, not well and his diary entries in late 1854 refer to his son being troubled with a bad leg. If both the Ashursts were away from the office, new business may not have been so brisk.

The early 1850s was also a troubled time for the Ashurst family. In 1848, against the advice and wishes of her family, Eliza, the eldest daughter, who was 35 years old, married a French artisan whom she had met in Paris during the revolution in June that year. In 1850 she died in childbirth, much to the distress of her family who were unable to reach Paris, when news of her condition reached them, in time to see her before she died. A year later they had her body brought back to England and reburied in the plot that Ashurst had bought in the new cemetery at Highgate. Opened in 1839, the original 20-acre site had been, in the eighteenth century, part of the grounds of the mansion belonging to Sir William Ashurst, Lord Mayor of London in 1693 (and an ancestor of William Ashurst – see Chapter 1).

There had also been a disagreement between Ashurst's sons-in-law, Stansfeld and Hawkes, over the business of the Swan Brewery; brewing they found to be no more lucrative than the law and the partnership broke up with the departure of Hawkes for Newcastle. At the same time the Hawkes's marriage, which had been unhappy for some time, broke down and the couple separated. In 1852 Mrs Ashurst's health gave rise to concern and, although somewhat recovered in 1853, she was not well enough to accompany her husband on his long-wished-for first visit to America. Like many others of his generation, 'America was to him [Ashurst] a promised land: a visit to the great republic was the cherished ideal of his life'. In September 1853, when his visit ended and he left America for home, Ashurst's own health was 'feeble' according to his old friend, Lloyd Garrison, with whom *inter alia*, he had been staying.[32]

Despite the opening of the railway at Hornsey, which at last made the Ashurst home at Muswell Hill more accessible – a mere three-quarters of a mile walk from the station – the Ashursts gave up the house early in 1854 and moved south of the river, to Wood Vale in Forest Hill. Their stay there was short for, in October 1854, Mrs Ashurst died. It seems that Ashurst had already decided to retire from professional life; his diary entries in November and December 1854 record trips to town to sort out

The first page of a diary kept by William Henry Ashurst in 1854–5.

his affairs and call in some of the debts owing to him. A large amount was outstanding in charges to James Morrison and, early in December Morrison's son, Charles, agreed to pay Ashurst an annuity of £400 a year. Ashurst also spent some time looking for a new house. 'What we want,' he wrote in his diary on 4 December 1854, after a wasted trip to Blackheath to see a house that was suitable but already let, 'is a house near a station and that station a good one, with plenty of town accommodation, yet on a hill.'

In the event, as his health deteriorated early in 1855, Ashurst gave up the search for a new house and lived for several months with his daughter Caroline and her husband, James Stansfeld. He continued to keep his diary until the spring, when he moved to Wimbledon to join his son and daughter-in-law who had just moved there. Mazzini visited him there in 1855; he wrote to Emilie who was by then in Genoa, describing the house as beautiful but remote, and a long way from a station. He went on to say: 'Your father is rather better in some respects, but he seems to me more and more entangled in his speaking.'[33] Ashurst died on 13 October 1855 and was buried in Highgate Cemetery.

In his will Ashurst left the business, the Old Jewry building and its contents to his son William. The remainder of his estate – totalling between £35,000 and £40,000 – was to be put into a trust, administered by his two old friends and fellow radicals, John Dillon and Peter Taylor, for the benefit of all his children and their families. Ashurst's investments, many of them made in the 1840s, took some time to realise for, apart from his insurance policies and investments in some railway shares, he had bought a number of reversions and mortgages and invested in all kinds of property. He owned, for example, 12 freehold pews in the Chapel of St George in Plymouth, which produced an annual rent of some £43. They were sold by auction in November 1859 for £299 10s. Ashurst had spent more than £400 on an electric light patent in 1849, but his executors found it to be 'valueless', and the Gutta Percha patents (see page 70) which he owned and bequeathed specifically to his son were refused by the latter and sold for £300. Ashurst's investments, while partly a matter of choice, also illustrate well the limited investment opportunities there were at the time. By contrast those of his son in the 1870s – most of them in company shares and property – evidence the widening of investment opportunities that took place between the 1840s and the 1870s.

Ashurst & Son

Following Ashurst's retirement and the dissolution of the partnership formed in July 1854, the practice was carried on by Ashurst junior and John Morris, and there are signs in the surviving documents that the practice soon began to recover from the doldrums of the early 1850s. Apart from Morris and Waller there had been in 1853 only seven clerks in the office, compared with about a dozen in the heyday of Ashurst's practice in the 1830s and 1840s. Their salaries in 1853 ranged from £1 11s 6d (£1.57) down to the seven shillings (35p) a week earned by the office boy. The average weekly salary bill was £15 in that year. By 1855 the number of staff employed had risen to 11 and the firm was paying out a total weekly salaries bill averaging £25.

Scanty information survives as to the lives and families of these men (and boys), often struggling to maintain and improve themselves in respectable employment. Most of them lived close to the City so that they could walk to work, for such transport as there was – mainly horse-drawn omnibuses – was too expensive for a clerk on a daily basis. Not untypical was David Harris, a clerk in the office in 1843, when he witnessed the affidavit certifying that William Ashurst junior had paid the necessary stamp duty on his articles, but no longer with the firm in the 1850s. Harris lived in Upper Rosoman Street, Wilmington Square, a

The firm's wages books give an indication of its size at various times.

street named after the manager of Sadlers Wells and close to the junction of Rosebery Avenue and the Farringdon Road, an easy walk to the office, then in Cheapside.

Perhaps some of them would have described their situation in the same way as Charles Dickens's Mr Guppy in *Bleak House*:

My present salary, Miss Summerson, at Kenge and Carboys [solicitors in Lincolns Inn], is two pounds a week. When I first had the happiness of looking upon you, it was one-fifteen, and had stood at that figure for a lengthened period. A rise of five has since taken place, and a further rise of five is guaranteed at the expiration of a term not exceeding twelve months from the present date. My mother has a little property, which takes the form of a small life annuity; upon which she lives in an independent though unassuming manner, in the Old Street Road. She is eminently calculated for a mother-in-law. She never interferes, is all for peace, and her disposition easy. She has her failings – as who does not? – but I never knew her to do it when company was present; at which time you may freely trust her with wines, spirits or malt liquors. My own abode is lodgings at Penton Place, Pentonville. It is lowly, but airy, open at the back, and considered one of the 'ealthiest outlets'. Miss Summerson! In the mildest language, I adore you. Would you be so kind as to allow me (as I may say) to file a declaration – to make an offer!

The move from managing clerk to partner enabled John Morris to marry in 1854, his proposal not meeting with summary dismissal, the fate of Mr Guppy's. His wife, Sarah Taylor, came from Leicestershire.

For seven years, Ashurst junior and Morris were in partnership at 6 Old Jewry and during that time the firm acted on some new company issues: in 1861 there was the London and Colonial Bank and, in the same year, the Paris Land Company (John Dillon was a director of it) and in 1862 there was the Greenland Company, 'for trading in furs, skins, oils and other Produce and working Mines of Copper and Silver-Lead and Tin under special concessions granted by His Majesty the King of Denmark'.[34] Ashurst dealt with the company work and continued to act for many of his father's radical clients and friends such as Peter Taylor and George J Holyoake; to the latter Ashurst lent money to help his publishing ventures. Like his father, Ashurst was a member of the Reform Club (the annual subscription had increased to 10 guineas by 1859) and he was also a member of, and solicitor to, the Whittington Club. This had been established in premises on the Strand in 1846 and, uniquely, offered full and equal membership to women.

The firm's journal for 1859–60 evidences many clients from the 1840s for whom the firm still acted, including Morrison Dillon & Co. and individual members of the Morrison family, as well as new clients such as the printers Petter & Galpin (see Chapter 3), the printers and publishers, Ward & Lock and the jewellers, Mappin & Webb. Morris also concerned himself with matters such as Chancery litigation, which took him to New York in 1858 and Admiralty law on which he had lectured to students at the Law Society in 1859. It was Morris who dealt with Emilie Ashurst Hawkes's divorce, after the passage of the Act in 1857 which for the first time made a divorce obtainable without an Act of Parliament. He travelled to Italy in May 1861 to tell Emilie that she was free to remarry.[35] In June that year, at Kensington Registry Office, she married Carlo Venturi (1829–66), a Venetian, who was a friend and follower of Mazzini.

In October 1862 the post of Solicitor to the Post Office became vacant when its incumbent died and William Ashurst was invited to accept the appointment. Given his connection with the Hill family as a schoolboy and his father's work for the introduction of the penny post, no appointment could have been more attractive to him. His withdrawal from the firm marked the end of the direct participation of the Ashurst family in the firm, although their connection with it continued for many years as Morris continued to act for members of the family. Ashurst was Solicitor to the Post Office until he died, in July 1879. According to his obituary notices, 'he gave himself up to the work of the office with great energy' and:

It fell to him, in addition to its ordinary duties, to do much laborious and anxious work in connection with the establishment of the telegraphic system and the important legislation, negotiations, and arrangements it involved. In all this work he exhibited great ability, combined with urbanity of manner, which made him popular with his professional brethren, even when he was opposed to them. Notwithstanding these important engagements connected with his office, he was ever ready to lend a helping hand towards the forwarding of all movements connected with popular progress and philanthropic objects.[36]

It is appropriate at this point to round off the accounts of the members of the Ashurst family. William junior and his wife Bessie had no children; Bessie died in 1896. Of the Ashurst daughters, only one, Matilda, had more than one child; Matilda and Joseph Biggs had four daughters but none of them married. Caroline Ashurst Biggs (1840–89) was a well-known feminist activist. Matilda herself died in 1866.

Emilie Ashurst Venturi lived until 1893. Her second marriage was short for her husband died in 1866 and Emilie (who had no children) spent the rest of her life working for radical and reform causes. Shortly before her death she was involved in Irish matters and before that, in the late 1870s and the early 1880s she worked with her brother-in-law, James Stansfeld in the campaign to repeal the Contagious Diseases Acts of the 1860s. Intended to protect members of the armed services, the legislation subjected women suspected of being prostitutes to detention without trial and compulsory examinations. Stansfeld abandoned a promising ministerial and Cabinet career to lead the campaign and, in 1886, the Acts were repealed. His wife, Caroline Ashurst Stansfeld died in 1885; the Stansfelds had one son, Joseph, whose descendants are today the only link with William Henry Ashurst.

CHAPTER 3
Exit Ashurst: enter Morris, Crisp & Morris

IN 1863 JOHN MORRIS became, by his purchase of the goodwill of the practice and the lease of the offices at 6 Old Jewry, the senior partner and, in effect, the sole proprietor of the firm established by Ashurst senior in 1822. At the age of 39 (he was not 40 until 12 December that year) his accession to the senior partnership of a distinguished City firm epitomised the kind of professional success, achieved by a combination of hard work and ability, so admired in the second half of the nineteenth century. Morris's chosen profession, which he himself characterised as 'the green pastures of the law', had offered him opportunities for advancement which he had not been slow to take. Depicted by Walter Morrison, son of the firm's most long-established client, as 'as high-minded a man as Mr Ashurst himself', neither his professional nor what is known of his private life evidence a commitment as wholehearted as that of Ashurst to radical causes, but the times were different. That Morris had also a keen eye for business and investment opportunities in the City and overseas, was to be amply demonstrated over the next 40 years.

Of Morris's standing and ability as a lawyer, the rapid growth of the firm's business, particularly during its first decade under his control, is a considerable witness. Walter Morrison's description, even allowing for some hyperbole in a public speech on a celebratory occasion, suggests the qualities accounting for his success:

He is a great Lawyer; possibly some of us have known Counsel who although not very learned in the Law have managed to get on to the Judicial Bench, but knowledge of Law is only part of the equipment of a great Solicitor ... We all admire Mr Morris'[s] calm judgement and thoroughness on any questions that may be submitted to him. He is a man who will tell his clients where the weak point is, if there should be a weak point, just as well as he will tell them the strong points of their position ... We all appreciate Mr Morris'[s] resource, his tact and his diplomatic ability. If you were ever to get into a tight place, I do not know anyone better in the City of London to get you out of it … Then I may speak of his administrative ability, which is great indeed, and which I do not think is an accompaniment of many lawyers engaged in their own professional business.

The terms on which Morris purchased the goodwill of the practice and the lease of 6 Old Jewry reflected both the size of the practice (in January 1863, 16 clerks were employed) and the value put on it, together with the expectation of the returns it would make. By an agreement signed on 21 January 1863 the partnership between Morris and Ashurst junior was dissolved on the latter's departure to take up his appointment as Solicitor to the Post Office. For the goodwill and the lease Morris was to pay Ashurst £15,000 in ten half-yearly instalments of £1,500 each, payable on 1 May and 1 November each year. Interest at 5 per cent a year was also payable on the amount outstanding from 1 May 1863. As security, several of Morris's insurance policies were assigned to Ashurst.

The agreement imposed certain conditions on Morris, as long as money was owing to Ashurst, that is until the end of 1867. Morris was not to draw more than £1,000 a year from the firm; this was, however, hardly a severe restraint for a man accustomed to earning, until relatively recently, a quarter of that sum. An income of £1,000 a year was, at that time, more than sufficient to sustain a comfortable middle-class standard of living. Ashurst's consent had to be sought and given to any partner Morris took into the business and half of any premium paid by a new partner had to be made over to

John Morris, 1823–1905, joined the firm as a clerk in 1841 and was admitted a solicitor in 1851. He was a partner 1854–1905 and senior partner 1863–1905.

Ashurst Morris Crisp

Ashurst. As to the name of the firm, the 'Son' had to be removed from the present title of Ashurst, Son & Morris and, only for the next ten years and as long as Morris himself was a partner, could 'Ashurst' be used as the first name of the firm.

Under the style of Ashurst & Morris the firm began the year 1863 in the City, then in the middle of a financial boom which lasted until 1866. The boom was stimulated and sustained largely by speculative activity on the Stock Exchange in the shares of many of the nearly 700 new companies registered in 1863, a number that rose to more than 900 in 1865.[1] Incorporation and flotation on such a scale were new, the result of changes in the law over the previous two decades (see page 35) and, as an increasing number of existing and new businesses chose to incorporate, company work became the most significant part of the practice of Morris and his partners for the rest of the century. According to Morris's own account, until 1862 the company work of Ashurst, Son & Morris had been largely the responsibility of Ashurst junior, helped by one or more of the clerks. Morris said that he then 'knew little or almost nothing about Company Law. I doubt if I had ever attended a Board Meeting, partly perhaps owing to my then slight deafness.'

This wallet was, according to its inscription, owned by John Morris when he first joined the firm in its Cheapside office.

Whether the new partner who joined Morris in 1863 was experienced in company law or not we do not know. Finlay Knight had been admitted in 1842 and, after his arrival, the firm practised, for the two years he was a partner, as Ashurst, Morris & Knight. It had a number of clients issuing prospectuses in those two years, including the Central Railway Company of Venezuela, the English & Russian Bank, the Kyffhauser Mining and Smelting Company and several hotel companies both at home – the Ramsgate and Broadstairs – and overseas – the Mediterranean and the Cannes companies.[2] In 1864 the firm's oldest client, the textile business of Morrison & Dillon, was sold to the newly incorporated Fore Street Warehouse Company which remained a client. The second generation of the Morrison family developed other extensive business interests (see Chapter 4) for which the firm acted.

The increasing amount of company work in the 1860s was concerned not only with the formation and flotation of companies and the drafting of articles of association and prospectuses. Over-ambitious plans, combined with the ups and downs of the trade cycle meant that some companies found themselves unable to continue in business and others were obliged to curtail their operations and sometimes seek a financial reorganisation. It was for this work that Morris proved to have a particular talent and, by the end of the decade, it had earned him (and the firm) a considerable reputation.

The first such scheme to come his way was the capital reorganisation of the Grand Trunk Railway of Canada, on which he was asked to act in 1863, probably through the firm's long connection with the Morrisons. Charles Morrison, the eldest son of James, had taken on most of his father's business interests which had included, since the 1840s, considerable investments in American railways.[3] The building of the American railways had provided a market for British investment, iron and engineering and the Grand Trunk was no exception to this. An ambitious project, the railway was intended to link the provinces of Canada with each other as well as with American agricultural centres in order to carry their grain to Canadian sea-ports. Conceived in the early 1850s, the company was formed in 1853 and, with the backing of British engineers and banks, most of its capital was raised in Britain by an issue of shares and debentures totalling nearly £3m.

However, political and financial problems bedevilled the railway's construction in Canada, delaying its completion and denying shareholders the anticipated returns. An attempt to raise more money by a further issue in 1860 was a failure. In 1861 Edward William Watkin, an entrepreneurial railway manager, was recruited from the Manchester, Sheffield & Lincolnshire Railway Company to become President of the Grand Trunk. It was with Watkin that Morris worked on the capital

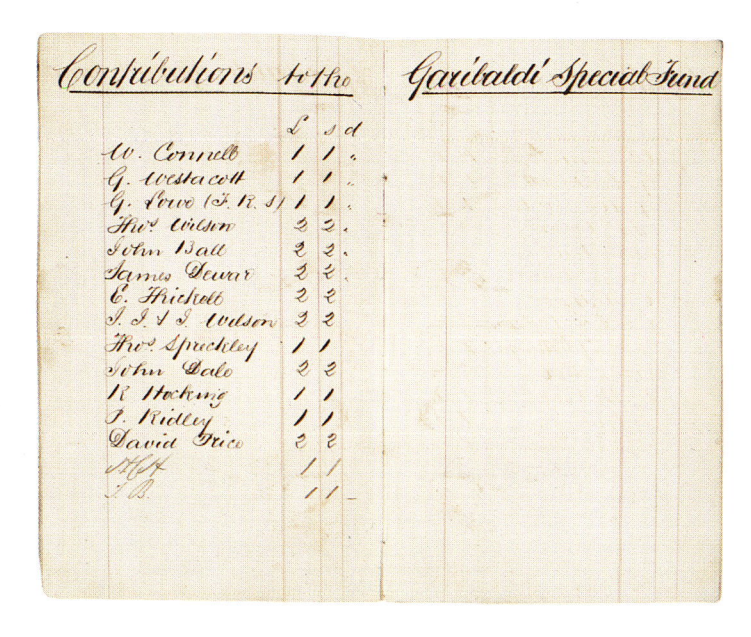

In 1860 the friends of Mazzini and Italian nationalism and unity in Britain established the Garibaldi fund to raise money for the military campaign. Prominent among them was William Ashurst. The notebooks detailing some of the contributions have survived among the firm's archives.

reorganisation, embodied in the Grand Trunk Arrangement Act of 1863, legislation which in Morris's own words, 'became in effect a second charter for that … company'.[4]

British investors, however, continued to pour money into American railways whose demand for capital seemed almost insatiable. By 1876 more than £100m of British money had been so invested and by the mid-1880s that amount had doubled. A good deal of British money went into the Erie Railway which had a chequered history, particularly under the control, from 1867 to 1872, of the notorious Jay Gould, an American stockbroker and speculator. In 1875 the Erie was forced into receivership and a London Committee formed to protect the interests of the British investors. Sir Edward Watkin was chairman of the Committee which also included among its members the merchant banker, Robert Fleming, who became a close friend and business associate of Morris. Through Watkin, Morris was called upon in 1875 to draft a 'friendly' reorganisation, that is a reorganisation of its capital structure, by agreement and compromise between the various holders of securities as opposed to reorganisation by foreclosure and sale.[5] Such arrangements became more common over the next two decades and Morris acted on a number of them.

It was not only, however, railway companies in the USA that provided the firm with work. The volume of traffic in London's busy streets and the congestion caused by the increasing number of horse-drawn omnibuses using the roads had led politicians, promoters and engineers to turn to the development of underground railways. The first of these – and the first in the world – the Metropolitan Line, opened to passengers in January 1863.[6] Its successful construction gave an immediate impetus to the promotion of other lines and, in the parliamentary session of 1863–4 the firm acted on the promotion of a Bill to extend the line so as to link its ends into an 'Inner Circle'. Other companies also promoted Bills with similar objectives at the same time but Morris's clients were successful in gaining parliamentary sanction to build the line between Westminster and High Street Kensington (later to become part of the District Line). In Morris's words, their success 'open[ed] up the whole of the South Kensington region, which up to that time had been chiefly market gardens or slums – the latter predominating'.

The main line railway companies also sought, at this time to bring their lines closer into the capital, among them the Great Eastern which had originally terminated at Mile End and, since 1840, at Shoreditch. To complete its City extension to a new terminus at Liverpool Street, the company required new capital at a time when its financial problems had already taken it into receivership. The firm acted for the receivers and was instrumental in the granting of a new Act in 1864 and ensuring that the capital could be raised. Morris recalled that the Great Eastern's 'then Chairman, (… Lord Salisbury) sent me a special letter of thanks for our part in it'.

In 1865 Finlay Knight's name disappeared from the firm and from the Law List; presumably he retired or died but his departure left Morris as the only partner in a busy and growing practice. This time he did not look outside for a partner but chose instead a qualified solicitor who had been working for the firm for some eight years. Thomas Morton Harvey

Building the District Line Railway in 1871. The firm had been involved with the establishment of the railway and acted for it when the early section linking Westminster and South Kensington was built.

Ashurst Morris Crisp

Liverpool Street Station, the new terminus for the Great Eastern Railway opened in 1874. The firm was involved in securing the necessary legislation in the 1860s.

had been admitted as a solicitor in 1847. He had joined the firm, then Ashurst, Son & Morris, in July 1857 on a weekly salary of £2 17s 8d; by early in 1861 he was being paid £4 4s 7d a week and in 1865 he became Morris's partner. In the 1866 Law List the firm appeared under the style of Morris & Harvey. By the terms of the agreement with Ashurst in 1863, this suggests that either Morris had been able to accelerate the payments and now owned the firm or that Ashurst had not approved the admission of Harvey as a partner. From 1866 until 1872/3 the firm seems not to have used the name 'Ashurst' in its styling, at least in the Law Lists, but in the 1873 List it re-emerged as Ashurst, Morris & Co.

Looking back many years later, Morris described the years from 1865 to 1875 as 'the most busy period of my professional life'. The great boom in incorporation and issue work of the early 1860s ended, at least for a time, in the wake of the failure of the discounting house of Overend Gurney & Co., long considered to be the largest, richest and most important discount house in the City. On Thursday, 10 May 1866 – a fine, hot day – Overend Gurney & Co. suspended payment with liabilities 'exceeding anything on commercial record' – the estimates varied from £10m to £18m. The following day, Friday, became known in the City as 'Black Friday'. Bank rate was raised to 9 per cent and 'distress and terror' spread in the City, according to contemporary accounts. Crowds of people poured into the City and blocked Lombard Street although as one writer wryly noted:

These persons were for the most part mere idlers, drawn thither by curiosity, desiring to see what a panic looked like, and themselves creating the very thing they wanted to see. Most probably, not one in a hundred of that multitude were concerned personally in the calamity which had occurred – those who had really suffered were not likely to spend their time gazing up at a harmless building; but great mischief was caused.[7]

Others rushed to withdraw their deposits from joint stock banks they now believed to be threatened. The English Joint Stock Bank had to suspend operations and only after the raising of the Bank Rate on Saturday to 10 per cent and the suspension of the Bank Charter Act did the panic begin to subside.[8] At the end of May, however, the Consolidated Bank undertook the protection of the Bank of London's creditors after it had suspended, an act considered by the *Bankers' Magazine* to be one of insanity given the Bank of London's large and unsecured lendings to American railways. The Consolidated's directors, 'a few days later ... apparently alarmed by the magnitude of the engagements they had accepted, abruptly closed their own doors'.[9] On 7 June, Agra and Mastermans Bank, a colonial bank with a large business in India, stopped payment. Morris became deeply involved in the drafting of a scheme of arrangement for the Agra Bank which, with the approval of Vice-Chancellor Wood (later Lord Chancellor Hatherley) enabled the bank, some six months later, to be brought out of liquidation and reconstituted. A similar scheme led to the re-opening of the Consolidated Bank, which then flourished independently until 1896, when it amalgamated with Parr's Bank.

The collapse of Overend Gurney & Co. so soon after its incorporation, which had taken place only in July 1865, not surprisingly created a lack of confidence in the process of incorporation. The partners in Overend Gurney had, some time before incorporation, diversified their investments: '... they covered the sea with their ships, ploughed up the land with their iron roads',[10] and over-extended their capital. As the post-mortem revealed, the firm had already been bankrupt when it was incorporated.

Dealing with these 'important and exceptionally difficult cases' was a strain, Morris admitted, some 40 years later. What kept him 'as fresh as a lark' (a description of him given by the chairman of the Consolidated Bank) were his long weekends in the country. Morris had by then acquired a country house, Abbotscliff, near Folkestone in Kent and, he recalled, 'it was a common habit for me to get off by the late mail train on Friday night and stop until the first train on Monday morning, thus sleeping three nights out of seven in that bracing air'. He had also, in the early 1850s, adopted a system of daily physical exercise developed by the Swede, Ling, to which he adhered for the rest of his life and to which he attributed his health and strength. His regime at the age of 80, when he was in partial retirement, was an adaptation of that he had followed since the 1850s and he described it thus:

Rise between 5 and 6, exercises 30 minutes, lying down again until 7.15, not for more sleep, but as affording a spare hour or so at the best working time of the day, which I would not lose on any account; then half an hour in the open air. Breakfast and reading the papers 8.30 to 9.30; the rest of the day to dinner time, general occupations (including more exercises). Dinner at 7.30. Reading &c. afterwards; retiring at 10 o'clock.

Wherever he went, he continued with his exercises and, as his partner Frank Crisp (see below), related, this could and did on at least one occasion lead to misunderstanding. During a visit to Egypt in 1902 Morris was:

camping out up country in the desert. One morning, early, his Secretary heard a great commotion, and looking out of his tent saw a ring of Arabs, and in the middle Mr Morris, in a nearly nude state going through his exercises. The Arabs were, as they thought, cooperating by frantic invocations to Allah, evidently under the impression that the exercises were a form of religious worship at sunrise. We must all regret, I certainly do, that we could not have a photograph of this unique scene.

By 1867 Morris and his wife, Sarah, had six children, five sons and one daughter. The education of his children and the maintenance of two houses – Morris's London home then was in Park Street and in 1871 there were three servants in residence there, a cook, a parlourmaid and a manservant – suggest that his professional success was increasingly remunerative.[11] The acquisition of a country house is one indication of Morris's growing prosperity; another is to be found in the fact that in 1868 he could afford to invest £5,000 in the business of one of his clients, the publishing house of Cassell & Co.

John Cassell, who had for some years been involved in the production of temperance journals, along with marketing 'non-alcoholic' tea and coffee, brought out the first issue of a new weekly newspaper, *The Standard of Freedom,* in May 1848. Soon afterwards Cassell became a member of the Association for Promoting the Repeal of Taxes on Knowledge (the taxes on paper and the stamp duty on newspapers), a cause with which William Ashurst senior had been closely associated; in December 1852 Ashurst had accompanied the Association's Committee to a meeting with Lord John Russell at the Foreign Office. The Association had become a client of Ashurst and then, in the early 1850s, of John Morris. When Cassell & Co. became a client of the firm is not certain; Cassell's early success led him to expand quickly. In 1851 he moved his publishing house into the Belle Sauvage, an old coaching inn at the bottom of Ludgate Hill and in his enthusiasm to publish 'good educational and recreational reading for the working man' he expanded his list so quickly that he was bankrupt in all but name by 1855.[12]

At this point Petter & Galpin, a printing business which was also a client of the firm, effectively bought Cassell's business, forming a new partnership with Cassell and continuing to use his name for the publications although he was effectively barred from control. Cassell died in 1865 and, with the business now prospering, Petter & Galpin decided to expand with the launch of a new daily evening paper, *The Echo*; it was to the financing of this that Morris contributed his £5,000 in 1868. The first issue of *The Echo* appeared on 8 December 1868, its leader promising a fearless examination of institutions while demanding, at the same time, universal education and the ending of sectarian domination of education. Although the paper gained a high reputation, it did not acquire a circulation to match and, in 1875 it was sold by Cassell & Co. It subsequently passed through the hands of several proprietors, all of whom failed to make money out of it, before it finally stopped publication in 1905.[13] Fortunately for John Morris's investment, much of Cassell's output was profitable, at least until the 1890s.

Barely had the City begun to recover from the damage caused by Overend Gurney when, in August 1869, the Albert Life Assurance Company failed. Although by no means on the same scale, the collapse of the Albert, it was estimated, affected more than 25,000 people.

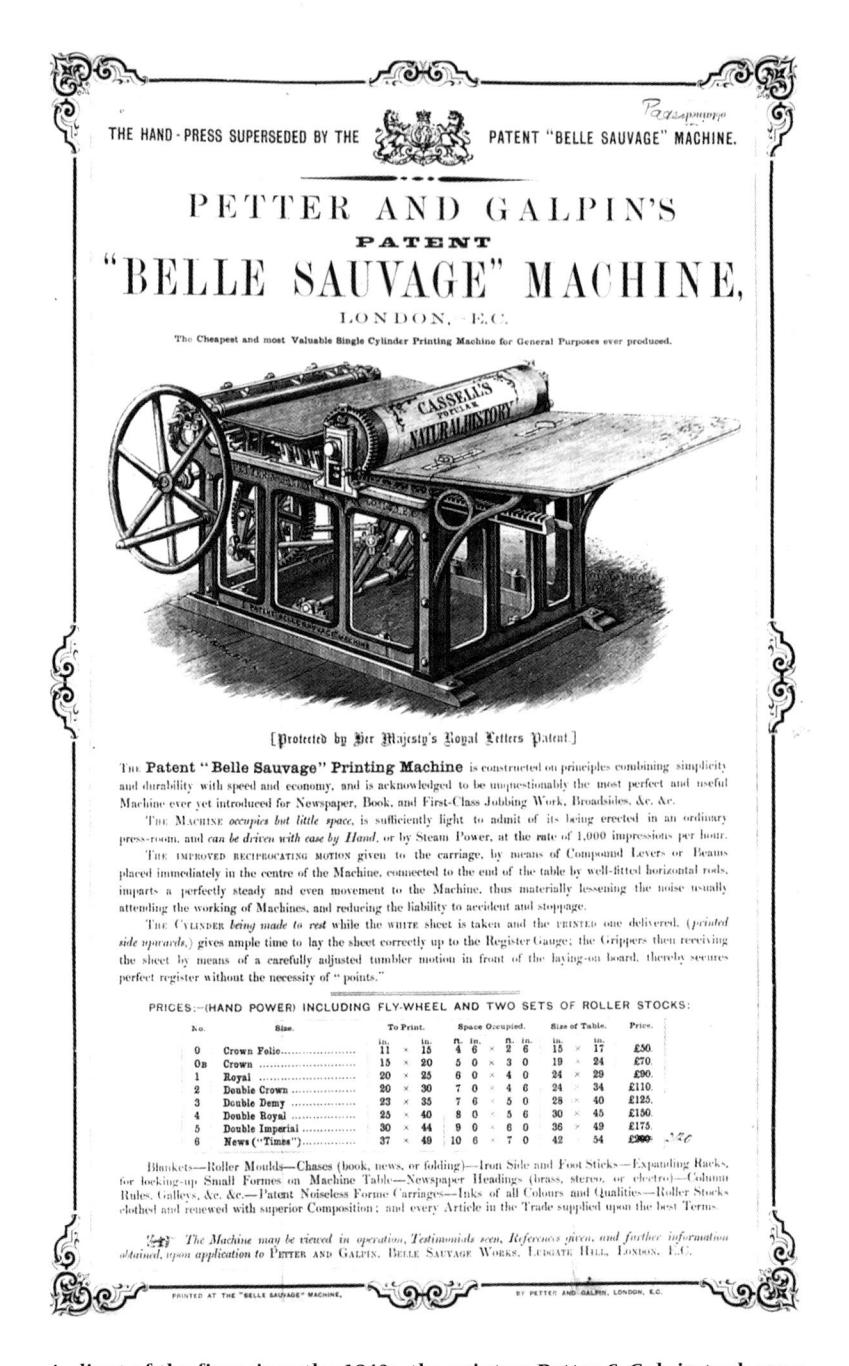

A client of the firm since the 1840s, the printers Petter & Galpin took over the publishing business of John Cassell in 1855, and the firm continued to act for both businesses through the nineteenth century.

Established in 1838, the Albert had been an acquisitive and under-capitalised company; its failure was attributed to poor management – and worse – by the angry shareholders and policy-holders of the parent and its many associated companies. Efforts to devise a satisfactory reconstruction to take the company out of liquidation failed.

The firm acted for the company in this crisis and Morris himself was involved in 'getting a special Act passed referring the winding up of the whole of these Companies [the Albert's 30 or 40 associated companies] to the arbitration of Lord Cairns, with the fullest powers'.[14] Shortly afterwards Morris was instrumental in drafting the Bill which became the Joint Stock Companies Arrangement Act 1870, making it possible for a scheme of arrangement to be approved by the Court when 75 per cent of the creditors agreed rather than seeking total unanimity as before. It was, Morris claimed some 30 years later, a matter of pride to him that the Act had benefited businesses in liquidation and their creditors. In the matter of the Albert Life, Morris's clerk, J. Green assisted him with this work, attending a meeting in the Vice-Chancellor's Court, representing the company, on 8 September 1869 to oppose the winding-up order. Green, who had been with the firm since 1865, was an admitted man, paid a managing clerk's salary of some £4 a week, as had been Morris and Harvey before they became partners.

Serious as the collapse of the Albert Life Assurance Company was, it did not, more than momentarily, disturb the equilibrium of the City's financial life. The growth of business in the City in the late 1860s and early 1870s arose from a combination of factors; more foreign loans were floated on the Stock Exchange and the cable link to the United States (laid under the Atlantic in 1866) brought faster communication between the old and the new worlds and a greater volume of trading and commerce with the USA. By 1871 some 42,000 telegrams a year were being exchanged between London and New York. These developments were part of a process which, by the early 1870s, culminated in a recognition that the City's significance as an international financial centre had markedly changed. The *Quarterly Review* noted in 1872: '… the unquestioned stability and credit of English institutions, the benefit of firm and equal laws, and the facilities and inducements of the freest ports, the lowest tariff and the cheapest manufacturers in the world, … render London the place of ultimate settlement of the largest part of the business of both hemispheres'.[15]

These changes inevitably led to more work for City lawyers and were reflected in the expansion of Morris & Harvey's practice and establishment. By the late 1860s the firm's surviving salary books indicate that a considerable growth had taken place. In January 1869 there were 39 clerks employed in the offices at Old Jewry, more than double the number of six years before; the weekly bill for salaries in 1869, at some £60, was double the amount it had been in 1861 and 1862 and the increase came from employing more rather than paying more; not untypical of the firm's employees was Mr Kitsell, who had been earning £1 9s a week in 1853, an amount that by 1869 had increased to £1 10s, a rise over 16 years of one shilling! Between 1850 and 1873 prices rose steadily and in many industries wages also rose, keeping pace with the price increases. The salaries of law clerks, however, seem to have remained remarkably stable through the nineteenth century and the clerks were probably eager to augment their incomes with overtime. In some weeks when the office was particularly busy, a further £5 or more was paid for overtime work, distributed between a number of clerks. The 39 clerks listed in January 1869 did not include the qualified men and the articled clerks so that in all the office strength was probably three times the size it had been in 1862. The firm now occupied all of 6 Old Jewry, 'a rabbit warren of

The number of clerks employed by the firm in the 1860s grew as the wages books clearly show.

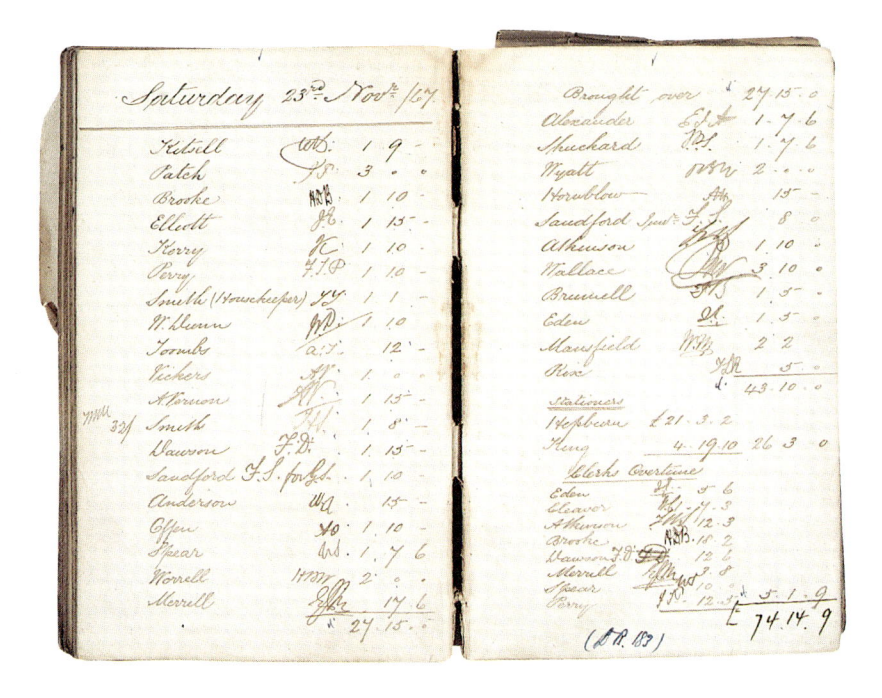

rooms at different levels',[16] whereas in the Ashursts' days it used only the back of the building and the front was let to another tenant.

The increasing volume and complexity of the practice are reflected in a change in the way the firm's books were kept at around this time. Since the 1830s the firm had operated on Ashurst's system although whether it was of his own devising or common practice at the time it is impossible to say. The starting point for all transactions was the waste book in which all letters, visits, notes, cash in and out etc. were entered on a daily basis. From this record, credit and debit entries were made in the firm's ledgers under appropriate clients' names, and accounts such as office expenses, disbursements, house accounts and individual partners. In the 1860s, probably in 1865 at the start of Morris's busiest decade, the waste books were given up and the firm moved on to a system of more elaborate cash journals in which daily entries were made and from which the matters recorded were transferred to the ledgers. By the early 1870s the volume of transactions was such that a cash journal sometimes only sufficed for a period of six months – for example, April–September 1872 – whereas the earlier series of waste books and ledgers, even in the relatively busy days of the late 1840s, covered several years.

Among the articled clerks were two who were nearing the end of their articles and were both admitted as solicitors in 1869. George Davis had been with the firm since 1861 and, following his admission in Michaelmas Term 1869, he became a partner. His fellow articled clerk, Frank Crisp, was admitted in Hilary Term 1869 and he became a partner in 1871. The 1870 Law List described the firm as Morris, Harvey & Davis. In 1872 the listing changed to Morris, Harvey, Davis & Crisp. This did not, however, prove to be a long-lived partnership. It was dissolved in 1874 and Davis left the firm to establish himself in practice first at 52 Moorgate Street and later in Coleman Street. It seems likely that Davis was supported and encouraged by John Morris to set up on his own, that he was given some clients' work to start him off, shared on an agency basis with Davis paying agency fees to the firm; while partnership agreements were then more fluid than they later became, such an arrangement for sharing clients and fees was, it seems, rare if not unique (see also Chapter 4). Harvey remained at 6 Old Jewry until 1879 but was not a party to the new partnership agreements of the 1870s.

Of Crisp, who over the next 50 years became one of the most eminent and distinguished company lawyers in the City, much more is known. Born in 1843, he was the only son of John Shalders Crisp, a printer and the grandson of John Childs of Bungay in Suffolk, also a printer and a long-established client of Ashurst and the firm (see Chapter 2). John Crisp, a native of Norwich, had been apprenticed to Childs and married his only daughter, Harriet Childs. John Morris, on a business visit to Childs in 1847 or 1848 had met Frank Crisp as a child and recalled that:

during his [Childs'] reading of a chapter of the Bible before the daily family prayers he ordered the servant to take out his little grandson, then about four years old, because he was inattentive. I said to Mr Childs afterwards that I thought it was a little strong to order the removal of the boy because he moved his feet, to which he bluffly replied 'Sir, train up a child in the way he should go.'

Crisp's parents lived in Nelson Square, 'a quiet secluded spot on the East side of Blackfriars Bridge', conveniently located for John Crisp's work with the publishers, Ward & Co. (also clients of the firm), in Paternoster Row. Frank Crisp was educated privately, from 1854 (when he was 11 years old) to 1857 at Central Hill House in Norwood, South London where William Hainworth was then the headmaster. For board and tuition Crisp's father paid the sum of 19 guineas for the half-year but there were also extras, with varied instruction including drilling, dancing, playing the flute and surveying. Crisp then completed his schooling with two years at University College School in Gower Street. Originally he was attracted to engineering as his profession, but in his last months at school he decided instead upon the law.[17]

His introduction to the office was recalled, some 40 years later, by John Morris.

… his uncle, Mr Charles Childs, came to me and asked if I would allow him to come to our office as an articled clerk. I said 'What sort of young fellow is he?' 'Well,' he said, 'he is such a many-sided boy that it is not easy to describe him; but I may say that at home we call him "the cat".' 'Why?' I said. He replied: 'Because, like a cat, he always falls on his feet.' That was quite enough to satisfy me.

My young friend came, was articled and entered on his duties at the office, to which he was most assiduous, until one day, he came and asked me for two or three days' leave of absence, as he was going up for his examination at the London University. I said: 'What do you mean? You cannot get a degree at the London University without great proficiency and giving much time to it.' However, he not only got through all right, but took his degree in all the examinations in the first class.

By 1867 Crisp was earning a salary of £250 per annum and in that year he married Catherine Howes. Crisp was, by all accounts, a glutton for work all his life. He passed the Law Society examinations in 1869 with honours.

Morris was by no means the only one to see the possibilities in Crisp. Some 50 years later, a friend of Crisp recalled that around 1870 there was a memorable encounter between Crisp and Baron Bramwell (1808–92), 'as shrewd a judge of men as of their affairs'. They met by chance 'during a vacation in Switzerland and [Bramwell] formed and – with wonted virility – expressed a high opinion of his abilities and confidently predicted a brilliant future for him'.[18]

It was to Frank Crisp in 1873 that John Morris's nephew, William Morris, was articled. William Morris was the elder and only surviving son of John Morris's brother, William, known in the family (to distinguish him from its many other Williams), as William of Hove, the town in whose development he was much interested and in which he chose to live from the 1880s following his retirement after a long and successful commercial career in London.

William Morris senior was *inter alia* a promoter of tramway companies in London and in many other European cities. The development of the horse-drawn tram had taken place in the United States where tramways had spread rapidly in the 1850s. The rails enabled a heavier load to be pulled by the horses than in an omnibus and the ride was smoother. It was also considered to be a safer mode of transport than the omnibus because the tramcar was fitted with a brake, rather than having to rely, as did the omnibus, on the driver pulling up the horses.

As a boy Frank Crisp was a pupil for three years at Central Hill House, a private school in Norwood, South London. This school bill shows boarding and tuition fees and extras.

But the first attempt to introduce trams to central London in the early 1860s met with fierce opposition and failed.

However by 1868 when John Bright, a tramcar enthusiast, became President of the Board of Trade, public opinion was changing. Three companies put forward Bills in 1869, two of which, the Metropolitan Street Tramways and the Pimlico, Peckham and Greenwich Street Tramways, were clients of John Morris. Moreover his brother, William, owned half of the issued shares of the Pimlico, Peckham and Greenwich Company, with Danish and American investors holding the rest. Parliament authorised all three companies and the first section of the Pimlico, Peckham and Greenwich Street Tramways which ran between Blackheath Hill and New Cross, opened in December 1869.[19]

The Glasgow Tramway & Omnibus Company was floated in 1871, as was the Edinburgh Tramways Company, two of the first of a large number of tramway companies for which the firm acted over the next two decades, many of them promoted by William Morris senior. The British and Foreign Tramways Company, of which Morris senior was a director, was floated in 1872 with the firm acting jointly with Baxter, Rose, Norton & Co.; its prospectus told would-be investors:

The intention of the Company is generally to invest its own capital in the construction and development of the Tramways selected by it, and to dispose of the same from time to time when tested by the experience of actual working, in which way the public will be protected against unsound and merely speculative projects.

Three members of the Morris family were partners in the firm.

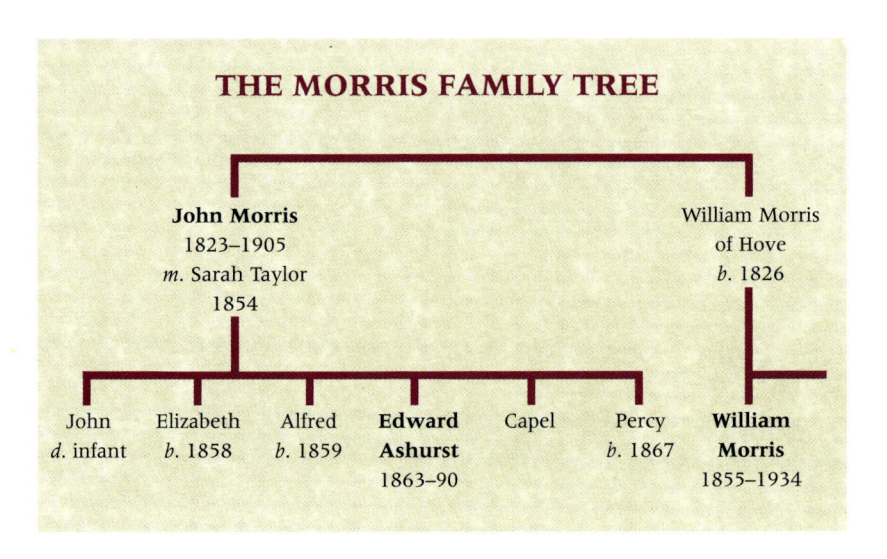

THE MORRIS FAMILY TREE

- **John Morris** 1823–1905, *m.* Sarah Taylor 1854
- **William Morris of Hove** *b.* 1826

Children of John Morris:
- John *d.* infant
- Elizabeth *b.* 1858
- Alfred *b.* 1859
- **Edward Ashurst** 1863–90
- Capel
- Percy *b.* 1867

Child of William Morris of Hove:
- **William Morris** 1855–1934

It was, in a way, a kind of investment trust in tramways; the prospectus went on to say that the directors were to be paid a fixed sum of £150 a year each plus 5 per cent of the profits in excess of 10 per cent.[20]

William Morris senior's son, William, with whom we are largely concerned, was born in 1855 and educated in Norwich and then in London at King's College School, at that time still the junior department of the College (the move to Wimbledon was not made until 1897). He first thought of accountancy as his profession and spent some months in an accountant's office before taking articles in his uncle's office at 6 Old Jewry. Early in 1874 he was ill with 'some slight bronchial trouble' and, in his own words:

Sir Andrew Clarke was consulted. He said there was nothing serious, but 'to make assurance doubly sure,' as he put it, he advised a voyage to Australia. Accordingly in February, 1874, I sailed from Gravesend for Sidney in Devitt and Moore's Hawkesbury, *1,200 tons. The passage was made in 77 days which was considered very fast, as the ordinary passage from London to Melbourne took about 90 days.*

It is interesting to note that there was at that time only one regular mail a month, by P and O to Australia, also that there was then no liner afloat of more than 5,000 tons.

After spending about six months in Australia I returned home by way of India, China, Japan, America and Canada, arriving at Liverpool in the middle of 1875.

He returned to Old Jewry to take up his articles again and his office diary for the following year, 1876, brief though the entries in it are, offers some insights into the work of an articled clerk at that time as well as into the firm's clients.

In 1876, the first day of January was a Saturday and found young Morris in the office as usual; throughout the nineteenth century City solicitors' offices stayed open on Saturdays, the only concession sometimes

The tram became a very popular mode of city transport in the 1870s, in European cities as well as in those of Britain. The firm acted on the flotation of a large number of tram companies.

being that they closed a little earlier than on a weekday. Much of his work seems to have been on his father's business affairs which had been handled by the firm for some time past. On Tuesday 4 January he recorded 'drafting and settling agreements between WM and Bache nearly all day'. (No further identification of Bache except that he was 'of Madrid' appears in the diary.) Later in January Morris was working on the affairs of the Thames Iron Works, drafting a case for the opinion of counsel.

Another client of the firm with whose affairs young Morris became concerned in 1876 was the Alexandra Palace Company. The success of the Crystal Palace Company in creating a venue for family outings in south London had led to a desire to emulate it in north London and in May 1873 the Alexandra Palace had opened to the public; the building had been used by the international exhibition of 1862 and then been reconstructed on a new site. However, 16 days after it opened, it burnt to the ground and the company which owned it decided to rebuild. The Palace, with its hall, concert room, reading room and theatre set in seven acres of grounds had re-opened in 1875 but it continued to be dogged by financial problems. Morris was working on a debenture issue for the company.[21]

Morris worked on various other company matters for clients as well as on the drafting of wills and dealing with probates. Much of his time was spent in the office but there were occasional visits to other City solicitors and to barristers' chambers. The Easter weekend gave him Friday and Monday as holidays but other than that he spent six days a week in the office until 4 August when his summer holiday started. He returned to the office on 25 August, sadly not recording how or where he had spent his three-week leave. He took a long weekend at the end of September, being absent on a Friday and a Monday and on 15 November recorded that he went into the Common Law department. At the end of the year the Christmas break was short. He was in the office, he recorded, until 1 p.m. on 23 December, a Saturday, and he was back for a normal day on Wednesday 27 December. Morris was admitted as a solicitor in 1879.

In the 1870s the pace of incorporation quickened again and the firm handled more issues on the Stock Exchange. In 1872 it acted, again jointly with Baxter, Rose, Norton & Co. on the flotation of the British & Foreign Water & Gas Works Company, and two years later there was another joint appointment with the same firm for the flotation of the

Saratov Water Works Company. Another of the City's textile businesses was incorporated in 1874 when the assets of the Wood Street Warehouse, owned by the Pawson family, were sold to the London Warehouse Company.[22]

The firm had, in these years, an increasing parliamentary practice, sufficient apparently to justify the opening of a separate Westminster office at 22 Abingdon Street in 1872. It was manned by six clerks, five of whom certainly came from Old Jewry, and there was a housekeeper. The office handled the work in promoting Bills for the Manchester Hydraulic Power Company in 1872, for the North Wales and Chester & Birkenhead Railway and a large number of provincial tram companies. By June 1873 the number of clerks had risen to a peak of nine but thereafter started to decline. A year later only four clerks were employed in the Abingdon Street office and in September 1874 it was closed.

John Morris's busiest professional decade had ended with the reconstruction of the American railway company, the Erie, in 1875 and in the course of that he had made another visit to the USA. Now in his early fifties and notwithstanding his healthy regime of diet and exercise, he succumbed in 1876 to a bout of illness and spent a period of time at home in Park Street; his nephew, William, recorded in his diary a visit there on professional matters on 30 March. The time at home, however, gave him space to reflect, not least on the extent of the energy and ability shown in the last five years by his young partner, Frank Crisp. As a result, he wrote to Crisp from his home in April in the following terms:

Notwithstanding your strongly expressed repugnance to anything being done during my illness to put into a proper shape our partnership re-arrangements, consequent on the dissolution with Davis & Harvey, I cannot refrain availing myself of a bright day to do what ought to have been done long before.

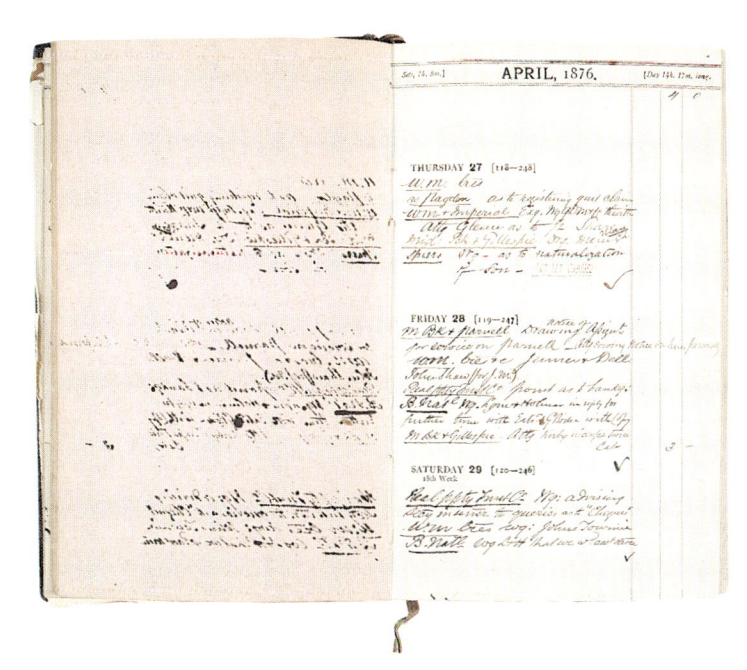

William Morris (1855–1934), a nephew of John Morris, was articled at the firm. This is an extract from his office diary of 1876, indicating some of the work he undertook as an articled clerk.

> *When the change before referred to took place I told you I wished to increase your share to a 7th – I subsequently determined (& I think so told you) to increase it to a 5th as the best acknowledgement I could make of your wonderful devotion to all the duties cast upon you.*

Morris went on to outline the details of the new partnership agreement which was to be drawn up in the office. It was to date from 30 September 1874 and to last for 14 years. He would, he said, 'continue to find the capital for the business & ... be free from obligation to give more personal attention to it than I think fit and to be at liberty to engage in any other business'.

In further recognition of Crisp's position, he would give 'all power of dissolution' to Crisp and 'the power whenever you think fit of having your name introduced into the Firm'.[23] In the Law List issued in January 1878 the entry for the firm was, for the first time, Ashurst, Morris, Crisp & Co. Over the next two decades Crisp's work as a company lawyer grew and did much to enhance the reputation of the firm. Before we explore that, however, it is appropriate to examine some of the changes in the City in the 1880s and the new clients for whom John Morris and his nephew William acted.

CHAPTER 4
The firm and the Morrises in the 1880s

Ashurst Morris Crisp

IN THE LATE 1870s and the early 1880s 'new technology' – to use the terminology of the late twentieth century – in the shape of the telephone and electric lighting arrived in the City. It was not inappropriate that the partners in the firm of Ashurst, Morris, Crisp & Co. were instrumental in securing the adoption of these inventions; it was the firm's founder, William Ashurst, who had argued that 'New discoveries will only open new fields of activity and usefulness ... the more communication is facilitated, and mind communes with mind, the greater will be the happiness resulting to man'.[1]

The exploitation of the invention of the telephone was enthusiastically taken up by John Morris within a year or so of its invention, when few appreciated its potential. The term 'telephone' had, since the 1850s, described instruments used to carry the sound of speech across short distances such as one room to another or across the inner quadrangle of a building. The first such instruments were large, concave reflectors but they were soon followed by the development of 'speaking tubes', a device which claimed to enable conversations in noisy environments – on trains, in omnibuses, on ships and in the theatre – to be heard.

'Railway Conversation Tubes', advertised by the manufacturers as 'small and cheap' enabled travellers 'to converse with ease and pleasure ... notwithstanding the noise of the train. This can be done in so soft a whisper as not to be overheard even by a fellow-traveller. They are portable, and will coil up so as to be placed inside the hat.' The tubes were made of gutta percha, a rubber-like substance manufactured from tree-sap, a patented process owned (in part) by the Gutta Percha Company; established in 1845, the company had been a client of the firm at that time and William Ashurst senior had become interested in it, buying a share in the patents (see page 42).[2]

Credit for the invention of the 'electric speaking telephone' in Boston in 1876 belongs to Alexander Graham Bell who, in 1877, visited England to publicise his invention. Queen Victoria, although finding the instrument 'extraordinary', soon had it installed on the Isle of Wight, at Windsor and in Buckingham Palace. The early telephone was, as George Bernard Shaw wrote, 'of such stentorian efficiency that it bellowed your most private communications all over the house instead of whispering them with some sort of discretion'. Shaw thought this made it particularly inappropriate for the City, where he was at the time working, but the Bank of England was quick to adopt the instrument, installing a line between Threadneedle Street and its West London Branch in Burlington Gardens in 1878. More typical was the reaction of a Norwegian bank manager who, after a demonstration of the new apparatus in 1880 dismissed it briskly, saying 'Gentlemen, this is a very amusing toy, but it will never have any practical significance.'[3]

John Morris, however, took the view that the advantages of the instrument far outweighed the disadvantages and the scheme that resulted in the establishment of the Telephone Company originated, he claimed, in the office at 6 Old Jewry, with '11 friends and myself subscribing £1,000 each'. The Telephone Company set up the first exchange in the City in 1879. Demand spread rapidly despite the fear that conversations on the telephone were not as private as direct personal contact and the perception that such instant communication would create more pressure in business; as *The Times* noted, shortly before installing the instrument itself:

It is a common complaint that the conditions of modern life, and especially of mercantile life, have been rendered well nigh intolerable by the telegraph; and the addition of the telephone must inevitably 'more embroil the fray'.

Ashurst, Morris, Crisp & Co. installed the telephone at Old Jewry, almost certainly the first firm of City solicitors to do so; its number was 15. For every one of those in the City like Walter de Zoete, a member of the Stock Exchange from 1867 until 1909 who was 'renowned for his conservatism, his phenomenal memory and his refusal to use the telephone', there were many more who did use it, if not all enthusiastically. In 1885 the firm acted on the flotation of two newly formed companies, the South of England Telephone Company and, overseas, the Telephone

John Morris was one of the promoters of the company which introduced the first telephones to the City.

Company of Austria.[4] The Telephone Company, as part of first the United and then the National Telephone Company continued to be a client until it was taken over by the Post Office in 1911.

The arrival of the telephone in the City completed London's position at the hub of the world's communications systems and underpinned, along with the telegraph system, London's domination of the world's commerce. Both the international shipping market and trade in most leading commodities and precious metals were, by the 1890s, controlled from London, the single world centre for the increasingly complex transactions of international commerce.

This the City did partly through its communications facilities; partly through its access to high-quality, continuous commercial intelligence; partly through its adaptability and accumulated expertise; partly through its ability to continue to attract talented incomers.[5]

While John Morris played a significant role in the introduction of the telephone to the City, it was his nephew, William, who acted as midwife to a number of electrical enterprises both before and after he became a partner in 1883. The widespread use of electric lighting required not only a public supply of electricity but also the development of a suitable light bulb and the difficulty of providing both meant that half a century elapsed between Faraday's demonstration of the possible in 1831 and its implementation in the 1880s. Arc lighting – formed by an electric arc between two carbon rods – had been increasingly used since the 1860s for lighting public places but its 'overbearing and flickering light' was unsuitable for domestic or office lighting. Candles, oil lamps and, increasingly in towns and cities, gas, provided light in the nation's homes and offices.[6]

In the late 1870s Joseph Swan, 'a prosperous self-educated Newcastle chemist and inventor' was working on the development of his discovery that

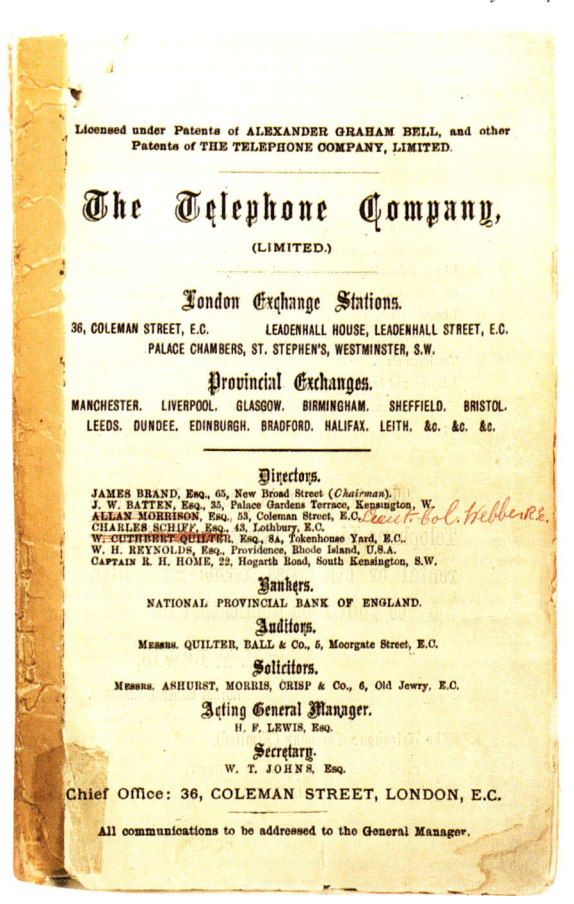

The firm was solicitor to the Telephone Company and an early subscriber to the service it offered, as the first London Directory shows.

'a carbon filament in an evacuated glass globe would glow when an electric current was passed through it'. Similar experiments were being carried out in the USA by Edison at the same time. Both men took out patents in 1881 and 1882 and established companies to exploit them, in Edison's case in the UK as well as in the USA; the firm acted in 1882 on the Swan Company's first prospectus and issue of £500,000. Almost inevitably litigation started between Edison and Swan as to who had the prior claim on the invention. A year later the litigation ended with the amalgamation of the companies to form the Edison and Swan United Electric Light Company Ltd which became, and remained a client of the firm.[7]

Electric lighting of the home and office was now possible but it was a luxury, even a status symbol, for the wealthy who could afford to install their own generators to provide a supply of electricity. In 1881 electric lighting was installed in the House of Commons and the Savoy Theatre, with the Mansion House, the British Museum and the Royal Academy quickly following suit. At the same time moves were afoot to secure the legislation allowing companies and local authorities to dig up the streets to lay cables supplying electricity to homes from a central station (as power stations were then known). The Electric Lighting Act of 1882 gave local authorities the right to establish electricity generating and distribution undertakings themselves or to empower private company undertakings to do so by licence, provisional order or special Act. Its sting in the tail was a clause which gave municipalities the option of purchasing privately owned undertakings after 21 years.

A flurry of activity in the shares of electricity companies on the Stock Exchange as well as something of a rush to apply for provisional orders took place; in 1883 there were more than a hundred applications. William Morris noted in his own account of his working life:

In 1883 I succeeded in obtaining four Electric Lighting Provisional Orders for:-
- *(1) Hanover Square District,*
- *(2) Victoria District,*
- *(3) South Kensington District,*
- *(4) Strand District,*

but the financial people allowed the Orders to lapse because of the 21 years' purchase Clause in the Act of 1882. What a gold mine was lost there!

In this view he reflected the conventional wisdom of the time, that the legislation deterred would-be electricity entrepreneurs. Historians

FACING PAGE

The potential of electric lighting was known from the 1830s and Ashurst himself had financially supported this patent in the 1840s. After his death it was judged to be valueless by his executors.

have since suggested that the economic depression of the 1880s and the immature state of the technology were as much if not more responsible for the slow development of that decade.[8] In 1888 a new Electric Lighting Act extended the period given to private undertakings before local authorities had the right to purchase to 42 years and that, combined with economic recovery, helped to speed up the pace of electricity installation.

The firm acted on the formation in 1887 of a new company, the London Electricity Supply Corporation, which took over the small Grosvenor Gallery Company, established originally by Sir Coutts Lindsay to supply the Gallery in New Bond Street and then a small area around it. With a capital of £1.25m, the new company's 1889 prospectus, on which the firm acted, offered 50,000 6 per cent preference shares of £5 each, raising £250,000. Adding lustre to the cluster, the company's chairman was the Earl of Crawford and its directors included Lord Wantage, who was also, with an investment of £220,000, its largest shareholder. From 1886 to 1891 the pioneering electrical engineer, Sebastian de Ferranti was the company's chief engineer and he designed for it the then largest power station at Deptford. The main cable which brought power into London was laid alongside the railway lines and it continued in use until 1933.[9] In 1891 William Morris registered the City of London Electric Lighting Company which, by 1894 was also offering to sell or hire to its customers 'electric cooking and warming appliances'. Morris continued to act personally for the company until 1924.

Admitted as a solicitor in 1879, William Morris became a partner in the firm on 1 January 1883. Partnership agreements for that period have not survived but we can estimate the size of his share of the partnership from the accounts. At that time it was customary for the senior partner to take the lion's share and it seemed that John Morris did so. Frank Crisp began with a share of one-seventh, raised in 1874 to one-fifth; the accounts of the mid-1880s suggest that William Morris's share was less than that, something of the order of 10 per cent when he first became a partner (see below). Morris had, however, been sufficiently confident of his future to marry six months before he became a partner.

On 3 January 1882 Florence Terry, 'the adorable Flossie ... most lovely and beloved of all the Terry girls', wrote in her diary one word, 'Engaged'. William Morris, or 'Willie' as he was known to his fiancée and her family, was regarded by the impecunious Terrys as a 'wealthy

**The firm
and the
Morrises**
75

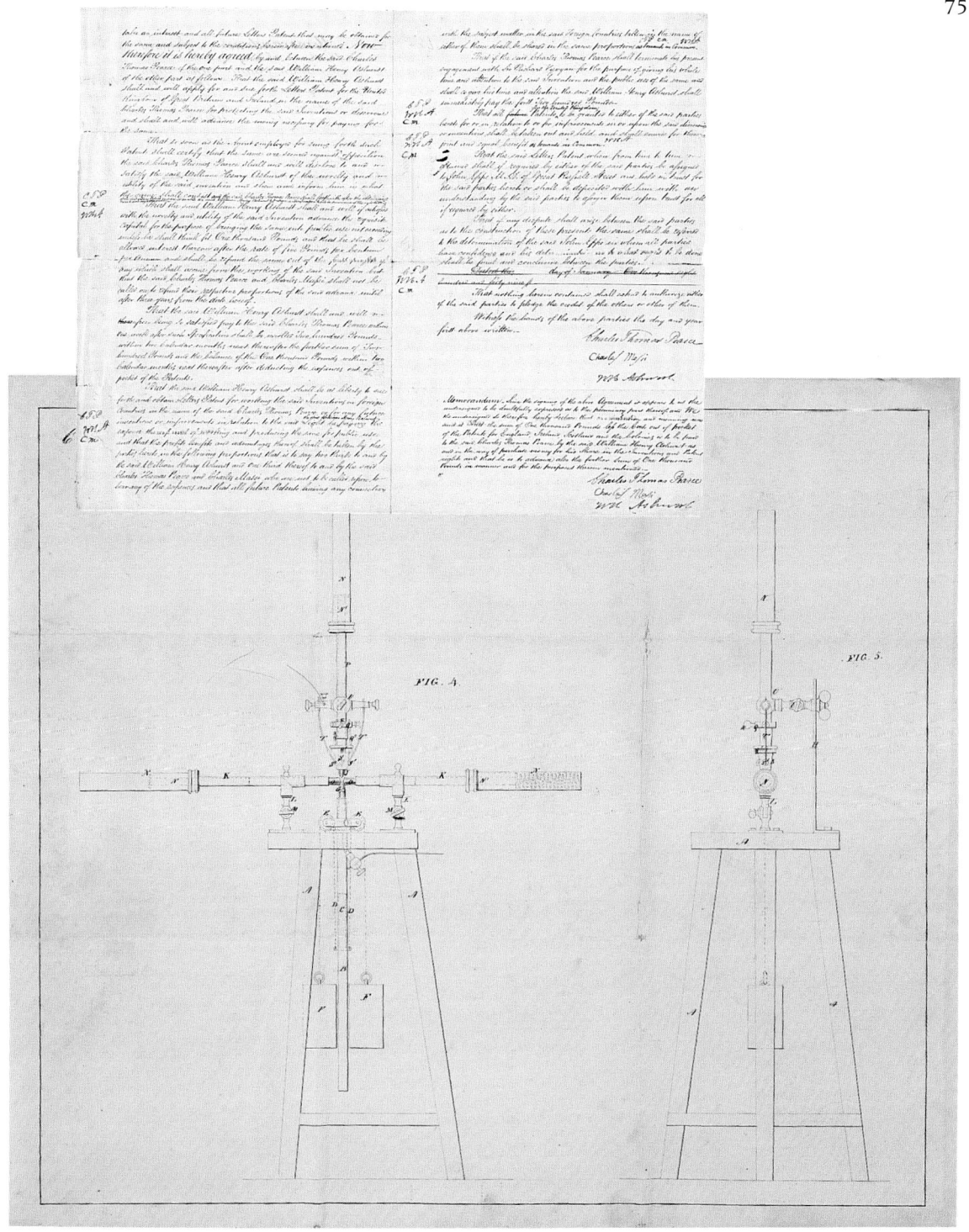

young lawyer' and, 'tall, dark, austere and handsome, with brown eyes and thick black hair (he went to a fancy dress ball in Turkish costume, and looked more Eastern than any pasha)', had been the subject of entries in Florence's diary for some time before the engagement.[10]

Born in 1855, the eighth (and sixth surviving) child of Benjamin and Sarah Terry, Florence was some eight years younger than her more famous actress sister, Ellen, although by Ellen's own account, united with her in being 'the lawless ones of the family'. The Terry parents moved up in the world in the 1860s, largely thanks to the earnings from the acting career of their eldest daughter, Kate and then to her fortunate marriage to the wealthy businessman, Arthur James Lewis. A silk mercer, he was a partner in Lewis & Allenby, sufficiently prosperous then to fund his purchase of Moray Lodge, Kensington in 1862. Thackeray, Trollope, Millais, Leighton and Arthur Sullivan were among the distinguished guests who attended his evening entertainments. An amateur artist himself, Lewis founded in 1863 the Arts Club, also frequented by the alumni of late Victorian London cultural life.[11]

Florence Terry and her sister Marion, had been sent to boarding school. Sunnyside, at Knight's Park, Kingston-on-Thames was a 'refined' establishment, 'for the daughters of Gentlemen'. Florence made her debut on the stage in London in the early 1870s, captivating audiences with her 'gay approach, her lightsome charm'. Provincial tours followed – Benjamin Terry saw the provincial theatre as invaluable training for his daughters – and then she returned to London. From 1879 she played supporting roles at the Lyceum, managed by Henry Irving who had in the previous year successfully invited Ellen Terry to join him there as his leading lady.

With her sister Marion, Florence enjoyed a busy social life interspersed with stage appearances, including assisting with amateur productions at Whistler's White House and at the miniature theatre Dickens had established at Tavistock House, once the home of Emilie Ashurst and her first husband. Florence's retirement from the stage shortly before her marriage took place, was marked, on 21 June 1882, by an event at the Savoy Theatre, ablaze, no doubt, with its new electric lighting; the programme featured Ellen, Florence and Marion in a popular play of the time, *Broken Hearts*, as well as the trial scene from the *Merchant of Venice* with Henry Irving playing Shylock, Ellen as Portia, Marion playing the Clerk and Florence herself as Nerissa, a role in

**The firm
and the
Morrises**

77

Florence Terry's last stage performance before she married William Morris in 1882 attracted considerable attention and comment in the theatrical press.

which her performance at the Lyceum had been reviewed as 'pretty and engaging'.[12]

William Morris bought a house in Kensington – number 13 (later renumbered to 49) Campden Hill Road, not far from Moray Lodge. The social whirl continued for Florence Morris, as a newspaper cutting preserved by her husband evidences – it was fashionable during the season to visit the art galleries and one newspaper reported in 1885:

Three years ago the winter exhibitions displayed almost as many button-hole bouquets as there were women ... and yet hardly a flower was to be found in the galleries a fortnight ago. Miss Marion Terry and her younger married sister [Florence] were two of the exceptions, as they wore lilies of the valley and maidenhair in large, flat, spray shape on their cloaks of Paisley shawling, made with sling and dolman sleeves respectively, and trimmed with brown fur. Miss Marion Terry's bonnet was of chenille-spotted brown felt, and her dress crimson satin. Her sister wore a large black velvet hat and feather, with a greenish aigrette.

The Morrises were, it seems, a happy couple with Florence becoming 'an accomplished hostess and a scrupulous housewife' and gracefully enduring her husband's reading aloud to her; he was, apparently, 'very fond of the sound of his own voice'. There were five children of the marriage (four survived to adulthood), a daughter and four sons. William Morris bought a house in the country – Bennets at Harpenden in Hertfordshire – for his wife and the children to use in the summer. But following the death while an infant of her third son, Hugh, Florence's own health deteriorated and on 15 March 1896, at the age of 41 and following the premature birth of her fifth child, she died of peritonitis.

After the death of Florence, her sister Marion moved into Campden Hill to look after the children. A year later a suggestion in the *St James Budget*, a London evening paper, that she and William Morris were about to marry resulted in a libel case brought, and won by Marion. The suggestion was in any case impossible since it was then illegal for a man to marry his sister-in-law. The case was conducted for Marion Terry by Sir George Lewis, solicitor to the great and the good (and some of the not-so-good) of Victorian society.

William Morris did in time marry again, a marriage which cemented – and complicated – his relationship with the Terry family. For his second wife he chose Gertrude Emily Neilson, a widow whose daughter, Julia, was married to Fred Terry, Florence Morris's younger brother; having been Fred Terry's brother-in-law, Morris became his stepfather-in-law. It was to his step-daughter, Julia, that Morris gave financial assistance to finance the theatrical company that she and her husband ran. For some years Morris also acted for the Lyceum Theatre, managed by Henry Irving from 1872 until his death in 1905.[13] This cannot have been an easy task for, despite his great popularity with theatre-goers and his international reputation, Irving's grandiose productions usually exceeded his budgets; to what extent Morris's involvement with the Lyceum and the Terry productions derived from an interest in the theatre and an ambition to be a 'theatrical angel' and to what extent it simply sprang from loyalty to the family he had married into, is unclear. That loyalty was certainly strong, for in 1898 when Arthur Lewis's business, Lewis & Allenby, went bankrupt and Moray Lodge, the family home, had to be sold, Morris bought a house in West Kensington for the Lewises, settling it on his sister-in-law for her lifetime.

At Ashurst, Morris, Crisp & Co., William Morris's work was a mixture of parliamentary and company work. The two came together, as we have seen, in the work for the electric lighting and supply companies. Morris also had many of the tramway companies whose origins were explored in the last chapter as clients. He acted for the Calcutta Tramways Company, formed in 1880 and floated with an issue of £350,000 in 1881 and for the East India Tramways Company, floated in 1884. Morris himself later recalled that he had acted for 'the Portsmouth, Gosport, Southampton, Plymouth, Cardiff, Grimsby, Thanet, Chatham, Hastings, Belfast, Lanarkshire, Paisley and Brisbane Companies'.

In the partnership agreement he drafted in 1876 John Morris had inserted a clause stating that he would be 'free from obligation to give more personal attention to it [the firm's business] than I think fit and to be at liberty to engage in any other business'. Such a stipulation was not uncommon, giving the senior partner — in this case now in his fifties — a lesser role in the day-to-day business of the firm, while at the same time giving the junior partners greater responsibility. Over the next two decades the business of the firm, particularly the company work carried out by Frank Crisp (see Chapter 5) grew considerably while John Morris had more time to devote to the clients and businesses that particularly interested him.

Among these were the overseas investments and interests, particularly in South America, of the Morrison family, descendants of the firm's first client. It was James Morrison's eldest son Charles (1817–1909) who devoted himself principally to developing the merchant banking business he inherited on the death of his father in 1857. He had considerable interests in North America but it was in South America in the 1880s that he built a new commercial empire, ably assisted and fronted by John Morris. From the 1850s Charles Morrison suffered from chronic cystitis,

a condition which reinforced his strong personal disinclination towards publicity. Rather than sit upon the boards of companies in which he was interested, Morrison preferred to engineer directorships for his closest colleagues.[14]

British trade with Argentina, a Spanish colony since the seventeenth century, dated back to the early nineteenth century. Until the building of the railways, however, in the 1860s, largely financed, engineered and managed from London, any development of the country and its trade was inhibited by its sparse population, poor communications and political instability. The railways changed all of that. By 1872 over 700 miles of railway were open and more were under construction; more than 40,000 immigrants arrived in Argentina that year and exports of wheat, sugar and wine were growing. A decade later refrigeration added meat to the list of significant exports; the first shipment of refrigerated meat from Argentina arrived in London in January 1884.[15]

The chief vehicle of Morrison's investment in Argentina and South America in the early 1880s was the River Plate Trust, Loan & Agency Company, floated with a nominal capital of £1m in 1881 to take over the assets of the ailing Mercantile Bank of the River Plate. 'The principal business of the Company,' the prospectus stated, 'will be the raising of money here on debentures and lending it again in the River Plate at the much higher rates of interest prevailing there, thus occupying the position of middleman between lender and borrower.' In 1884 John Morris became chairman of the Trust Company, a position he continued to hold for more than 20 years until his death.

The Trust company under Morris became the centre of a network of Anglo-River Plate mortgage, investment, utility and railway companies employing a total capital in excess of £10m and linked by directorships, common management services and overlapping investment patterns.

In 1886 Morris, then aged 63, made the long journey to Buenos Aires to see for himself some of the activities of the company in which he was so interested, not only as solicitor and chairman but also as an investor.

He was following in the footsteps of royalty for in 1880 a five-day visit to Buenos Aires had been made by Prince George, Duke of York (later George V), accompanied by the Duke of Clarence and Prince Louis Battenberg, a visit intended to signal the respectability of British interest in the area.[16]

Morris's visit enthused him with the commercial prospects in South America and in 1888 two more companies were established; the largest was the River Plate and General Investment Trust Company, closely related to the Loan & Agency Company and with Morris as a 'Trustee' (in effect, a director) taking the chair at its meetings. The second one was the Mortgage Company of the River Plate of which Morris was also chairman. There can be no doubt that the Morrison South American interests brought a great deal of work into the offices of Ashurst, Morris, Crisp & Co. as well as to John Morris himself. With the London office of the Trust, the firm was responsible for handling:

the promotion of companies [there were in all more than 30], *the detailed administration of syndicated issues of equity and debenture capital, the payment of coupons, and a thousand other varied services which today might be undertaken by accountants, management consultants, and merchant and commercial bankers.*

An article in the Buenos Aires daily newspaper *El Nacional*, in April 1888, summed up Morris's influence and connection with Argentinian business and commerce, albeit with a degree of hyperbole:

In the last ten years nothing worth the name of 'business' has been done in the River Plate without John Morris being consulted first. Across his dusty threshhold have passed the undertakings [of Argentina's major entrepreneurs] *and many others. This man ... is the real builder of all the railways in the Argentine Republic and the principal medium of South American progress ... When Mr Morris has a mind to it his clients will gather in 24 hours to form a syndicate for any undertaking, whatever may be the capital required, and – still more curious – they will do it without taking the trouble of confirming that the business is a good one: Morris has arranged matters, and that is enough.*[17]

Busy then as the firm's office was with Morris's South American work and the rest of the corporate practice, litigation also came to form a steady and increasing part of the firm's practice in the last three decades of the nineteenth century. Much of it related to and reflected the firm's large corporate practice (see also Chapter 5), with cases requiring the clarification of points of company or commercial law as well as the settlement of commercial disputes, but there were also cases concerning fraud. While serving his articles in 1877, William Morris had been involved in getting up 'the evidence for the prosecution of Baxter Langley, the Chairman, Swindlehurst, the Secretary, and Saffery, the Accountant, for conspiring to defraud the Artizans', Labourers' and General Dwellings Company'.

The company had been founded and incorporated in 1867 by William Austin, a drain-laying contractor, to build housing for the industrious poor in London. It had a capital of about £300,000 but the fraudulent activities of its officials had brought it to the verge of bankruptcy, Morris recalled. Following the conviction at the Old Bailey of Langley, Swindlehurst and Saffery, who were all sentenced to terms of imprisonment, recovery and expansion became possible. In 1882 the company bought 100 acres of land in Hornsey on which, over the next 50 years, it built the Noel Park Estate. In 1884 its capital was increased to £1.75m, with an issue of £500,000 of preference shares which helped to fund the building, between 1885 and 1892, of some 1,500 block dwellings – in these two or three flats shared facilities such as lavatories and sinks – for the 'labouring poor' in central and west London.[18]

Occasionally there were cases completely unrelated to company law. In 1884 Ashurst, Morris, Crisp & Co. defended Miss Louisa Devey, executrix of the late Lady Lytton in two actions brought against her by the Earl of Lytton as executor of the late Lord Lytton. Edward Bulwer Lytton (1803–73) was a man of varied talents, encompassing both 'literary labour' and politics, the latter as an MP and as Secretary for the Colonies 1858–9. He had married in 1827 Rosina Wheeler (1802–82), a young Irish woman 'of excitable temperament', also a writer. In 1836 the couple separated with considerable acrimony. Lady Lytton's novel, *Chevely or the Man of Honour*, published in 1839, portrayed her husband, clearly recognisable, as the villain. In 1883, the only son of the marriage, Robert, now Lord Lytton, published a life of his father. The publication stirred Miss Devey into announcing that she would publish the letters in her possession to vindicate the character of the late Lady Lytton and in October 1884 an article was published, with extracts from the letters, in the *Pall Mall Gazette*.

Perhaps finding the public washing of dirty linen dating back some

50 years distasteful, Bacon VC began his judgment by noting that the case had been argued 'at most immoderate length'. The Earl of Lytton was partially successful in that Bacon granted that he had the right to ask for the letters not to be published but he had, the judgment concluded, no right to the possession of the letters which should remain in the hands of Miss Devey as Lady Lytton's executrix.[19]

The Lytton case was heard in the Chancery Division of the Supreme Court, established by Lord Selbourne's Judicature Acts of 1873–5 which had brought together the formerly separate courts. It was also Selbourne who had been responsible for the decision to build the new Law Courts in the Strand. They were opened, with due pomp and ceremony, in the presence of the royal family, the Archbishops, the Prime Minister, the judges and members of both branches of the profession on 4 December 1882. A *cause célèbre* of the time, the litigation between Richard Belt and C B Lawes, proved to be the last case to be heard in the courts at Westminster and in the new courts. Our interest in this unusual case stems from the fact that, according to Morris family records, Edward Ashurst Morris, son of John Morris, and then an undergraduate at Trinity Hall, Cambridge, appeared as a witness in the case.

Lawes, a Cambridge man who combined a prowess in athletics and rowing with sculpting had written an article in *Vanity Fair* saying that Belt, a sculptor then highly regarded and remunerated by the fashionable world, employed others to execute his commissions. Belt sued Lawes but after a month in court during which the luminaries of the artistic world gave evidence on both sides, the jury could not reach a decision; it was then that Hardinge Giffard (later Lord Halsbury) suggested that Belt should be given the materials and asked to perform in court. This then took place and the jury, satisfied with the end product, found in favour of Belt and awarded him £500 damages.[20]

Edward Ashurst Morris, named after his father's mentor and, apparently commonly known as Ashurst, was born in 1863 and was John Morris's third son. His abilities manifested themselves early for when the boy was only 14 years old, his father identified him as the son most likely to follow in his footsteps. In a letter he wrote in April 1876 to Frank Crisp on partnership matters, he said, 'I have great hopes that my 2nd son [the eldest son born to John and Sarah Morris died in infancy] Ashurst will if spared be a great acquisition to the business & at the present time he

Ashurst Morris Crisp

is the one I have in my mind to come in and help you by & by [sic].'[21] Edward Ashurst Morris was educated at Charterhouse, Westminster and in Germany before he went up to Trinity Hall in 1880. When he completed his studies at Cambridge in 1883, he was articled to his father and, after serving three years (the five-year term had been reduced to three for graduates in the 1840s), he was admitted as a solicitor in 1886. He became a partner on 1 January 1888. The firm then had four partners, 28 weekly paid clerks and an unrecorded number of managing clerks and articled clerks. Of the former there were at least seven, recorded in the surviving weekly salary books with the clerks who worked for them, but there is no mention, for example, in the book covering this period, of John Stevenson (see Chapter 6) who had been given his articles and was admitted as a solicitor in 1886. There were certainly other qualified staff who, like Stevenson, were paid monthly, for in 1882 the firm paid out a total of some £6,500 on wages and salaries and the total paid to the clerks only represents between a half and two-thirds of that. This suggests that in all the firm probably employed between 40 and 50 men and boys, a large establishment in the profession at the time.

Edward Ashurst Morris, 1863–90, son of John Morris, became a partner in the firm in 1888. This photograph was taken at the time of his wedding in July 1889.

One of the firm's senior qualified men left at the same time as Edward Ashurst Morris became a partner. William Capel Slaughter was born in 1857, served his articles with the firm of Wilkinson & Drew in Bermondsey Street and, following his admission as a solicitor in July 1879, joined Ashurst, Morris, Crisp & Co. He left with the blessing and perhaps even at the suggestion of John Morris to establish his own practice, for it must have been clear that there was no scope to offer him a partnership at 6 Old Jewry.

The firm's partnership agreements from that period have not survived so there is no knowing whether at that time they had written into the constitution, as did some other City firms, that partnerships were to be the preserve of the owning families. John Morris's second son, Alfred, was already settled in the Army and his fourth boy, Capel was also settled with an estate in Kent, but his youngest son, Percy, born in 1867, had, after his schooling at Eton, followed in his brother's footsteps, going up to Trinity Hall, Cambridge in October 1887. At that time in his life he and his family may have been undecided as to which branch of the profession he would follow and, as long ago as 1876, John Morris had made it clear to his then only partner, Frank Crisp that any of his sons who wished to come into the firm should be able to do so. In the event, Percy Morris chose the Bar and he was called at the Inner Temple in 1894 and practised in the Queen's Bench Division.[22]

The agreement between John Morris and William Slaughter, dated 2 January 1888 (in the first instance for a year but it was then renewed and continued for some years – the precise date of its termination is not known), 'provided that, of those clients whose affairs Slaughter handled, some were to be handled by him in the name of Ashurst Morris Crisp & Co. as their agent, while the remainder were to be handled by Slaughter in his own name and on his behalf'. The firm's ledgers suggest that this kind of arrangement had been made by Morris before. George Davis had worked for the firm and been a partner from 1869 to 1874 before leaving to set up his own practice; the accounts for the early 1880s indicate that he was still paying agency fees to the firm as too was John Vernon, who had also been with the firm through the late 1860s and early 1870s. Vernon was mentioned in a letter Morris wrote to Crisp in April 1876 as a possible junior partner but it seems that he chose or was directed instead to set up on his own.

There is further substantiation of this in one of the letters Morris wrote early in 1888 to a client, W Woolley of Imperial Mercantile, clarifying the position of Ashurst, Morris, Crisp & Co. *vis-à-vis* Slaughter:

I think you might like to know that our arrangements with my friend Slaughter are such that whenever you would wish him to undertake any matter in conjunction with us, you have only to mention it to me, and I can arrange it with him without the least difficulty, as we have a general understanding that he will continue to attend to any matters in connection with our firm ... Of course we cannot object to you giving him any matters quite independently of us, but I think you have more than once expressed your satisfaction at the way in which the Imperial Mercantile matters were conducted, whereby the details were worked out by Davis, but retaining our position as consulting solicitors, and that is the position which we should occupy in any new matter of the class I have referred to, if taken in conjunction with Slaughter.

Such an arrangement clearly worked to the benefit of all concerned, since Ashurst, Morris, Crisp & Co. had clients and enough to spare and young men who had shown themselves to be able and ambitious were trusted by John Morris to do their best for the firm, the clients and themselves. There was a very large gulf, in terms of financial reward, between the top salary achievable by a managing clerk (today's assistant solicitor), however good a lawyer he was, and the returns to a profit-sharing partner in good years. Partners of course took the risk that in a bad year their income might drop dramatically; there were few, if any, bad years for City solicitors in general and for Ashurst, Morris, Crisp & Co. in particular, in the last two decades of the nineteenth century (see Appendix 1).

It is tempting to suggest that, like many of John Morris's business practices, that of setting up young men who had worked well for him in their own practices, dated back to William Ashurst senior, who had perhaps adopted such a means of helping men like William Shaen (see Chapter 2) in that way. At this distance of time and in the absence of any documentary proof, however, this can only be speculation. Morris's enthusiasm for following the customs of his former principal is well-attested, not least in a letter he wrote to Crisp in 1876, in which he affirmed his wish to follow the precedents 'established by the late Mr A[shurst] as to all his partnership arrangements'.[23]

William Slaughter took offices at 18 Austin Friars and in 1888 he was joined there by another recruit from Ashurst, Morris, Crisp & Co. William May had been articled at the firm in 1885, his father paying 300 guineas for the privilege; that amount was the same as William Ashurst senior had charged for articles in 1839. May had been educated at Charterhouse, where he must have been a near contemporary of Edward Ashurst Morris but thereafter their paths had diverged as May went on to Oxford. As he was completing his articles, May recorded in his diary that the alternative to joining Slaughter appeared to be 'staying on as a salaried menial after articles are out' and, as Slaughter's partner which he became on 1 January 1889, he had no cause to regret the move.[24]

Ashurst, Morris, Crisp & Co.'s balance sheets and profit and loss accounts show that between 1881 and 1885 the average annual net

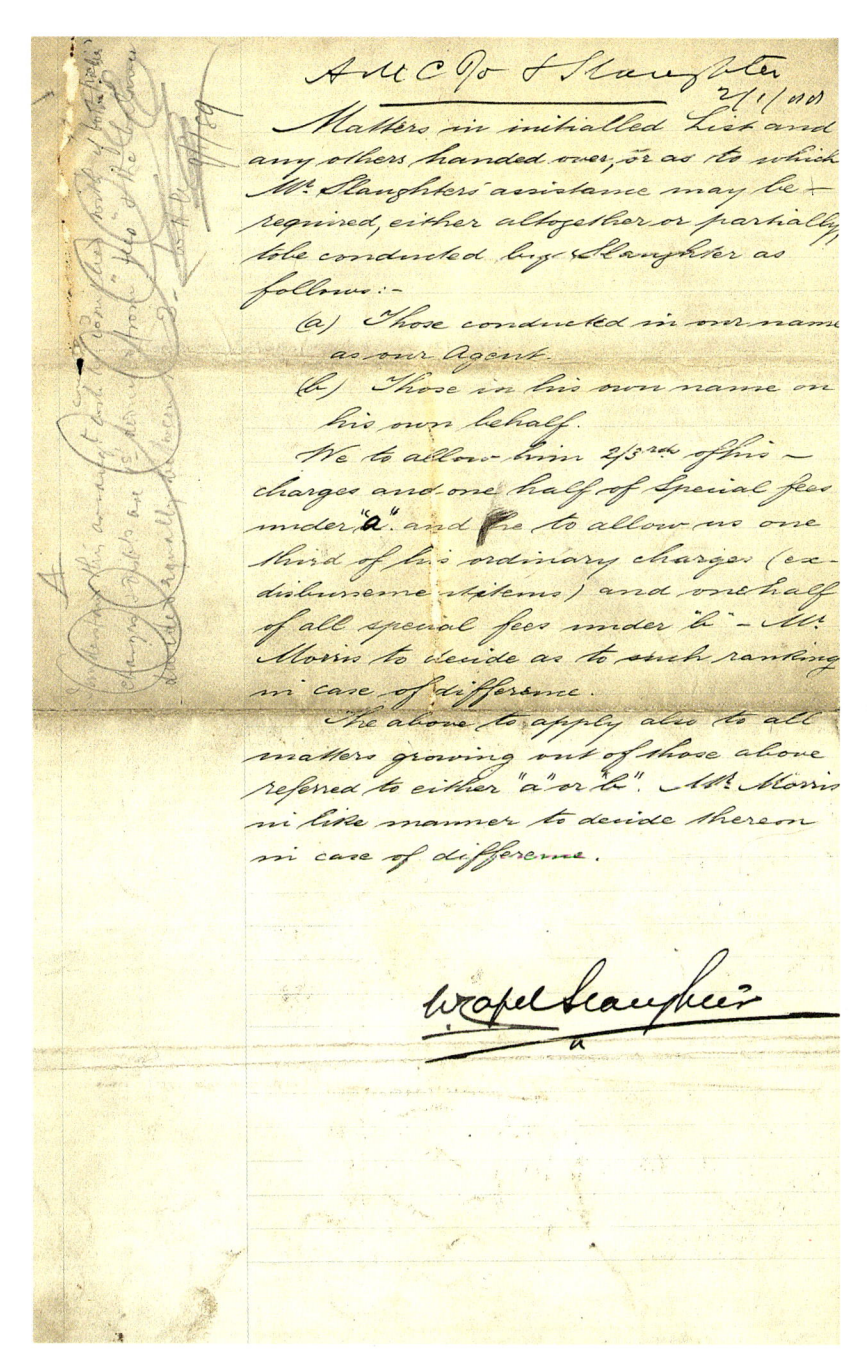

The letter setting out the arrangement between John Morris and William Slaughter, enabling the latter to establish his own practice.

Ashurst Morris Crisp

profit was £22,900 (see Table 4.1). On the evidence we have for City solicitors, this suggests that the firm was the most profitable in the City. It was considerably – some £9,000 – more a year than the average annual profit made by Linklaters (now Linklaters & Paines) which, between 1881 and 1886, was £13,500 a year. With its three partners, Linklaters was very much the same size as Ashurst, Morris, Crisp & Co.[25]

The annual net profit figure, however, only shows part of the story. At that time billing was much more relaxed than it became a century or so later; it is difficult to establish on precisely what principles bills were made up and sent out but it seems clear that the annual net profit figure was based on monies which had come in during that calendar year less expenses, but not necessarily on work done that year. The firm's 1882 balance sheet shows £62,000 owed to it in its ledgers and, among its assets,

In the late nineteenth century, the firm's staff enjoyed an annual outing.

a further £100,000 undivided profits 'of the old firm'. Because of the slow billing and the length of time taken to recover the charges, the firm could be running several sets of accounts at the same time, some for partnerships dissolved years previously but still accumulating funds from work done years before. Partners could, therefore, if they had also been members of a previous partnership, be drawing on several funds for their annual incomes and interest was paid on undivided profits outstanding.

Thus in 1885 the balance sheet shows John Morris's drawings (plus interest) from three separate partnerships: first, from the partnership with Harvey, Davis and Crisp which had been dissolved in 1874 (which still had credited to it undivided profits of £101,942 and from which portions were also payable to Davis and Harvey), second, from the partnership of Morris and Crisp which lasted from 1874 to 1883 and third, from the then current partnership which also included William Morris and dated from January 1883. Frank Crisp was in the same position, while William Morris had a share only from the current partnership. Table 4.2 overleaf shows the amounts from the three partnerships described above.

Table 4.1 Ashurst, Morris, Crisp & Co.: Net profit, 1881–85

Year	Net profit (£)	Equivalent in 1995 £
1881	24,330	973,200
1882	27,242	1,089,680
1883	17,882	715,280
1884	21,589	863,560
1885	23,508	940,320

William Morris's share in 1885 was £2,489 (= 1995 £99,560). It seems unlikely that the partners – particularly John Morris and Frank Crisp – actually drew out such large amounts, although the accounts clearly describe them as partners' drawings. To have such large sums credited to them, however, is a more than sufficient indication of the size of the business they were carrying on and the rewards it offered.

By the mid-1880s John Morris was a wealthy man for as well as his profit share in Ashurst, Morris, Crisp & Co. he had investments such as those in the companies forming the Morrison South American empire, which were at that time paying well. By 1888 the firm had been in the 'rabbit-warren' at 6 Old Jewry for some 40 years; the building itself was old, in City terms, since demolition and new building had been going on almost continuously since the late 1860s. Over the last 15 years or so the firm had also grown considerably and the Old Jewry offices were becoming cramped; perhaps too Morris had in mind the enterprise of his former principal, Ashurst, in having built his own office in the 1840s. It was on Morris's own account, rather than that of the firm, that he decided to invest in new buildings to be developed in Throgmorton Avenue.

The foundation stone for Number 17, to become the firm's new offices, was laid on 21 September 1889 by Mrs Ashurst Morris.

Three months earlier that year Edward Ashurst Morris had married; his bride was Minnie, daughter of Sir John Henry Puleston, the English partner of McCulloch & Co., a leading US banking house. Sir John was a well-known City figure and MP for Devonport. Later, after McCulloch & Co. closed their London branch, Puleston opened his own private bank; it was described by another noted City man, the company promoter, Osborne O'Hagan (see Chapter 5) as 'small and insignificant' in its activities. O'Hagan was even less complimentary about its owner. At the time of the wedding, however, Puleston was riding high and the marriage, which took place on 2 July at the Chapel Royal, was a major social event; nine bridesmaids, including one of Frank Crisp's daughters, attended the bride. The press reports were fulsome, characterising it as 'one of the most popular weddings of the season'. *The Citizen* went further:

The large and distinguished gathering that crowded the Royal Chapel at Whitehall was a deserved tribute to the power of the one family and the popularity of the other. There were some dozens of peers and peeresses, quorums from nearly every party in the House of Commons and journalism, la haute finance *of both England and America – in short, everything in London that is wealthy, fashionable, and powerful was represented.*

Nor did the wedding pass unnoticed by the staff of Ashurst, Morris, Crisp & Co. For the firm's clerks and some visitors, numbering some 50 in all, there was a banquet in the evening in the Holborn Restaurant, presided over by the father of the groom, John Morris. On the table in front of Morris was 'the fine piece of plate which the shareholders of the River Plate Trust, Loan & Agency Company recently presented to him

Table 4.2 Partners' shares of the profit plus interest, 1885

	John Morris £	Frank Crisp £
1	32,331	8,450
2	115,433	31,198
3	17,673	5,738
Total	165,437 (= 1995 £6.6m)	45,386 (= 1995 £1.8m)

NOTE The inclusion of interest in the amount credited to each partner makes the total of the three exceed the figure given as profit in Table 4.1.

in recognition of his successful management of that undertaking'. The seven-course banquet was followed by speeches and songs led by the senior clerk, H D Brooke, and the evening ended with Auld Lang Syne.[26]

The young couple, gifted by much of London society with the necessities and luxuries required in life, judging by the extant lists of wedding presents and their donors, took up their residence at 44 Cadogan Square. In 1890 their first child, a daughter, was born. Named Joan Alice, her godparents were Lady Burdett-Coutts, Dowager Lady Williams-Wynn and Mr Peter Reid.

In 1890 the firm moved into its new offices and, at the same time there opened in the basement of the new building in Throgmorton Avenue, another of John Morris's interests, the new vaults for 'the protection of scrip, valuables and documents' of the City Safe Deposit Company, of which Morris was chairman. To celebrate the opening 'a select number of gentlemen known in finance, law, politics and literature'

The firm and the Morrises

On 21 September 1889 the foundation stone of the firm's new offices in Throgmorton Avenue was laid. Members of the Morris and Crisp families and their wives attended this social function. A green glass jar, containing coins of the time and a copy of *The Times* **for that day was buried at the ceremony. The time capsule was recovered in 1986.**

Ashurst Morris Crisp

John Morris leased numbers 17 and 19 Throgmorton Avenue, known as the Garden House, as new offices for the firm. The building was designed by the architects Messrs Davis and Emanuel and built by Messrs Colls & Son. Ashurst, Morris, Crisp & Co. moved into the building in 1890 and stayed until 1981. The lease proved to be a financial benefit to the firm in the 1950s and the 1960s.

The firm and the Morrises

were taken on a tour of inspection of the building, including its vaults and the firm's new offices, characterised by 'magnificent staircases ... lofty and well-lit rooms'. Afterwards the visitors were entertained at dinner in the nearby 'noble hall of the Carpenters' Society'. *The Sun* reported the event: 'Everybody was there [enjoying the] splendid dinner, perilously seductive wines: and much speech-making.'

It was a great occasion to mark a significant move in the firm's history and the end of a most successful decade of practice. More and better was to come but for John Morris personally, the year 1890 ended on a low note. On 17 December his son Edward Ashurst Morris died, at the age of 27, of typhoid fever. He was buried in Highgate Cemetery and two windows were erected to his memory, one in St Margaret's Church, Westminster and another at Frimley in Surrey. Despite his youth and short career, Edward Ashurst Morris had, it seems already made his mark in the world. An obituary in the *Financial Times* noted: 'He was of a genial and generous disposition and much esteemed by all who came into contact with him in either a business or private capacity ... He took considerable interest in company matters and was himself a director of the Law Debenture Corporation.'[27] In the years that followed John Morris's partner Frank Crisp became to him a 'life-long friend and more than son' and it is Crisp's professional career and life we now explore.

CHAPTER 5

'The Lord High Accoucheur of joint stock companies'

Ashurst Morris Crisp

IN 1891 THERE were, according to the census taken in April that year, more than 2,000 firms of solicitors practising in the City. Some were sole practitioners but few, if any, were as large in terms of establishment, clients and profitability as Ashurst, Morris, Crisp & Co.; its status and reputation – it was described by the *Financial News* in 1887 as 'the most eminent legal firm in Europe' – were unchallenged.[1] Its pre-eminent position among the City firms, *primus inter pares*, will be amply evidenced in this chapter. It is also well illustrated by the fact that no other City firm had such a wealth of clients that it could afford to hand over a clutch of them to one of its own assistant solicitors to help him in setting up his own practice, the favour bestowed, as we have seen, upon William Slaughter.

The firm's reputation in the rapidly growing area of company work had been built initially on John Morris's expertise in company liquidation and reorganisation work. William Morris's work in advising the tramway and electricity undertakings and drafting and securing the passage of the Acts of Parliament they required had also attracted new clients. Far and away the most significant contributor to the growth of the firm's corporate practice had been Frank Crisp, who was 48 years old in 1891 and had been a partner for 20 years. Crisp 'and the new Limited Liability law developed together', *Vanity Fair* noted, in the text accompanying that accolade of the time, the publication of a Spy cartoon of Crisp; of the joint stock companies formed and floated in the 1870s and the 1880s, the writer continued, 'few ... and unimportant, are brought out without his manipulation'. According to Crisp's close business associate and friend, the company promoter, Henry Osborne O'Hagan (see below), it was with his 'usual sagacity' that John Morris recognised the ability of his young assistant, Crisp. O'Hagan continued: '... great as John Morris was as a corporation lawyer, he was quickly outdistanced by his young partner, who, owing to his great abilities and his commanding personality, soon became the firm'.[2]

'The Lord High Accoucheur'

The number of businesses seeking incorporation multiplied during the last two decades of the nineteenth century. As an increasing number of joint stock companies showed a successful survival record, the distrust of incorporation and limited liability faded, along with the memories of the Overend Gurney crash which had itself created much of the suspicion. Businesses grew larger and needed access to capital and there were more owners of capital seeking investment opportunities. Severe competition in some industries was, as ever, a powerful stimulus to mergers which again required larger amounts of capital. By the late 1880s about 2,500 new companies a year were being registered, and ten years later, that figure had almost doubled.[3] The figures only give an indication of the increasing trend towards incorporation, since by no means all the companies that were registered got beyond that stage and some that did only had a short life.

Many family businesses operating as partnerships chose to incorporate in order to limit their liability, but at the same time wished to ensure that ownership and control stayed in their own hands. They did not, therefore, always seek the investment of the wider public in their businesses, through a flotation on the Stock Exchange, or, if they did they offered only preference shares, keeping the ordinary shares and effective control in family hands (as did Van den Berghs – see below). It was often possible to draw on new sources of capital through private placements with family, friends or investors introduced by professional advisers. They remained, in effect, private companies (and are difficult, if not impossible, to trace as clients), although recognition of the private company as such in law did not come until 1907.

Other family firms looked to mergers and amalgamations, accompanied by a flotation on the Stock Exchange, to secure their future. Such a one was Wickens, Pease & Co. Ltd, of Cheapside, whose telegraphic

This **Spy** cartoon of Frank Crisp was published in *Vanity Fair* on 31 May 1890. Crisp was known as an enthusiastic collector of microscopes.

address – BONELESS – aptly described the nature of its business: '... the company has been formed for the purpose of acquiring by purchase as going concerns, carrying on and further developing nine well-known old established businesses of bone boilers, bone crushers and tallow melters', the prospectus issued in 1886 informed the public.[4] At the first general meeting of the company's shareholders, held on 28 April 1886, a resolution was passed that Messrs Ashurst, Morris, Crisp & Co., the solicitors to the company, should be paid an annual fee, exclusive of disbursements, of £105 (100 guineas), the fee to cover attendances at Board meetings and 'all ordinary business matters but not conveyancing matters, contentious business or special journeys'. Surviving documents indicate that there were similar arrangements for annual retaining fees made with many of the firm's corporate clients.

Company registration and issue work included the preparation of a Memorandum and Articles of Association and the drafting and printing of a prospectus. Of Frank Crisp, perhaps tongue-in-cheek, it was said, that 'he kept a printing-press on the top floor of the office mansion and his clerk-compositors could if called upon run off at an hour's notice the requisite printed paraphernalia and propaganda to register a company the same day that instructions to do so had been received'.[5] Company registration and flotation were already recognised as the preserve of the City firms of solicitors, but it was not until well into the twentieth century that they were sometimes separated from other corporate work. At this time, therefore, it can safely be assumed that any company whose flotation or issue was handled by Ashurst, Morris, Crisp & Co. would also, like Wickens, Pease & Co., come to the firm for all their legal advice.

A much larger client formed and floated also in 1886 was the Nobel–Dynamite Trust Company, with a nominal capital of £2m of which £1.5m was issued. In the 1870s the Swedish entrepreneur and inventor, Alfred Nobel, had established companies in Britain (Nobel's Explosives Company of Glasgow), in France and in Germany to exploit his discoveries of dynamite and other high explosives in each country and in its colonial markets. By the early 1880s these companies were competing fiercely with each other and with other companies established after Nobel's dynamite patents ran out in 1882. The results of the 'rigours of free competition' in the shape of falling profits soon persuaded the German companies, more serious competitors than elsewhere, that some kind of cartel agreement was desirable; such agreements which either fixed prices, shared profits or markets or some blend of all of these, were then common in German industry and protected by German law.

The major German companies came to terms among themselves in 1885 and followed this in 1886 with a further set of complex agreements with the French Nobel company and with Nobel's Explosives Company of Glasgow. Effectively, this international diplomacy resulted in a carving up of the world into markets designated as each company's territory in which each sold its products at agreed prices. The Nobel-Dynamite Trust was a holding company, created to buy out the shares of the German companies and Nobel's Explosives Company. Further agreements which followed the formation and flotation of the Trust regulated the trade even more closely and, in 1897, a market-sharing agreement with the US industry in the shape of the Du Pont company satisfactorily ended most of what had become severe competition between the Americans and the Europeans.[6]

The Trust was 'a very advanced form of business organization … There was [then] nothing like it in England' and its international industrial diplomacy was the training ground for Harry McGowan who, as Lord McGowan, later exercised the skills he had then learned, as chairman of Imperial Chemical Industries. For the next two decades the Nobel-Dynamite Trust ran a very successful and very profitable international business from its small office in London. As its solicitor, Frank Crisp continued to be intimately involved with its affairs.

Not all of Crisp's clients were as successful; the Salt Union was formed in 1888 as a result of what was described as 'reckless competition which

The Nobel–Dynamite Trust was formed in 1886 as a holding company for the British and German explosives manufacturers to contain their competition. It became part of a complex business empire, advised by the firm and particularly by Frank Crisp.

injuriously affects the salt industry'. Following an unsuccessful attempt by the salt-makers to regulate prices voluntarily, 'their affairs [were] ... taken up by a London syndicate – a rare example of City financiers taking a hand in provincial business – and a company ... [was] promoted to buy out and merge most of the Cheshire firms, along with others in Worcestershire, Middlesborough and Ireland'. The Salt Union Ltd, claiming to control about 90 per cent of the UK's salt output and with a capital of some £3m, was floated on the Stock Exchange in 1888. It was 'much the largest and most lavish undertaking of its kind ever, up to that time, seen in England ... Neither *The Times* nor *The Economist* liked it, but investors loved it.' In the event, the financial press was right in its misgivings for after 1896 the Salt Union paid a dividend on its ordinary shares only once and, after 1898, it passed the dividend on its preference shares too.[7]

Company promotion was a lively activity in the City in the 1880s and 1890s, as the published recollections and memoirs of those there at the time, including those of Henry O'Hagan testify. O'Hagan was not, it seems, the financier promoting the Salt Union but he had by this time developed a close working relationship and friendship with Frank Crisp, who acted for him as his personal solicitor as well as in a number of company formations and flotations. Born in 1853, O'Hagan began his professional life in the City in 1868 as a junior clerk with a firm promoting Acts of Parliament and Board of Trade Provisional Orders authorising the construction of railways, tramways and other public works. He may well have first encountered Frank Crisp at this time, given the firm's connections with tramway companies (see Chapter 4). In the mid-1870s O'Hagan established himself as an independent company promoter.[8]

The activities of some company promoters ranged from the dubious to the downright fraudulent; the bankruptcy of Ernest Hooley, whose promotion of the Dunlop company in 1896 had made him famous and rich, was the event of 1898 in the City and he ended up in prison, serving a sentence for fraud. Horatio Bottomley, apparently a more lovable rogue, was characterised by O'Hagan as 'one who was unsuited to the paths of finance, and wanting in ballast'; he too spent time in prison during which, the story goes, he was seen by a visitor passing through who remarked, 'Ah Bottomley, sewing I see.' 'No,' replied Bottomley who, whatever his lack of ballast, apparently had a ready wit, 'Reaping.'[9]

In contrast to the Hooleys and Bottomleys of the City, O'Hagan 'was by general repute … genuinely seeking to convert only worthwhile concerns into public companies and trying to ensure a distribution of the capital sufficiently honest not to wreck the company's future prospects'. He introduced what became 'the standard practice of securing the underwriting of capital by means of the promoter (as *de facto* issuing house) farming it out on a commission basis'.[10] Frank Crisp was, by O'Hagan's own account:

the leading authority on company matters in the City of London, a man whose advice carried the greatest weight in the counsels of the great undertakings in the City, for his legal knowledge and acumen rarely led him astray when he was called upon time after time for an immediate opinion. On the rare occasions when he had gone astray – for he always checked the opinions he had given – he was man enough at once to revise his opinion, and in such a graceful and manly fashion as to raise him further in the estimation of his clients. It is true to say that when directors were in any difficulty, the coming into the room of Frank Crisp changed the whole atmosphere.

O'Hagan is by no means the only source to describe Crisp's strength

City clerks at lunch.

as a lawyer and the qualities which made his advice so widely sought and highly regarded. Another contemporary who described himself as a friend of many years summarised Crisp's abilities thus: '... his sound grasp of legal principles, his unwearying capacity for work, his easy assimilation of detail, his clearness of vision, and his quick-witted, sound advice ...'

Crisp was a Fellow of the Royal Microscopical Society from 1870 and a member of its Council from 1874 – his hobby was the study of 'many things which are quite invisible to the naked eye ... he owns an unrivalled collection of all that is microscopically interesting or useful'. An old friend and fellow Councillor, Dr B Dayton Jackson, characterised him thus: 'in Council ... many awkward questions were got over or smoothed away by his acute mind. His quick grasp of essentials and strong common sense enabled him repeatedly to brush aside legal cobwebs which would have hindered the work in hand.'

Common sense, combined with a comprehensive and confident but not obtrusive knowledge of the law, pithily delivered by a forceful personality gave Crisp his commanding position: he 'was known to his clients as a man of no hesitation. He would never give an opinion and it was his custom to tell his clients "It is so"; never would he descend to the uncertainty of "I am inclined to the opinion".'[11]

That the enterprises formed and floated by O'Hagan with Frank Crisp as their solicitor were diverse and international in character can be amply illustrated by some examples. In 1888 O'Hagan was consulted by two manufacturers of tobacco and cigars from Cuba, Gustav Bock and F de P Alvarez, and, after some negotiations, he agreed to buy both their businesses and amalgamate them. Crisp acted on the flotation, in November that year, of the new company, Henry Clay & Bock & Co. Ltd when £380,000 of a nominal capital of £500,000 was issued. Some ten years later O'Hagan turned his attention again to the tobacco industry of Cuba, proposing a further amalgamation of a number of smaller companies with valuable brand names with Henry Clay & Bock & Co.

The negotiations for the merger were lengthy, held up first by the Spanish-American War and then by the stance taken by the chairman of Clay & Bock, Lord Ebury. Described by O'Hagan, who had himself played a part in securing Ebury's appointment in 1888, as 'a man of some ability, but with a somewhat narrow mind', Ebury apparently believed himself to be a keen negotiator. O'Hagan commented dourly, 'Had he [Ebury] been offered the earth, he would have stipulated for a barbed-wire fence around it; and when that was conceded, he would raise questions about the stars and the planets.' Eventually, through Crisp, the consent of the directors of Clay & Bock & Co. was transmitted to O'Hagan and the new company, the Havana Cigar and Tobacco Company, was formed and floated. After some 15 years of successful trading, the Havana Company, like many other tobacco companies in the early years of this century, was taken over by the American Tobacco Company then headed by the aggressive James Buchanan Duke. Against the advice of both Crisp and O'Hagan, the Havana Cigar and Tobacco Company's directors initially opposed the take-over but eventually capitulated to it.[12]

Lord Ebury was also chairman of the English company of the Dutch margarine makers, Van den Bergh; he had been recommended to the family by the stockbroker, Panmure Gordon who was involved in its flotation and who also enjoyed a close relationship with O'Hagan. The company was formed in 1895 to buy the old family partnership but only the preference shares were issued to the public as the Van den Bergh family preserved their control of the business and its management by their ownership of the ordinary capital. Crisp was the new company's solicitor.

According to the *Financial Times*, Crisp's:

conduct of business at company meetings, where his portly figure is well-known, is a revelation even to his enemies. The manner in which, with a few well-chosen words, he will demolish the apparently invulnerable arguments of his opponents has to be seen to be appreciated.

At Van den Bergh's Annual General Meetings, Crisp's skills may well have been tested. Lord Ebury regarded himself as the representative of the Preference shareholders and spoke accordingly, regardless of the views of his fellow directors; 'one year the shareholders were treated to the unusual spectacle of a platform disagreement between the Chairman and his colleagues'. Ebury did not agree with the Van den Bergh policy of investing in wholesale grocery businesses, including those of the Lipton chain (which it was eventually to acquire), and there were 'stormy scenes'.

In 1902 Ebury 'whose sense of humour from time to time outran his discretion, alluded to a "hope expressed by one of the shareholders of

Lipton's that the gentleman upon whose aptitude for business that company mainly depends for its prosperity would not spend too much of his time in yachting".' Sir Thomas Lipton, now a millionaire, had launched his first challenge for the America's Cup in 1899; it had brought him a great deal of publicity and, not surprisingly, the comments of Van den Bergh's chairman were not well received. In fact they led to the immediate withdrawal of Lipton's custom from Van den Bergh, although in the event the damage was short term as the business was soon regained.[13]

The growth in the opportunities for food retailing in the latter part of the nineteenth century was underpinned by two social factors – the rapid increase in the urban population and the steady rise in real incomes and the standard of living. Benefiting from these changes was another client of the firm, a rapidly growing competitor of Lipton's, the partnership of Kearley & Tongue. Established in 1876 by Hudson Kearley (who later became well known as Lord Devonport, Minister of Food Control during the First World War), the partnership had, by 1885, opened 100 shops which traded under the name of the International Tea Company. By 1890 there were 200 shops, a larger chain than that of either Lipton or the Home and Colonial Stores, the latter a client of the new partnership of Slaughter and May.[14]

Both Crisp and John Morris were involved in advising Kearley & Tongue and the firm drew up a number of partnership agreements for them in the 1880s and the early 1890s. It was, according to O'Hagan, John Morris who sent Kearley and Tongue to him in 1895 to explore the possibilities of a flotation. Kearley was, said O'Hagan, 'a very difficult man' who regarded himself as something of a financier and, on the first visit on hearing that O'Hagan would expect fees of some £40,000, responded with 'I think we will say good day. We can convert ourselves into a company and save that money.' However, further consultations with Ashurst, Morris, Crisp & Co. brought Tongue and a reluctant Kearley back and O'Hagan's scheme was accepted. The International Tea Company was formed and floated in 1895 with a capital of £900,000.[15]

One more example of an industry in which O'Hagan was active in making promotions which also involved Frank Crisp will suffice. Until the 1880s the British brewing industry's family-owned partnerships had eschewed incorporation but:

On 25 October 1886 the death knell of the British brewing partnership was sounded. Guinness was sold to the public for £6 million. Scenes in the City were unprecedented ... In its wake, during the next few years, there was a rush by almost every major brewery to convert to limited liability.

In that same year Crisp acted on the flotation of Barrett's Brewery and Bottling Company, a London company which owned the Vauxhall Brewery, and in 1888 another brewing company was floated, Kenward & Court of Hadlow in Kent.[16] Much larger flotations, however, were made on the London Stock Exchange for the American brewers.

In the late 1880s O'Hagan's attention was drawn to the 'wonderful trade' of a number of US breweries. These were, he recalled, 'the huge lager-beer breweries which before the introduction of Prohibition were to be found all over the United States, each turning out hundreds of thousands of barrels of light and non-intoxicating lager beer, refreshing but innocuous ... earning hundreds of thousands of dollars a year'. In 1889 Crisp acted on the flotation of the Bartholomay Brewing Company of Rochester in New York State. The company was formed to amalgamate three large breweries in Rochester and its capital of £620,000 was oversubscribed, for, according to O'Hagan, the English brewers were eager to invest in what they saw to be a profitable venture. The £10 shares rose rapidly to £17. The success with the Bartholomay isssue was quickly followed, O'Hagan wrote, 'by the Chicago Breweries, the Chicago & Milwaukee Breweries ... the Indianapolis Breweries, the Milwaukee Breweries, the St Louis Breweries ... [and] the San Francisco Breweries', all of which became Crisp's clients.[17]

The firm and Crisp had other US clients too, railway and manufacturing companies and businesses concerned with commodities such as the Chicago and North West Granaries Company. By no means were all of Crisp's clients connected with the promotion activities of O'Hagan. Crisp had as clients a large number of mining companies, active in the USA, India, South Africa and Australia, whereas O'Hagan had, as he recorded, 'kept almost entirely out of the Mysore, the Transvaal and the West Australia mining speculation, as I had strong objections to mining'. Not surprisingly gold-mining, characterised by Charles Tennant (see below) as 'a lottery' attracted some of the more dubious characters in the City and the methods used and acceptable then offered plenty of scope for fraud. The process of bringing out a speculative company was described by Cecil Braithwaite of the stockbroking firm, Foster & Braithwaite (a client of Ashurst, Morris, Crisp & Co.) thus:

> ... it was quite customary for say half a dozen men to get together and form a Company. No prospectus was produced till many days after dealings had commenced, and the procedure was as follows. The Broker appointed by the promoting group went into the market and told his friends that he was bringing out a Company to exploit, we will say, a Gold-Mine. He – the Broker – explained what the Company was, and let his friends have some shares with probably a call of more. He then arranged to have the shares bid for in order to attract attention, his friends in the market having 'Bated [sic] the Swim' among their friends. At this stage the Company was not even registered. If the operation was successful, and a good market was established, a prospectus was then advertised, and nominally, the public had a chance of subscribing. I say nominally, because if the shares already stood at a good premium, the public had very little chance of obtaining any. A special settlement was then applied for, which unless there was opposition generally went through. If the efforts of the group in the market failed to make the shares go, and be popular, often nothing more was heard of it.[18]

Some 300 or so companies were clients of the firm and listed on the Stock Exchange in 1900; in 1996 the stock market listed clients of Ashurst Morris Crisp, Linklaters & Paines and Slaughter and May totalled 300. Almost a quarter of those listed in 1900 were directly concerned with mining and exploration for minerals and by far the greatest number of those were concerned with gold-mining. India had long been a source of gold and Crisp acted on the flotation of two Indian gold-mining companies in 1879, the Indian Glenrock and the South Indian.

In 1886 he had a more significant client in the shape of Gold Fields of Mysore. The company, which owned the Champion Reef mine, its potential as yet unrealised, had been formed in 1880 by Charles Tennant (1823–1906), the third generation of his family to be concerned with the St Rollox Chemical Works, at one time the largest chemical works in Europe. Tennant, known to his intimates from 1885, when Gladstone created him a baronet, as 'the Bart', had wide commercial interests encompassing the Nobel-Dynamite Trust Company (see above) as well as the mines of Tharsis in Spain which included the Huelva & San Juan Copper Company for which Crisp already acted.

Tennant was 'short and slight, but immensely vigorous', the latter not least in his creation of his family; he had 12 children with his first wife and, after her death he married again (at the age of 75) and fathered four more daughters. In the 1880s Tennant's daughters from his first marriage 'achieved a social triumph' in London; Charlotte married Lord Ribblesdale, Laura the Hon. Alfred Lyttelton and Margot, the youngest, married the Liberal Party leader and Prime Minister, Herbert Asquith.

In business, it was said of Tennant that, 'For those who lacked commercial courage he had nothing but disdain. It was one of his most successful tactics, when there were signs of failing confidence, to offer to buy out querulous shareholders at par.' These were the tactics he was obliged to employ with Gold Fields of Mysore when, after four years, no gold deposits had been found. However, when gold was found the company was reconstructed, with Tennant remaining as chairman and his son-in-law, Lord Ribblesdale as a director. Gold Fields of Mysore was floated with a capital of £220,000. From the late 1880s on its profits soared and it was able to pay dividends of over 100 per cent a year.[19]

Much of the success of the Mysore company was due to the development of the MacArthur-Forrest method of using a cyanide solution to extract gold from refractory ores. In this too Tennant took an interest and the use of the process in South Africa in the 1890s was a significant factor in the growth of the gold-mining industry there. Small-scale development of gold-mining had taken place in South Africa in the 1870s but it was not until 1884 that the existence of the huge gold-bearing deposits of the Witwatersrand began to emerge. In 1886 the Rand was declared officially public diggings and the first gold-induced investment boom began in 1888–9.

In 1888 Crisp acted on the flotation of the Durban-Roodeport Gold Mining Company, the issue being £61,500 of its £900,000 capital. The *Financial News* described it as 'a new departure ... in bringing out gold-mines' to the extent that it 'reduce[d] such investments ... to no more than ordinary risks'. This view was well-justified by the dividends, ranging from 40 per cent in 1892 to 60 per cent in 1894 and reaching 80

Sir Charles Tennant, known to his family and friends as 'The Bart'; Frank Crisp acted for a number of the mining companies with which he was concerned.

per cent in 1898. The original Roodeport farmland owned by the mine was only 343 acres although in the 1890s adjacent claims were acquired. Nearby the 3,000-acre farm of Vogelstruisfontein provided the basis for the gold-mining company of that name, also Crisp's client, floated soon after the Durban-Roodeport.[20]

In both these companies a large interest was held by Donald Currie, the Scottish entrepreneur and shipping magnate who, after some years spent working for Cunard, had established his own shipping company – the Castle Packet (in 1900 it merged to create the Union Castle Mail Steam Ship Company). Currie also had a large interest in the Namaqua United Copper Company; the firm had acted on its issue in 1887. The demand for copper boomed in the 1880s, principally driven by the increasing use of it in the new electrical industry and by the armaments manufacturers.

Currie's interests in South African gold and minerals and his companies to exploit them for which Crisp acted pre-dated the Kaffir boom of 1894–5 in the City. 'In the closing months of 1894 all eyes were increasingly turned to the South African mining market, otherwise known as the Kaffir Circus.' Many of the brokers and jobbers concerned in the dealing spilled over into Throgmorton Street, not far from the firm's offices in Throgmorton Avenue; the excitement and heightened activity came to a climax there in March 1895 during after-hours dealing, in the Battle of Throgmorton Street, when one of the leading jobbers, Harry Paxton was arrested and charged with disorderly conduct.[21]

By late in 1895 doubt about the future of deep level mining in the Rand and the growing political uncertainty in South Africa, which culminated in 1896 in the Jameson Raid, led to a falling off of the enthusiasm for South African mining shares. Even so, in 1900, Ashurst, Morris, Crisp & Co. still had nearly 30 clients involved in gold-mining in Southern Africa. However, the discovery of gold deposits in Western Australia in 1892–3 led to a new boom. Crisp acted for some 15 West Australian gold mining companies which issued prospectuses and were floated on the Stock Exchange at this time; some of them were picturesquely named – the Lady Emily, the Great Boulder Perseverance and the Shamrock Gold-Mining Company. Gold-mining in Western Australia proved to be both more successful and of greater longevity than it was in Queensland, where a brief boom between 1886 and 1889 had led to the flotation of 47 companies in London, few of which survived even to the turn of the century. Crisp had as a client one of the few successes, the Day Dawn Company, floated in 1887.[22]

Enough has been said to show that the firm's corporate practice encompassed a large and growing variety of economic activity. Alongside the new clients from brewing and mining, the firm continued to act for clients who dated back to the Ashursts' days. These included, for example, J & J Colman, whose East Anglian mustard manufacturing business dated back to 1814; under Jeremiah James Colman the business expanded and new products such as starch and cornflour were added. There were publishing companies too; to Cassell & Co., for which the firm still acted, were added George Routledge & Sons and Chapman & Hall; the latter, publishers of the novels of Charles Dickens and Anthony Trollope, was incorporated in 1880, with Trollope himself as one of its directors.[23]

There were also shipping companies as clients, including Leyland & Co., the Houlder Line and the Nelson Line. In the second half of the nineteenth century, Britain's mercantile marine was the largest and most powerful in the world. Its need for ships, along with the demand from the Navy for warships, created and supported a large and much respected shipbuilding industry. It was to that industry that, in the early 1890s, the Japanese turned in search of warships for its Navy. A contract was

Frank Crisp drew up the contracts for the construction in England of a number of battleships for the Japanese navy.

drawn up with Sir W G Armstrong's shipyard at Elswick, near Newcastle, for several ships to be built, among them the *Yoshino* in 1892, the *Yashima* in 1896 and the *Kashima* in 1905. Crisp drew up the contracts between the Japanese and Armstrongs for the ships; tradition has it that the *Yashima* contract was written on white silk.

At the centre of the firm's large and ever-growing corporate practice over these years was Frank Crisp, 'a robust Englishman, broad with grizzled iron-grey hair'. Frequently described as portly and, by O'Hagan, a large man himself, as 'of no mean weight' the two together provided the *Rialto*, the City's *Private Eye* of the late nineteenth century, with good material for copy. On one occasion, O'Hagan recalled:

> … there was talk of a big financial action being referred to my arbitration … Crisp was one of the solicitors in the case and Mr Danckwerts Q.C. (a very stout man), one of the counsel. 'It is said,' remarked the Rialto, 'that the large hall at the Law Institution has been secured. What with Mr O'Hagan … Crisp, and Mr Danckwerts, a bigger hall must be obtained.'[24]

Crisp, however, despite the many matters claiming his attention, 'never seemed in a hurry; he had such a competent corps of adjutants he had only to give a quiet word to his orderly (a commissionaire) and an adjutant hastened to his side'.[25] The impact of his activities on the office of Ashurst, Morris, Crisp & Co. must have been considerable, but his own routine was, it seems, unvarying. He arrived at the office from his home in Holland Park at 9.45 a.m. and worked through the day with only a bar of chocolate at lunch-time. He took tea and toast at 4 p.m. and then either worked on until 6.45 p.m. or, sometimes went to spend an hour with O'Hagan from 5 p.m. until 6 p.m. Dinner was followed by a return to the office at 8 p.m. and he worked on until 10 p.m., his clerks taking it in turns to stay late to take dictation.

This page of the firm's salary book shows the last entry for William Slaughter before he left to establish his own practice, later Slaughter and May.

In 1889, the last year for which the firm's detailed salary books survive, of the 34 weekly paid clerks, five were listed as working for Crisp; that number included the youngest, an office boy, Thomas Outen (whom we shall meet again in Chapter 6), who had only joined the firm in February that year and was then earning 10 shillings a week. There were also a number of more senior managing clerks who were paid monthly; their number and details have not survived but they included Arthur F Solomon who had joined the firm in December 1867 and worked for Crisp as a weekly paid clerk until the end of August 1888. He was then the highest paid clerk, on £4 a week and was promoted to a monthly salary.

In the early 1890s Crisp's routine changed following his purchase of Friar Park, a house and estate near Henley. From then he left the office on Friday afternoon for Paddington Station, travelling in a horse-drawn brougham and accompanied by his clerk taking dictation. He was met at Paddington on Monday morning and driven to the City, dictating through the journey. Crisp was a man 'of wonderfully methodical habit',[26] a characterisation borne out by his working practice and by surviving fragmentary evidence from the office, including his instructions, delivered in 1895, as to how the office accounts were to be kept.

He did not take a summer holiday but during the Long Vacation he left the office on Thursday evening bound for Friar Park and did not return until Tuesday morning. Friar Park, which will be described in the next chapter, represented a considerable investment to Crisp; by around 1900 he had, according to O'Hagan, spent some £150,000 on it. Crisp's private ledger for 1890 shows heavy expenditure on fencing, shrubs, garden furniture and greenhouses as well as furniture, lamps and paintings for the house. He could, however, well afford it for the returns from the practice continued to grow. Moreover with his intimate knowledge of the opportunities in the City he was able to enhance his income from the practice by skilful investment. Family tradition has it that he made – and lost – his fortune several times over.

The firm's accounts show clearly the growth of the practice measured by the number of clerks employed. In 1889 the firm paid out just over £6,000 in salaries, the sum including a special payment, it was noted, of £500 to 'Mr Slaughter leaving'. Two years later just over £8,000 went on salaries and in that year too some £300 was spent on 'new linoleum throughout the office and restoring furniture'. Through the 1890s the annual cost of salaries continued to rise, reaching in 1897 some £13,000, more than twice the amount it had been in 1889. Given that prices had fallen, it is unlikely that salaries had risen very much, if at all, and such

Ashurst Morris Crisp

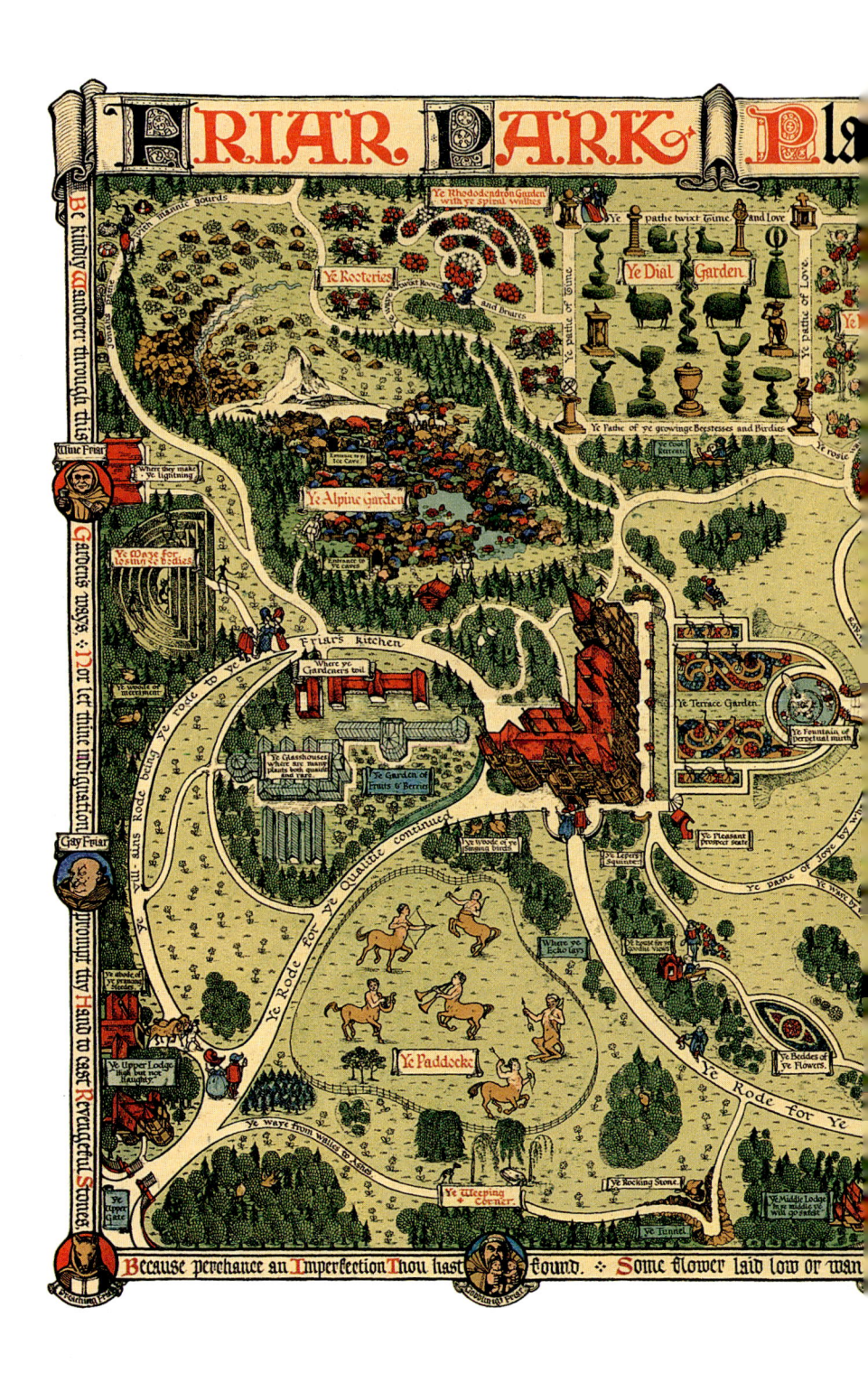

'The Lord High
Accoucheur'

113

Friar Park, near Henley became Crisp's hobby and passion from his purchase of it until his death. For some 30 years he lavished time and money on the creation of a house and garden to which he welcomed eminent visitors including royalty.

Despite his extensive practice Crisp found time to be active in local politics and affairs and was a generous contributor to local causes.

a sum indicates a very large establishment of qualified solicitors and clerks. By comparison, Linklaters' annual salary costs remained at around £6,000 throughout the 1890s.

The firm's annual profits also rose; over the four years 1895–8 they averaged £50,000 a year (the equivalent today of some £2m). That was three or four times as much as the profit being made by other City firms at the time; Linklaters' profits averaged £12,500 through the 1890s while at Freshfields, Edwin Freshfield told his son in 1891 that the firm's 'net income ... seems to be £15,000 a year'.[27] The annual net profit figure presented only part of the picture (see pages 88–9) and through the 1890s at Ashurst, Morris, Crisp & Co. undebited costs, that is work in progress, ran at more than £100,000 a year. There were also considerable reserves in the shape of the undivided profits which had accumulated from previous partnerships as well as from the present partnership (see Appendix 1).

Frank Crisp's share of the firm's profits increased steadily too; in the late 1880s he had a quarter share. A letter written to him in December 1888 from a relative living in Streatham confirms this:

I am of course much interested in all you tell me about yourself or your business growth. I never knew, I never asked & you never told me till a few weeks or months ago what was your exact engagement with Mr M.

I guessed – but without data – that you had one fourth of No 6 [Old Jewry].

Considering that you attacked sublunary things as late as 1843, your present position in the world does seem to me somewhat marvellous, and I should think such incomes are unprecedented, even in your profession, that is in the case of one so young & may I say so green.

I congratulate you most heartily in this last arrangement. Mind you carry corn.*

*Your grandfather, speaking to me of — said, 'he can't carry corn, & whether he has 500 or 5000 a year he will never have a penny.'[28]

Crisp's friend, O'Hagan, noted, 'Almost year by year Mr Morris, who was greatly attached to his colleague, conceded him a larger and larger share in the partnership, until Frank Crisp had one half ... After this [he] refused a still larger interest.'[29] The firm's accounts indicate that by 1892 the change had taken place and Crisp was then entitled to a half of the profits.

By 1897 it had become apparent that the firm needed another partner and in 1898 John Stevenson, who had been admitted as a solicitor

Ashurst Morris Crisp

in 1886 and who had been a managing clerk with the firm for some years – the precise date when he joined the firm is not known, nor are his antecedents – became a partner. He was probably a salaried partner for the first two years; the firm's accounts do not indicate his entitlement to a share of the profits until the end of 1899. With its four partners and large staff comfortably ensconced in Throgmorton Avenue, Ashurst, Morris, Crisp & Co. completed a most successful decade of practice in 1899 and faced the beginning of a new century.

CHAPTER 6
The Edwardian Era and beyond

Ashurst Morris Crisp

ON 27 JUNE 1900 the Central London Railway was officially opened by the Prince of Wales (soon to be Edward VII) and celebrated with 'a late luncheon in the generating station at Wood Lane'. The celebration may perhaps have been a little muted, for the electrically powered trains had not yet started to run on the underground railway, which had originally been scheduled for completion at the end of 1898. The line had been conceived in 1890, like many other transport ventures both at home and overseas, in the offices of Ashurst, Morris, Crisp & Co. Planned to run between the City and West London, under Cheapside, High Holborn, Oxford Street and the Bayswater Road, its prospects were promising, given that some 6 million passengers had travelled the route above ground in omnibuses during the last six months of 1889.[1]

In sharp contrast to the City & South London Company, which had pioneered the use of electricity but was proving to be singularly unprofitable, the Central London Railway project's future was sufficiently assured to attract the attention of the Rothschild-backed Exploration Company, then recently formed, as its name suggests, principally to develop mining interests. The syndicate formed to promote the Central London Railway included City financiers and bankers, Sir Ernest Cassel, Henry Oppenheim, Robert Fleming and Arthur Wragg as well as American interests.

William Morris acted for the group promoting the Central London Railway and became heavily involved, as he himself described, in alterations to the original scheme:

In 1891 I carried through the Central London Railway Act, which provided for a station in Cornhill, a very costly site. By arrangement with the Grosvenor Estate (Mr Boodle [of Boodle, Hatfield & Co., solicitors to the Estate]*) powers were obtained in this Act for the opening up of Davies Street and South Molton Street into Oxford Street, a very important street improvement.*

When the costliness of the Cornhill Station site seemed likely to prevent the construction of the Central London railway, I conceived the idea of making an underground station in front of the Royal Exchange with public subways and accesses from the streets. My friend, Mr J H Greathead, the Engineer ..., got out a Plan on the lines which I suggested to him.

In the Central London Railway Act of 1892 I introduced a Clause providing that three months before commencing any works within the City of London the Company should submit to the Commissioners (of Sewers) a comprehensive scheme and design for a central station and booking office and for public subways connecting Princes Street, Mansion House Street, The Poultry, Queen Victoria Street, Walbrook, Mansion House Place, Lombard Street, Cornhill and Threadneedle Street.

The same Clause provided that any other Railway Company having an underground station in the vicinity of the Mansion House should be entitled, subject to the written approval of the Commissioners, to have access by means of a subway from such underground station to the system of public subways.

I succeeded in obtaining the approval of the Commissioners of Sewers and the Corporation to the construction of what is now known as the Bank Station ...

My conception of the underground Bank Station has been utilised in other places – notably at Piccadilly Circus.

The layout of Bank station was the brainchild of William Morris for his client, the Central London Railway Company.

More than £2m was raised by an issue on the Stock Exchange in 1895 to finance the building of the line which started in 1896. In July 1900 the first trains ran, although Bond Street station was not completed and opened until September that year. The Twopenny Tube, as it soon became known following its adoption of a flat-rate fare, rapidly justified the hopes of those who had promoted and invested in it, attracting more than 100,000 passengers a day.[2]

William Morris's practice continued to reflect his interests, developed some two decades earlier, in transport and electricity. Increasingly the two came together, as the trams turned from horse power to electricity just as the underground railways were turning from steam to electric power. Extracts from Morris's own account of his professional life indicate not only the breadth of his client list but also the way in which his work for his clients adapted to reflect the challenges they had to meet. As he recalled:

In 1894 I acted for the London Street Tramways Company in the litigation which went to the House of Lords and which determined the principles on which Tramways were to be acquired by Local Authorities under the Act of 1870.

Subsequently I have acted in Arbitrations or arrangements for the sale of Tramway Undertakings to the London County Council and the Portsmouth, Plymouth, Cardiff, Grimsby and Belfast Corporations. I have also been concerned in the sale of various foreign and colonial Tramway Undertakings, including Madrid, Barcelona, Bucharest, Bombay and Brisbane.

In 1904 I became associated with the Anglo-Argentine Tramways Company ... negotiations had been started for absorbing various tramway undertakings in Buenos Ayres and I acted in the amalgamation with the Anglo-Argentine Company of ten separate Tramway Undertakings in that City. In 1908 a Concession was obtained under which a subway or underground railway was constructed through the heart of Buenos Ayres.

He did not mention, perhaps because of its lack of success, a scheme promoted in 1895 by the County of London Tramways Syndicate, also backed by the Exploration Company, in concert with the well-known mining house of Wernher, Beit & Co. The far-sighted scheme involved an attempt to amalgamate all the London tramway companies, introduce electrification to their operations and lease them in a complex scheme with the London County Council.[3]

Also among Morris's clients were two of London's 14 privately owned electricity undertakings. London was a special case as far as the supply of electricity was concerned; it was the only area in which more than one licence or order had been issued and, as a result, 14 private companies and 12 local authorities had established electricity supply undertakings. Competition was fierce and uneconomic. The County of London Electric Power Bill was introduced in 1905/6 in an attempt to create a more unified and sensible supply for the capital. The form in which it was proposed to do so was not, however, acceptable to Morris's clients:

I acted for all the Electric Lighting Companies in London in opposing ... the Bill. ... The Bill was not passed. In 1908 I opposed another similar Bill ... which was rejected ... and in that year I carried through the London Electricity Supply Act ... which was of great importance in that it provided that the London County Council could not purchase one Electric Light Undertaking without purchasing all.

Like the need for electricity, demand for housing in London spawned a number of corporate ventures. William Morris's involvement with the Artizans', Labourers' and General Dwellings Company has already been chronicled and in the 1890s two more housing companies for which he acted for the rest of his professional life were formed. Rowton Houses was registered by Morris in 1894. Lord Rowton, who as Montagu William Lowry had been Disraeli's secretary, had been concerned with the establishment of the Guinness Trust in 1890, to provide housing for the urban poor. Rowton's survey of London's common lodging houses, carried out for the Trust, persuaded him of the need for hostels for working men and the first Rowton House opened at Vauxhall in 1892. It offered a night's accommodation (including clean sheets, washing and cooking facilities) for 6d. In 1894, the year the company was registered, another hostel at King's Cross with nearly 700 beds (now the Mount Pleasant Hotel) opened. The company went on to open four more hostels: these were the 800-bedded Parkview House (now the London Park Hotel) at Newington Butts – where the charge was 7d a night – in 1897, at Hammersmith (1897), in Whitechapel (1902) and the largest, with over 1,000 beds at Camden Town (1905).[1]

In 1896 William Morris had been concerned with the establishment of the Wharncliffe Dwellings Company, formed to take over the buildings erected by the Great Central Railway Company in St John's Wood Road. The firm also acted for the Middle Class Dwellings Company and the Portman Estate Mansions Company. There were, too, other land and property development and investment companies among its clients; some were in London, for example, City and West End Properties, Consolidated London Properties and Metropolitan Properties while others were spread across the world, in the USA, Australia and New Zealand, Mexico and Africa as well as in John Morris's long-favoured area of interest, South America.[5]

In 1903 the senior partner, John Morris, reached the age of 80. His birthday was celebrated in style on 12 December with a banquet at the Hotel Metropole in Northumberland Avenue. Built in the mid-1880s, the 550-room hotel offered spacious accommodation for the guests to be received in the King's Hall. It was furnished for the occasion – to emphasise the longevity of the firm as well as that of Morris – with mementoes of the firm's history, including portraits of the founder, William Ashurst and of his grandfather, the distinguished judge, Sir William Ashurst. Among the guests was Ashurst's grandson, Joseph Stansfeld, the only son of his daughter Caroline and her husband, Sir James Stansfeld.

More than 50 guests attended the banquet in the Oak Room; they included Morris's fellow practitioners in the City, eminent members of the Bar and City bankers, accountants and financiers as well as his partners and his family. More than 40 further guests invited could not attend, prevented, in the case of a number of fellow octagenarians by ill health, or by other commitments. Their letters and the speeches which followed the dinner all paid tribute to Morris's longevity, abilities and achievements.

A year to the day later, on 12 December 1904, some 200 guests gathered again at the Hotel Metropole, this time in the Whitehall Rooms, to mark the Golden Wedding of John and Sarah Morris; the actual anniversary date had been in August but this gathering, orchestrated by Sir John Puleston (see Chapter 4), met to present the Morrises with 'a fitting Testimonial' subscribed for by more than 140 friends. John and Sarah Morris were presented with a portrait of themselves, painted by

Contributors to the presentation made to John Morris and his wife on 12 December 1904 to mark their Golden Wedding evidence the respect in which Morris was held in the profession and in the City.

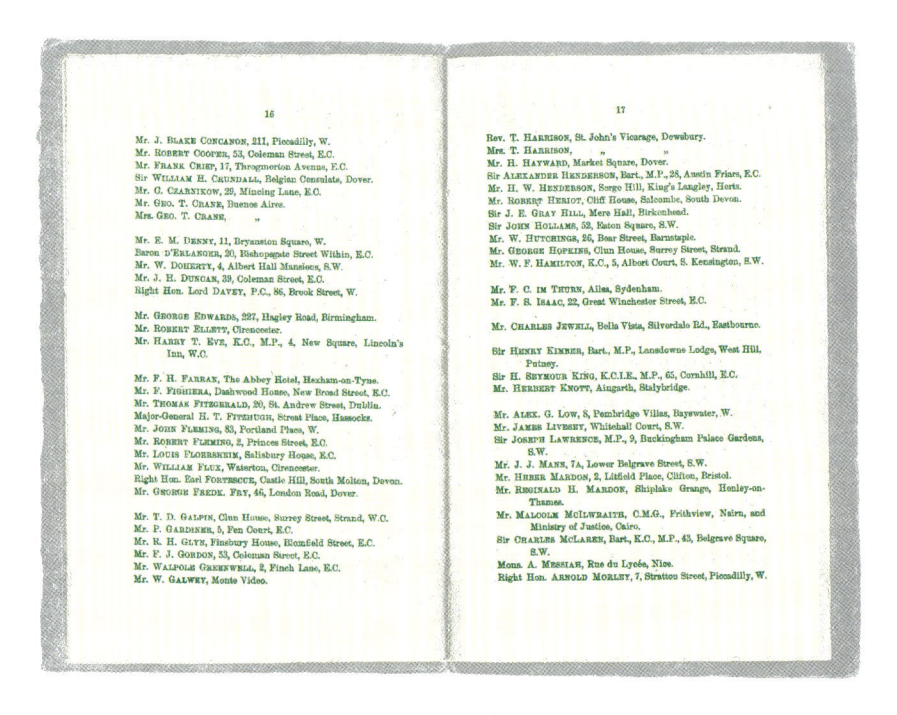

Hugh G Rivière (the completion of the portrait was the reason for the delay until December) and, as there had been funds to spare, they were also given 'an antique representation in ivory of Louis XIV, mounted in the pose of a Roman Emperor' and a diamond and pearl pendant for Mrs Morris. A further tribute to John Morris on this occasion was the presence of Charles Morrison, whose custom was, because of his poor health, not to attend such public functions. On both these occasions there were speeches and recollections of Morris's life and professional career, from which extracts have already been quoted.

Three months later, on 22 March 1905, John Morris died suddenly of heart failure at his London home. He was buried in Highgate Cemetery. Although one of his obituarists suggests he had made a partial retirement, there is no evidence that he had done so; indeed, he had been, according to the *Solicitors' Journal*, in the office only the day before he died. He had, however, while remaining the titular senior partner, increasingly handed over the reins of running the firm to Frank Crisp who now became, in name as well as fact, senior partner of Ashurst, Morris, Crisp & Co.

John Morris had spent 64 years with the firm, 51 of them as a partner and more than 40 of them as senior partner; it was an unrivalled record. He was, in the last two decades of the nineteenth century, largely and it should be said by his own decision — eclipsed by his younger partner, Frank Crisp. Morris's own abilities were summed up by the *Solicitors' Journal*: 'He was not only a skilled adviser who inspired the esteem and confidence of his clients, but also a man of far-seeing shrewdness and no little administrative ability.'[6] Moreover, the credit – and it should be a significant amount – for sustaining the firm and enhancing its reputation after the death of its founder and then the departure of his son to the Post Office, must belong to Morris alone.

Morris's death left the firm with three partners, Frank Crisp, William Morris and John Stevenson. The latter remains an insubstantial figure in the firm's history. His partnership lasted some 13 years, for ill-health forced him to retire in 1911 and he died the following year. According to one account, he was much occupied in company work and litigation during his time with the firm. With his managing clerk, George A J Smallman, he was concerned with the conduct of the litigation resulting from an action brought by Rhodesia Goldfields against the Globe &

Ashurst Morris Crisp

Sir John Crisp, son of Sir Frank and a partner 1906–50, senior partner 1934–50.

Phoenix Assurance Company, a case which lasted for about 12 years and, when it finally came to court, was at the time one of the longest actions heard.

Stevenson was a stickler for correct dress; he insisted that all his staff should wear the then regulation City dress – a morning suit and silk hat. It was *de rigueur* for this to be accompanied by a stiff collar. Soft collars, brown boots, flannel and light-coloured suits and bowler hats were rarely seen in the City and were regarded as negligent in the extreme. Better, it seems, the correct dress, even if the black coat was shiny, the collar frayed and the cuffs shabby – which, on a clerk's salary was sometimes all that could be managed – than the wrong clothes.[7]

In 1906 two new partners were admitted, John and Charles Crisp, two of the four sons of Frank Crisp. It had apparently been Crisp's intention that all his four boys, who had been educated at Eton, should go into the firm. The eldest son, however, Frank Morris Crisp, named for his father's partner and mentor, had artistic leanings and refused to become a solicitor. Another son, Bernard, preferred horticulture and became a partner in the firm of seed-merchants and market-gardeners, Waterer & Sons at Twyford.

John Wilson Crisp was a talented and keen oarsman; at the Henley Regatta in 1897 he was stroke for the winning Kingston Rowing Club four which beat Jesus College for the Wyfold Cup and for the eight which beat Christ Church, Oxford in the final of the Thames Cup.[8] He was also interested in coursing and won the Eye-Gold Cup and was runner-up in the Waterloo Cup with a whippet called *Clerical Error*. He was articled to his father after leaving Eton and admitted in January 1906.

Charles Crisp had a more technical turn of mind and was something of an amateur inventor. He went to Cambridge after Eton and then he, too, was articled to his father. He was admitted a solicitor in 1905. The two Crisp sons were by no means the only articled clerks at the firm. There had been a steady stream of them – one or two a year – in the 1890s, all paying a premium of 300 guineas, the charge made since the late 1830s. In 1903 a Mr Milburn was articled and in 1905 a Mr Fisher. Young men training for the Bar also found it useful to 'sit' for a time in a solicitor's office. In 1895 Mr Ford had paid £50 for a seat in the office and in 1903 a Mr Hedley paid a fee of £105 for the same privilege.

By this time, some ten years after his purchase of his country house, Friar Park, Frank Crisp's hobby had become something of a show-piece and it was open to the public twice a week. The original house had been considerably extended and rebuilt in neo-Gothic style, for entertaining and for the family; the Crisps had two daughters (one of them, Catherine, had married William Paterson in 1894; the wedding presents were kept in the firm's safe for a time) as well as the four sons. At Friar Park, Crisp and his wife entertained largely; one of his granddaughters recalled, 'The house was usually full at weekends, and at Christmas, Easter and Regatta week.' She went on to say of her grandfather: 'In an undemonstrative way he was devoted to my grandmother. She, as a good Victorian wife, was outwardly subservient, but had quite an influence on him without letting it appear so … As a whole, his family held him in great awe and respect, some fear and not much affection.'[9]

It was, however, in the grounds that Crisp indulged both his serious interest in gardening and what has been variously described as an eccentric and even bizarre sense of humour and taste for surprising, not always pleasantly, the 'IVs' – Ignorant Visitors – as Crisp characterised them. The grounds were dominated by a 100-ft scale model of the Matterhorn, built of Yorkshire mill-stone grit (20,000 tons of it were used) and topped with a piece of rock from the summit of the real mountain. Visitors were invited to view the Matterhorn through a telescope and saw a chamois grazing on the slopes; it was painted on the telescope. Beneath the mountain was a series of caves, illuminated with electricity and linked by an underground river. In the Big Cave there was a wishing well and a swan-shaped boat in which the visitor could paddle through to the ice cave or blue grotto where a model of a Chinese stork drank water when a button was pushed. There was also a vine cave (with glass grapes), a skeleton cave, an illusion cave (furnished with optical trickery) and a gnome cave; in the latter 'the little chaps were depicted taking snuff, examining a fly, opening a champagne bottle,

Sir Frank Crisp and a gardener at Friar Park with one of the follies.

and generally behaving in a very un-gnome-like fashion – not a fishing rod between them'.[10]

Away from Friar Park, the more Crisp became known in the wider world beyond the City, the more his services were in demand. In 1907 he drew up the agreements covering the cutting of the then largest diamond in the world. The Cullinan diamond, just over 3,000 carats, was discovered in the Premier mine in the Transvaal in 1905. The 'fine blue-white block … [was so large that it] would be a white elephant unless cut up'.[11] Presented to Edward VII by the Transvaal Government, it was sent to Amsterdam and cut into nine large stones and a number of small chips. Tradition has it that the expert cutter employed fainted after successfully completing his task, so greatly had the responsibility affected him.

At around the same time, Crisp made his expertise in company law available to the Board of Trade enquiry into the working of company law. Since the passing of the 1862 Companies Act there had been, from time to time, calls for reform and Bills drafted but all had been rejected. There was a powerful lobby of those who believed that incorporation with limited liability, whatever the opportunities it also offered to fraudulent promoters, had on balance 'conferred very great benefits on the country' and on the City.[12] The legislation which followed this enquiry clarified the status of the private company but made no other major changes.

Crisp drew up the contract for the cutting of the Cullinan diamond into the separate stones shown here.

Crisp was knighted in 1907, an honour which, according to several sources, had been offered to him previously but which he had always refused while John Morris was alive. It was, therefore, as Sir Frank Crisp, that he was appointed as solicitor in December 1908 to a new company, the Anglo-Persian Oil Company (now The British Petroleum Company plc (BP)). The oil industry, dominated at the beginning of the century by Russia and the USA was not unknown to the firm, which in 1900 had six oil companies as clients, two Russian, two Austrian and two in the Far East.[13] The origins of the Anglo-Persian company go back to the concession to explore for oil in Persia granted in 1901 to an Englishman, William Knox D'Arcy, who had already made his fortune in an Australian mining venture.

The exploration process, however, was long and expensive and even D'Arcy's resources were strained; he was obliged to accept financial assistance from the Burmah Oil Company. On 26 May 1908, oil in commercial quantities was found at Masjid i-Suleiman and the complex negotiations to form a company to exploit the discovery and the concession began. The detail and the complexity of the issues – the payment of royalties to the Persian Government, the rights of the Burmah Oil Company which had funded the discovery – have been recounted elsewhere. In these Crisp played a part and in April 1909 the Anglo-Persian Oil Company, with a capital of £2m, was incorporated. A few days later an issue of £600,000 in 6 per cent preference shares and £600,000 in 5 per cent debenture stock was made.

Some three years later the company was again in financial straits; at the same time the government wanted to secure a source of oil for the Navy. The two came together in 'protracted and complicated negotiations' over a draft contract drawn up by Sir Frank. The agreement was not finally signed until May 1914 but under its terms the government acquired, for about £2m, a controlling interest in the Anglo-Persian Oil Company, a shareholding that lasted until the 1980s. For the company the agreement was of the greatest significance: 'Without the security of the Admiralty contract it is almost inconceivable that the Company would have preserved its independent existence.'[14]

Of Ashurst, Morris, Crisp & Co.'s office staff in the years preceding the outbreak of war in 1914 not a great deal of detail is known. With four partners and its extensive list of clients, the size of its establishment had not diminished; the annual salaries bill drifted upwards and reached £15,000 in 1914. Profits in that year were £30,000, some £12,000 less than in 1913 but even so, they were still generally double those of Linklaters which also had four partners. Through all these years and up until 1917 undebited costs (work in progress) never fell below £100,000 and there were large sums in reserve and undivided profits (see Appendix 1). With the market for clerks 'notoriously overstocked' and

This lump of silver was originally a silver inkstand, presented to Crisp by clients when their case triumphed in the court of the first instance. The judgment was, however, overturned by the Appeal Court and the clients were very angry. They demanded the return of the inkstand but when the House of Lords upheld the original judgment, they presented it to him again! Sir Frank had it melted down and kept it on his mantlepiece to illustrate the uncertainties of litigation and, as the inscription on it reads, as a 'memento to the transient gratitude of clients'.

This Prospectus has been filed with the Registrar of Joint Stock Companies.

The List will be opened on the 19th April, 1909, and will be closed on or before the 21st April, 1909.

Anglo-Persian Oil Company, Limited

(Incorporated under the Companies (Consolidation) Act, 1908).

CAPITAL — — — £2,000,000,

DIVIDED INTO

1,000,000 Cumulative 6 per Cent. PARTICIPATING PREFERENCE SHARES of £1 each,

AND

1,000,000 ORDINARY SHARES of £1 each.

ISSUE OF

600,000 Cumulative 6 per Cent. PARTICIPATING PREFERENCE SHARES of £1 each at par,

PAYABLE

2s. 6d. per Share on Application.
2s. 6d. „ „ Allotment.

And the balance, as and when required, in Calls not exceeding 5s. each, at intervals of not less than two months.

The Preference Shares are entitled to a Preferential and Cumulative Dividend at the rate of 6 per cent. per annum on the amounts paid thereon, such Dividends for the first five years being guaranteed as hereinafter mentioned by The Burmah Oil Company, Limited.

After payment of the Cumulative Preference Dividend and payment of a Dividend on the Ordinary Shares for the year at the rate of 6 per cent. per annum, the profits in each year will be applied in payment of a further Non-Cumulative Dividend on the amounts paid on the Preference Shares at the rate of 2 per cent. per annum, and subject thereto a sum will be carried to a Special Reserve Fund out of the profits of each year, which fund will be applied only (a) in making up any deficit on the 6 per cent. Preference Dividend, and (b) in payment of the Capital paid up on the Preference Shares and the premium of 10 per cent. payable in respect thereof, but such Reserve may be used as part of the Working Capital of the Company.

Subject as aforesaid, the balance of the profits available for Dividend will belong to the holders of the Ordinary Shares.

On a winding-up the Preference Shares will be entitled to the preferential payment of an amount equal to 110 per cent. of the amounts paid thereon. The remainder of the surplus assets available for distribution will belong to the holders of the Ordinary Shares.

AND

£600,000 5 per Cent. FIRST DEBENTURE STOCK at par,

PAYABLE

£25 per cent. on Application.
£75 „ „ Allotment.

The Debenture Stock will be secured by a First Floating Charge on the whole of the Company's undertaking, and assets in favour of the Trustees named below, and will be redeemable at the Company's option at 5 per cent. premium, either in whole or in part, on the 31st December, 1920, or on any subsequent 31st December, on not less than six months' notice, and will be redeemed at the like rate on the Company going into voluntary liquidation for the purpose of re-construction or amalgamation. Commencing with the year 1920 the Company will redeem Debenture Stock to the amount of £20,000 annually, either by purchasing it in the open market, if obtainable under 5 per cent. premium, or by drawings in the usual way at 5 per cent. premium. The Company has the right to issue further Debenture Stock ranking *pari passu* with the above Stock provided the total Debenture issue equal to half the amount of the issued Share Capital for the time being.

Interest on the Debenture Stock will be payable half-yearly on 30th June and 31st December, the first payment being calculated on the instalments from the respective dates of payment. The Stock will only be transferable in multiples of £1.

Applications have already been received for 200,000 Preference Shares, and for £200,000 of Debenture Stock at par, and these Shares and Debenture Stock will be allotted to the applicants in full upon the terms of this Prospectus. Accordingly only 400,000 Preference Shares and £400,000 of Debenture Stock will be available for allotment otherwise.

The Directors will go to allotment only on subscription of the full amount of 600,000 Preference Shares and £600,000 of Debenture Stock.

No part of these issues has been underwritten.

Trustees for the Debenture Stockholders.

His Grace The DUKE OF SUTHERLAND, K.G., Stafford House, St. James's, London, S.W.
The Right Hon. The EARL OF LICHFIELD, 38, Great Cumberland Place, London, W.

Solicitors for the Trustees to the Debenture Stockholders.

FRESHFIELDS, 31, Old Jewry, London, E.C.

Board of Directors.

Chairman.

The Right Hon. LORD STRATHCONA AND MOUNT ROYAL, G.C.M.G., G.C.V.O., 28, Grosvenor Square, London, W.

Vice-Chairman.

C. W. WALLACE, Director The Burmah Oil Company, Limited, Winchester House, Old Broad Street, London, E.C.

Directors.

Sir HUGH S. BARNES, K.C.S.I., K.C.V.O. (late Lieutenant-Governor of Burma), East India United Service Club, St. James's Square, London, S.W.
JOHN T. CARGILL, Chairman The Burmah Oil Company, Limited, 175, West George Street, Glasgow.
W. K. D'ARCY, Chairman London Board Mount Morgan Gold Mining Company, Limited, 42, Grosvenor Square, London, W.
WILLIAM GARSON, Writer to the Signet, 5, Albyn Place, Edinburgh.
C. GREENWAY, Merchant (R. G. Shaw & Co.), Winchester House, London, E.C.
JAMES HAMILTON, Director The Burmah Oil Company, Limited, 175, West George Street, Glasgow.
H.S.H. PRINCE FRANCIS OF TECK, K.C.V.O., D.S.O., 36, Welbeck Street, London, W.

Bankers.

NATIONAL PROVINCIAL BANK OF ENGLAND, LIMITED, Head Office, 112, Bishopsgate Street Within, London, E.C., and Branches.
BANK OF SCOTLAND, Edinburgh (Head Office); Glasgow; London.
THE IMPERIAL BANK OF PERSIA, 25, Abchurch Lane, London, E.C.

Solicitors for the Company.

ASHURST, MORRIS, CRISP & CO., 17, Throgmorton Avenue, London, E.C.

Solicitors for the Vendors.

For THE BURMAH OIL COMPANY, LIMITED, and THE CONCESSIONS SYNDICATE, LIMITED—BOYDS, MILLER & THOMPSON, Glasgow.
For LORD STRATHCONA—SKENE, EDWARDS & GARSON, W.S., Edinburgh.

Brokers.

J. & A. SCRIMGEOUR, 37, Threadneedle Street, London, E.C.
S. M. PENNEY & MACGEORGE, 24, George Square, Glasgow.

Auditors.

BROWN, FLEMING & MURRAY, C.A., 175, West George Street, Glasgow.

Secretary.

S. ARTHUR SMITH.

Offices.

WINCHESTER HOUSE, OLD BROAD STREET, LONDON, E.C.

average wages and salaries not increasing, the 1890s and the years of this century up to 1914 have been characterised by one historian of the profession as the golden age for solicitors.[15]

One member of staff who joined as an office boy in 1909 at eight shillings a week – remuneration which had not changed since the mid-nineteenth century – wrote down some recollections some 60 years later. Of his eight shillings, a 2d tube fare and an 8d dinner – steak pudding with vegetables and a sweet – for six days a week would take some five shillings of his wage. He recalled that the only woman ever seen in the office was the housekeeper's maid who brought tea and toast to the partners and managers in the afternoon. Most letters and documents were still written by hand although one or two 'very cumbrous typewriters' had been installed in the office; they were known as 'caligraphic writing machines'. As in most other offices at the time, copies were obtained by using the letter-press; letters were inserted in a dampened tissue paper book and pressed to ensure that a copy was retained on the tissue paper.

For relaxation the firm supported a number of activities for its clerks; cricket and football teams were organised to play matches with teams from other City solicitors' offices. There was an annual outing, one year to Eastbourne and one year to Friar Park. And there was the Ashmor Musical Society which held three Smoking Concerts a year, usually in the Abercorn Room at the Great Eastern Hotel, 'at which the leading vocalists and musicians of the day would be engaged to provide the entertainment'. Established in 1899, the Ashmor Musical Society had been a great success, too much so it seems, for at a special meeting in December 1912, Mr Botwright (one of the firm's cashiers and a leading light of the Society) was obliged to announce to its members that it was 'the wish of Sir Frank Crisp (expressed with the concurrence of the other partners in the Firm) that no persons outside the office should be asked for subscriptions to the Society'. In these circumstances, the members decided, it was impossible to carry on. Out of the remaining funds of the society, presentations were to be made to Mr Botwright and to the Musical Director, James Honess (he was William Morris's clerk) and the balance was to be given to the Ashmor football club. The minutes concluded in a melancholy fashion: '... thus ended the last meeting of the Ashmor Musical Society which existed for nearly 13 years and which

FACING PAGE

The Anglo-Persian Oil Company (now The British Petroleum Company plc) was formed and floated on the Stock Exchange in 1909, the firm acting for it as the prospectus indicates.

from a small beginning grew to large proportions and gained a high reputation in the City of London for the excellence of its concerts'.

For some time Sir Frank Crisp had been acting as legal adviser to the Liberal Party, since December 1905 the governing party after a landslide election victory. In 1913 his services were called upon during what became known as the Marconi Scandal. In 1910 Godfrey Isaacs became managing director of the Marconi Company which, some two years later, was tendering for a contract to build an imperial network of wireless stations. Isaacs' elder brother, Rufus (later Lord Reading) was the Government's Attorney-General. The Isaacs were Jewish and rumours soon began to circulate suggesting that they and Sir Herbert Samuel, the Postmaster-General who was also Jewish, were involved in exercising undue influence in getting the contract for the Marconi Company. Soon it was also suggested that ministers – Isaacs, Samuel and the then Chancellor of the Exchequer, David Lloyd George – had been indulging in 'insider dealing' to profit personally from buying and selling Marconi shares.

In the longer term the various enquiries showed such allegations to be untrue, although some ministers had, unwisely, bought shares in the American Marconi Company which was quite unaffected by the UK government contract. In the short term it was a personal statement in the House of Commons by the Attorney-General, Rufus Isaacs, a speech in the drafting of which, tradition has it, Sir Frank played a part, which defused the tension and saved the government. Whatever Sir Frank's particular contribution may have been, he was certainly involved in advising the participants at a critical time in the party's affairs.[16]

Crisp's close connection with the Liberal Party is evidenced further by his inclusion in Asquith's 1911 list of 'men of Liberal conviction whom he proposed to enoble should the need arise' in the battle to secure the passage of the Parliament Bill. In January 1913 Crisp was made a Baronet. Writing to Venetia Stanley, the girl with whom he was then in love, on 18 February 1913, Asquith mentioned Crisp:

Your letter of Friday arrived here this morning and was as welcome as – I was going to say 'the flowers that bloom in the spring'. But looking out of the window upon our spacious lawns and parterres, I can only see a single yellow crocus ... Sir F Crisp, who promised to be our horticultural providence, has certainly not earned the baronetcy which was prematurely bestowed upon him on New Year's Day.[17]

The outbreak of war in August 1914 came as a shock to the City. It also took by surprise one of Crisp's clients – the Nobel-Dynamite Trust. Referred to initially by its secretary as 'unfortunate international complications' its members hoped, as did so many others, that it would be 'business as usual' and be over by Christmas. In the short term the joint German ownership was effectively put on ice and there was no direct contact with the German co-owners and members of the Trust.

In January 1915, however, an article on the Trust was published in *The Engineer*. Temperate in tone, it noted of the Trust that 'the many years' connection with Great Britain … constitutes a fresh example in which British enterprise has assisted … in fortifying the warlike equipment of a country whose hostility towards us has been manifest for a long time past'. Seeing this as a warning bell, Crisp wrote to his client immediately:

If the position of the Trust were ventilated publicly, the way in which the public would look at it would be that the Trust are the owners of the whole of the shares of four German companies who are engaged in making explosives … for … killing our troops, and those of our Allies and there would be I am afraid a howl of indignation throughout the country at the Directors of the Trust personally for not having as it will be said lifted a little finger to in any way remedy this state of things.

Prodded thus by their solicitor, the Trust directors moved swiftly and by September that year the Trust had been, through correspondence with a neutral middleman, liquidated.

Inevitably, the British company, Nobel's Explosives Company, earned a good deal of money during the war, even with the amounts creamed off by the excess profits tax that the government introduced. This fuelled the ambitions of its managing director, Sir Harry McGowan, to create a more widely based industrial group and gave him the wherewithal to achieve them. In 1918 Sir Frank Crisp acted on the formation of Explosives Trades Ltd, a merger, based on Nobel's Explosives Company, of all the companies in the industry. The company was renamed Nobel Industries Ltd in 1920, to reflect better its rationalisation of the explosives industry and its investments and acquisitions in motor components, leathercloth and paint. The new company, with its capital of nearly £16m, was a step on the way to the formation of ICI in 1926.[18]

The Asquith Cup was given to Sir Frank Crisp by Prime Minister H H Asquith and his wife, Margot (daughter of Sir Charles Tennant) in grateful recognition of the help and advice Sir Frank had given at the time of the Marconi Scandal.

As the war continued, the strains in the firm's office must have been considerable. As in other City offices, young men departed to the armed forces, many to be killed in action. For those at home there was still work to be done, even though the Stock Exchange was closed until 1915 and then only permitted very limited transactions, and there were far fewer men to do them. In many City solicitors' offices women were – albeit reluctantly – employed for the first time. There was personal grief and loss too; William Morris's youngest son, Frederick, who had already joined the firm, was killed in action. So too were five other members of the firm.

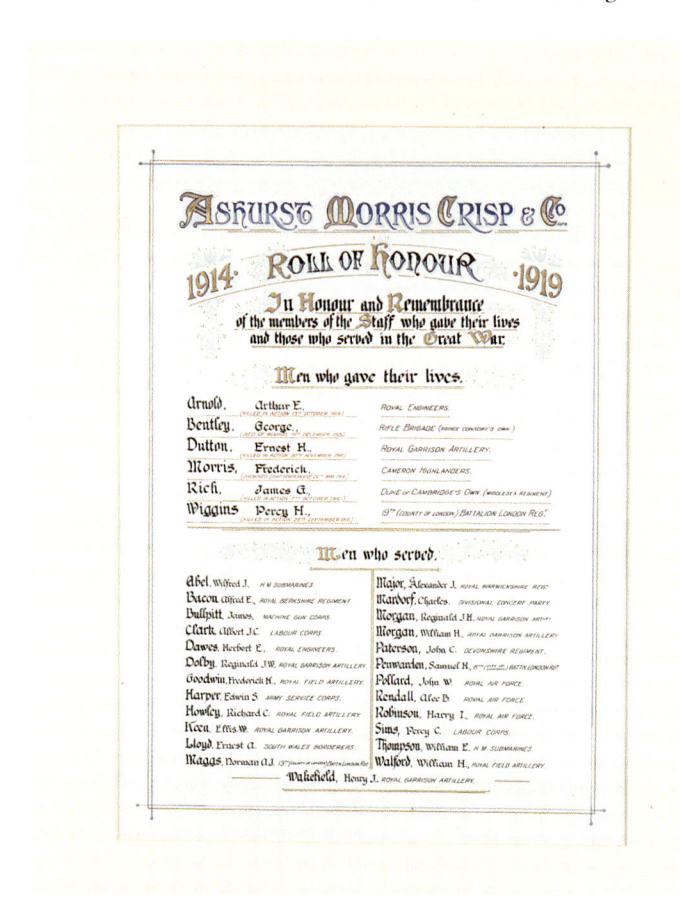

The firm's profits, however, held up well. They fell to their lowest, £20,600, in 1915, a figure representing about a half of the annual profit in good pre-war years; in 1916 Linklaters' profits bottomed at £6,500, also about half of pre-war profits. By 1918 Ashurst, Morris, Crisp & Co.'s profits were almost £29,000 again; the salaries bill that year was £12,500, less than pre-war and, given war-time inflation and pressure on wages and salaries, indicates a smaller establishment of clerks. By 1918, however, the signs that business was picking up again were sufficient for the partners to look to the future and in that year a new (and initially salaried) partner was admitted. Thomas Outen, who had joined the firm as an office boy in 1889, had shown both ability and a determination to get on and had been given his articles. He had been admitted as a solicitor in 1917.

Sir Frank Crisp was 75 in 1919. He continued to work as he had done for so many years. In April that year he was advising Courtaulds, the company built up by Samuel Courtauld, for whom Ashurst had acted in

Frederick Morris (b. 1892), was the only son of William Morris to join the firm. Like others he left for active service during the First World War and was killed in action. The Roll of Honour commemorates those from the firm who died.

the 1830s in the fight against Church rates. The precise date when Courtaulds became a client is not known. Crisp acted for the company in 1913, perhaps for the first time, when the company, hitherto a private and family-owned concern reorganised and restructured itself although it did not then make a public flotation.[19] The company's development of a new synthetic fabric, rayon, had earned it great wealth in the USA where it had established a subsidiary company as well as in the UK. It was on the problem of dealing with this that Crisp was advising the company in April 1919.

At the end of that month, however, at Friar Park, Sir Frank died. He was buried at Henley, where he had become a well-known local figure and a generous municipal benefactor, his funeral attended by many of his clients or their representatives, as well as local organisations and

Courtaulds established a subsidiary company in the USA in 1909 to exploit the development of rayon. The American Viscose Company's factory, shown here, was at Marcus Hook. It was very successful and profitable.

family. The obituaries of a 'great legal personality' were fulsome, all noting his 'unrivalled knowledge' of company law and, due in no small part to this, the firm's 'exceptionally large' corporate practice. It would be difficult to exaggerate Crisp's contribution to the growth of the firm and its standing in the City. His death, almost a century after the founding of the firm, brought to an end a period of almost 60 years with the firm, 48 of them as a partner – and the last 15 of them as senior partner. It marked the end of an era for the firm.

CHAPTER 7

The doldrums: 1919–46

THE SUDDEN AND unexpected death of Sir Frank Crisp at the end of April 1919 created a vacuum in the firm, where there was no successor ready groomed to take over his large portfolio of corporate clients or indeed his place in the City. William Morris, then 64 years old, who has been described at that time as 'a formidable-looking man, stout and red-cheeked like a character in a Galsworthy novel',[1] became the senior partner of the firm. He was a much respected figure in the profession, evidenced by his recent election (in March 1919) to the prestigious Lowtonian Society, the first member of the firm to be offered that privilege. The Society, a select dining club, had been founded in 1793 and was restricted by its constitution to 31 members. William Morris had, as we have seen, his own extensive practice built up over the years. Crisp's sons, John and Charles, had been partners for 13 years but junior partners, much overshadowed by their father. It does not seem that Sir Frank had bequeathed to them or fostered in them the qualities which had given him such professional eminence.

In Thomas Outen the firm had, as Sir Frank had rightly seen and as Outen himself was to prove over the next two decades, an able lawyer. He was, however, a man who lived only for his work, putting in long hours at the office and rarely, if ever, relaxing. At that time some solicitors entered their home address in the annually published Law List, perhaps hoping to attract additional clients. Characteristically, Outen did so as long as the practice continued; when he became a partner he was living in Stroud Green, in North London. In 1925 he moved to Stanmore.

It was, those who knew him recall, typical of Outen to begin a letter to the chairman of Courtaulds, one of Sir Frank's clients whose affairs he inherited in 1919, in this fashion: 'I had the following thoughts when lying in bed at 2 a.m.' He continued to elaborate on the thoughts for some 20 pages. Outen's ability and dedication won for him the respect of his clients but he did not wear his expertise lightly, as had his mentor, and he never developed either the presence or the authority of Sir Frank.

In the immediate aftermath of Crisp's death, the partners cast about for a suitable new partner. It was not an easy time to do so. The profession's manpower, claimed by its leaders through most of the nineteenth century to be overstocked, was seriously depleted during the First World War. More than 3,000 solicitors, representing almost a quarter of the profession, saw active service and more than a third of them were killed or seriously wounded. More than a half of the then articled clerks also served and almost two-thirds of them were killed or seriously wounded. The number of solicitors admitted during the war years dropped and, in the years immediately after the war, there was no compensating increase in either admissions or articled clerks.[2]

The partners in Ashurst, Morris, Crisp & Co. thought they had found a suitable candidate in Arthur Manfred Wintle Wells, a barrister, with whom they quickly agreed in June 1919 that, having left the Bar, as soon as he had qualified as a solicitor, he should become a partner; in the meantime he was to be paid a salary of £1,000 a year. The agreement stipulated that when Wells became a partner, he was to share a quarter of the partnership profits with Outen, Wells taking three-twentieths and Outen two; William Morris, John Crisp and Charles Crisp were entitled each to a quarter of the profits. Wells was admitted as a solicitor in July 1920 but the new partnership did not last long; in October 1920, for reasons which are not now known, it was dissolved, apparently amicably. A new agreement between William Morris, the Crisp brothers and Thomas Outen was drawn up, giving Morris a 25 per cent interest, the Crisps 30 per cent each and Outen 15 per cent.

It was not, however, only the problem of finding a worthy sucessor to Crisp that the firm faced. Although he was 75 when he died Crisp had, it seems, either not received or not taken notice of any intimations of mortality and his personal and professional affairs were not as well-ordered as might have been expected. His will, unaltered since 1871, was

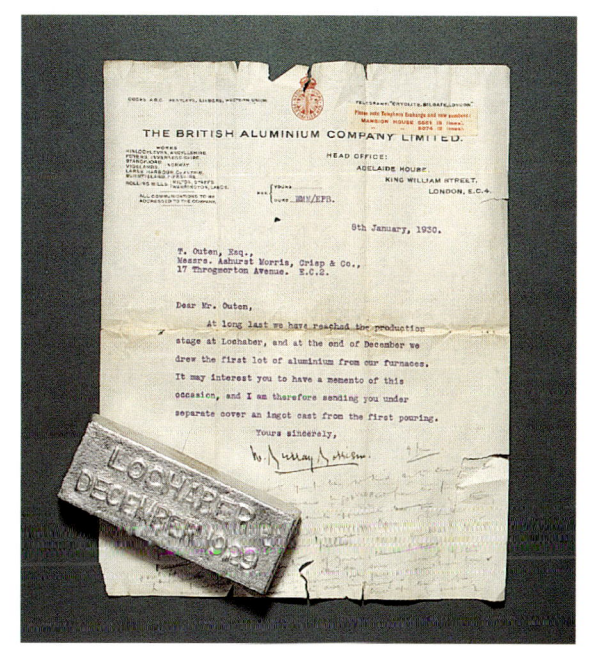

The British Aluminium Company, a client of the firm, proudly presented Thomas Outen with an ingot from the first pouring.

William Morris, a partner 1883–1933, senior partner 1919–33.

a simple and extraordinarily brief document for any man, let alone one believed to be very wealthy. 'Made on a sheet of notepaper, and contains less than 100 words', as *The Legal Journal* reported, with a note of incredulity, it read: 'I give devise and bequeath all my property whatsoever over which I have now or may hereafter have any disposing power to my wife Catherine for her own use absolutely.'[3] There was no executor appointed, so his eldest son, Frank Morris Crisp had to apply for letters of administration. Frank Morris Crisp was now Sir Frank since he had inherited his father's baronetcy; he was, according to family tradition, grateful that he had escaped by a whisker being 'Lord Bung'. Apparently Sir Frank Crisp had, early in 1919, accepted a peerage offered by Lloyd George and decided to be known as Lord Bungay. He died before it could be conferred upon him.[4] Sir Frank's estate was valued for probate at £179,214 (gross), £71,139 (net) but was subsequently revalued to a mere £2,000. Friar Park had to be sold, raising £70,000 for the estate but the family's London house, in Lansdowne Road, was secured for Lady Crisp.

There were financial repercussions for the firm too, as a result of Crisp's death. Income tax had risen sharply during the war to become, for the first time, noticeable; in 1915 it was raised to 3s 6d in the pound, in 1916 to five shillings in the pound and in 1918 to six shillings in the pound. Additionally in 1918 supertax was imposed for the first time on higher incomes at up to six shillings in the pound. By 1922 it had become apparent that the firm faced large tax bills; Thomas Outen, who was dealing with the matter, wrote bitterly to his partners in August that year: '… the result to me of my becoming a partner will apparently be that every penny I scraped together while I was a manager will have to go to pay these infernal taxes – which is not a very pleasant result after having worked like a nigger for over 3 years (to say nothing of all my hard work of previous years)'.

Although the firm's profits had, like those of all City solicitors, inevitably fallen during the war when business and commercial activity had been at a low ebb, money had continued to come in on bills and work done in previous years. The problem was compounded, as the firm's accountants explained to the partners in 1925, by the method chosen for assessing liability:

Contrary to the usual Income Tax procedure of assessing businesses on the average of three years' profits, your Firm has been assessed on the average of three

The
doldrums

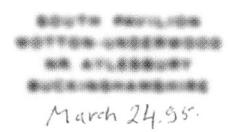

139

[Address redacted]

March 24. 95.

Dear Miss Slinn,

I remember meeting Mr Morris on one occasion when he invited me to his grand flat in Portland Place having suddenly decided to give me a present of £100 on the occasion I think of my 21st Birthday! He was a rather formidable looking man, stout and red cheeked like a character in a Galsworthy novel, and was I think with his third wife who had been Miss Halibut. Florence Terry died before I was born, but Gertrude, his second wife lived in a handsome house on Campden Hill when I met her several times - once on a Christmas Day visit. She was a handsome and agreeable lady. But I never met 'Uncle Willie' then.

Olive his daughter, was outlawed by him for many years owing to her liaison with Charles Hawtrey the well-known actor, by whom she had three children - Anthony, one of them, went on the stage and was in the same company as I was at the Old Vic in 1929. I never knew him well, but he had some success as a director and manager of the

her daughter, the actress Julia Neilson, married Fred Terry, who became Willie's son-in-law after previously being his brother-in-law owing to his marriage to Florence Terry!

Embassy Theatre in Swiss Cottage. My brother worked with him there. I am not sure when he died. There is quite a bit about Olive in Marguerite Steen's book 'A Pride of Terrys' which you might be interested to read. Olive lived at Smallhythe in her later years and became custodian of the Ellen Terry Museum there. I knew her very slightly but she was elegant and amiable. I think that is all I can tell you.

Tony Hawtrey married Marjorie, an actress and later gave up the stage and suddenly reappeared in Washington as a Cook Housekeeper at the British Embassy when I happened to meet her. I know in 1954 if they had any children.

Yours sincerely
John Gielgud

Sir John Gielgud was William Morris's godson; he remembers him in the 1920s as rather like a character from a Galsworthy novel.

years' net cash receipts. This method of assessment was agreed to by the Inspector of Taxes a number of years ago and unfortunately now gives rise to inequalities when changes in the members of the firm occur, more especially in the case of the retirement or death of a partner holding a considerable share in the business of the firm.

Crisp's share in the partnership had been 55 per cent and as long as money continued to come in from the old firm, his estate was due that proportion of it. Equally, counsel advised when consulted by the partners, his estate must be liable for a proportionate share of the tax bills. It was not therefore until 1930 that Crisp's estate and the firm's tax affairs were finally settled to the satisfaction of all concerned.

In the City the post-war return to normality had been signalled in March 1919 when the Treasury's control of new domestic issues was lifted. In the year-long boom that followed some £400m new capital was raised by flotations on the London Stock Exchange but thereafter new issue work declined as the economy slid into a slump.[5] The liquidation of British overseas investments that had taken place during the war reduced the number of foreign business enterprises financed from London, many of whom had, as we have seen, been the firm's clients. The City journalist, A S J Osborn, noted the change in *The City News* in 1928: 'The Foreign Market does not quite assume the importance of pre-war days when we were almost exclusively financiers to the world.'[6]

However, among those client companies that did survive were a number of South American enterprises, including the Buenos Ayres & Pacific Railway Company for which the firm continued to act until after the Second World War. It was on behalf of the railway company that Outen became involved in a lengthy arbitration in the 1920s concerning a tunnel built through the Andes. Frederick William Cowham was Outen's litigation managing clerk and it was he who, in an expedition unusual at this time, spent some nine months in Argentina gathering the evidence which enabled the firm to win the case for its client. Cowham had been with the firm for some 30 years – he joined it in August 1889 on a weekly wage of £3 which had, by 1925, trebled; he continued to work with Ashurst, Morris, Crisp & Co. until after the Second World War.

Cowham was typical of the unadmitted managing clerks on whom the partners – in City firms generally as well as at Ashurst, Morris, Crisp & Co. – relied for the transaction of business. Often joining their firms as office boys, they developed by the time they were in their forties, an unrivalled knowledge of custom and practice in the Courts. They also knew the highways and byways of the City, the gossip and the *on-dit* of the profession, the Bar and the City more fully than their principals.

The firm's total manpower shrank in the 1920s, according to the account of one of its then clerks, and it was able to sub-let the first floor of Garden House (17 Throgmorton Avenue), including the room which had been Sir Frank Crisp's, to a firm of stockbrokers instead of using it itself, as it had done since 1890. Although qualified solicitors were less readily available than before, with unemployment at 1m from 1921 on, there was no problem in employing staff so that the reduction came from choice rather than necessity. It suggests, along with the other evidence, that the practice became smaller in the 1920s, although the client lists which can be extracted from the *Stock Exchange Year Books* of those years indicate a still extensive practice. The fee income and net profits in the 1920s are considerably less than in the 1880s and 1890s, the more so when the fall in the value of money over the war years is taken into account. The average profit in the five years 1923 to 1927 was just over £21,000 and the annual salaries bill in those years averaged £15,000 (see Appendix 1).

The firm's figures, however, are broadly in the same range as those of, for example, Slaughter and May, which also had four partners, and whose profits were £20,356 in 1919 and £25,757 in 1920. Among other City firms, Linklaters & Paines, as the firm had become following a merger, was now a much larger firm with nine partners, and its profits averaged, through the 1920s and the early 1930s, £54,000 a year. Taken down to fee income earned per partner, that does not represent earnings much greater than those at Ashurst, Morris, Crisp & Co. or at Slaughter and May. What made the difference, it seems clear from looking at the profits of a new firm

Bill Rowe (born in 1894) joined the firm in 1925, as a liftman, after seeing active service during the First World War. He stayed as a general 'odd-job' man until the 1960s, resisting all attempts to retire him.

specialising in the work, was acting on new issues. Clifford-Turner & Hopton, acting on more than 40 new issues in the boom of 1919–20 produced profits in 1920 (with only two partners) of £36,284. In 1922, when the boom was over, their profits dropped back to £18,000.[7]

Without Sir Frank Crisp, work – and especially that connected with incorporation and flotation – did not come to the firm in the same quantity. The connection he had forged with the Nobel-Dynamite Trust and Explosives Trades (see Chapters 5 and 6), for example, was lost; when Nobel Industries (as Explosives Trades had become) merged in 1926 with Brunner Mond and two other smaller companies to form Imperial Chemical Industries (ICI), Slaughter and May were appointed as ICI's solicitors and the more recently established firm of Clifford-Turner, Hopton & Lawrence acted on the incorporation. This was business that the firm could have counted on receiving in Sir Frank's time. Inevitably, in the circumstances, there were one or two clients who left the firm when Sir Frank was no longer there to attend to them personally; in 1919 the Anglo-Persian Oil Company took its main corporate work to Linklaters & Paines and the merchant bank, Morgan Grenfell, did likewise to Slaughter and May.

These were, however, the exceptions rather than the rule and the firm's clients in the 1920s included most of the mining, land and development, plantation and South American companies for which it had acted since the 1880s and 1890s. There were some changes; Prohibition introduced in 1920 in the USA had an impact on the business of the US breweries which were clients of the firm and some of them diversified into other activities. The New England Breweries changed its name to the New England and General Trust, to indicate its new business as an investment trust; Bartholomay Brewing diversified first into ice-cream production and, in 1931, also into an investment trust.[8] There were, too, new clients. Thomas Outen started to act for the International Harvester Company's British subsidiary and for the Royal Bank of Canada.

Strange tasks have been and are sometimes entrusted to City solicitors. It was, according to an earlier historian of the firm, in 1922 that Outen:

was asked to undertake a most delicate matter. The daughter of an American millionaire had fallen in love with her Swiss riding master who was somewhat older than she. Her father would not consent to the marriage until his daughter had reached her 18th birthday.

She was therefore sent over to this country with a Chaperone, presumably to try to break off the attachment, however the Swiss riding master also came over here and there were many consultations between the young couple and Mr Outen in this office. The same day as the daughter reached her 18th birthday, Mr Outen received a cable from her father consenting to the marriage taking place.

Tremendous publicity was being given to the romance by the newspapers, both in America and here, and Mr Outen's task was to get the couple married as quietly as possible.

With the very able and wiley [sic] assistance of Mr Cowham, the newspaper representatives were put on to a false trail of the heiress having gone to Paris for her trousseau, in the meantime, the bridegroom (who had been residing with Mr Cowham for the past three weeks) and his bride were quietly married in the local Registry Office.

More mainstream to the firm's practice than the love life of American heiresses was the development in the interwar years of what have become known as the 'new' industries, broadly characterised as chemicals, rayon, electrical engineering, entertainment and motor manufacturing. There were just under 1m motor vehicles on the roads in 1921, more than 2m by 1931 and 3m, two thirds of which were private cars, by 1938. William Richard Morris (Viscount Nuffield, 1877–1963) had produced his first motor-cars in 1913 and, during the 1920s he emerged as the foremost British car manufacturer. He was also manufacturing lorries, vans, taxis and luxury cars as separate businesses. In 1926 they were all consolidated into Morris Motors Ltd, a transaction on which Ashurst, Morris, Crisp & Co. acted; in the following year Morris acquired the Wolsey manufacturing company. There was no large flotation when Morris Motors was formed; of the new company's £3m issued capital only some preference shares were issued to the public. Morris himself continued, for another decade, to own £2m in ordinary shares.[9]

Another developing industry was that of aircraft manufacture where again the firm had a significant client. Charles Crisp's interest in technical matters and innovation has already been noted and, according to one account, he invented and patented a sparking plug. It was, no doubt, in pursuit of these interests that he became acquainted with Richard Fairey, founder of the Fairey Aviation Company. Born in 1887, Fairey was obliged to leave school at 15 when his father's business failed. He trained as an electrical engineer and it was while he was working at

Finchley Power Station that he began to work on model aircraft. In 1912 he joined Short Brothers and, as the need for aeroplanes grew rapidly during the war, in 1915, with the blessing of Shorts and the promise of an Admiralty contract, Fairey formed his own company. Charles Crisp, described by Fairey's historian as a friend of the founder, was its solicitor.[10]

The immediate post-war years were difficult for the aircraft industry as a whole as orders from the government disappeared; the Fairey Company was voluntarily liquidated in 1921 and reconstructed. The mid- to late-1920s, however, saw the economy staging something of a recovery from the slump. With the outlook improving, a new Fairey company was registered in 1929, with a nominal capital of £500,000 in 10 shilling shares. Later that year the company bought a 150-acre site near Harmondsworth in Middlesex for £15,000 where it laid out a private aerodrome. That site eventually, and after creating a good deal of work for the firm, formed the initial nucleus of Heathrow Airport (see Chapter 8).

The increasing commercial activity had played a part in the decision, in 1926, to admit a new partner to the firm. Appelbe Chisholm Adams was 48 years old; educated at Harrow, he was admitted a solicitor in 1906, and, after a brief period as a partner with Farrar, Porter & Co. of 2 Wardrobe Place, he had joined Stephenson Harwood & Co., according to their records as a managing clerk. From 1910 to 1915 he did, however, have an entry in the Law List at their offices in 31 Lombard Street, but it was not until 1915 that he became a partner. He was away for a period of war service 1917–19 and then returned as a partner. Following the merger of Stephenson Harwood with Tatham & Lousada, he became a partner in the new firm, Stephenson Harwood & Tatham in 1920 and it was from there that he came to Ashurst, Morris, Crisp & Co. Surviving descriptions of Adams indicate that he was 'a marvellous company man', with a good deal of experience in preparing company prospectuses, and was 'charming ... friendly and popular'. Although 'given to the use of extremely coarse language [he was] ... extremely good-natured and sociable', the latter especially so when taking liquid refreshment after office hours.[11]

The detailed arrangements that the partners made with Adams show that he was not regarded as a full partner. He brought with him clients of his own for whom separate press-copy letter books and account books

The doldrums

The Ashmor Sports Club dinner, 1937.

were to be kept; these were to be open for inspection by the principal partners (Morris, the Crisp brothers and Outen) but Adams was not to have access to the firm's books or accounts. Adams was entitled to 50 per cent of the profits from work for his clients and a share of the firm's profits equal to the proportion that two-thirds of his own profits bore to the firm's profits. These complex arrangements did not, however, last for long. Adams died of cancer in 1927 and the firm again consisted of only four partners.

Of those four, the senior partner, William Morris, was now 71 years of age. His health was uncertain and he no longer worked full time at the office. As he himself wrote in 1932:

In 1924 and again in 1925 I had severe illnesses. My Doctor advised that I should restrict my business activities and take things more easily. Since 1925 I have taken in hand very little new work, but I continue to act for certain concerns with which I have been long and intimately associated and in connection with various trusts and family businesses.

In January 1921, at the age of 65, Morris had married again; his third wife, Emma Heilbut, was a wealthy widow. After the marriage the Morrises lived at Gordon House, Sunningdale, an 11-bedroomed detached country house set in grounds of nearly one and a half acres bordering the Sunningdale Ladies Golf Club. They also had a flat in town.

The badge of the Ashmor Football Club, probably based on John Crisp's whippet, Clerical Error *which had enjoyed considerable success in the field.*

Morris's days in the office were attended with a good deal of ceremony. He arrived at 11 a.m. and the beadle who looked after Throgmorton Avenue, alerted by the firm's liftman, would make sure that the Avenue in front of Number 17 was clear for the arrival of Morris in his Rolls-Royce car. At 4 p.m. the Avenue was cleared again for the Rolls to collect Morris and take him home. Similar routines were observed nearby for Lord Faringdon's day at the stockbroking firm, Greenwoods; he arrived in his Cabriolet Daimler – he kept his Rolls in the country.[12]

Morris reduced his share of the profits in 1926 from 25 per cent to 15 per cent, and the agreement between the partners in that year gave Thomas Outen the extra 10 per cent. Effectively then, the firm had three full-time partners and this may, in part have dictated the agreement with Adams. After his sudden death, however, the partners carried on until January 1931 when Outen's son, Roland, aged 29, who had been articled to him and admitted in 1924, became a partner. The two Crisps and Outen senior all reduced their shares slightly to give Roland Outen a 5 per cent share in the partnership. He was guaranteed an income of £1,000 a year (the amount his father had been paid in 1918 as a salaried partner) in the event of his 5 per cent share of the profits falling below that sum.

From the mid-1920s John Crisp was busy with the affairs of a client inherited from his father who turned out to be a bane rather than a blessing for the firm. Clarence Charles Hatry (1888–1965) was a company promoter and financier whose interests lay in devising, promoting and organising the financing of schemes of amalgamation and rationalisation. Following the failure of his family business Hatry established himself in the City, first as an insurance broker. In 1916 he took over the Commercial Bank of London, reconstructing it in 1920 as the Commercial Corporation of London to act as the vehicle for his further acquisitions and promotions. It collapsed in 1923.

Undeterred, Hatry went on to establish a group of interrelated companies and finance houses centred on the Austin Friars Trust and including Corporation & General Securities, the Drapery & General Investment Trust (to amalgamate department stores which he successfully sold to Debenhams), the Photomaton Parent Corporation and the Associated Automatic Machine Corporation, for all of which the firm acted. Hatry was, according to the Marquess of Winchester who became his close business associate:

> ... *an example of the alert business brain having an unusually quick perception of any proposition, a marvellous gift for sifting the intricacies of a Balance Sheet, a power of putting his case with a clarity of expression rarely found apart from legal training, coupled with an apparent frankness which amounted to a charm of manner.*

Many of Hatry's schemes for industrial rationalisation were sound and sensible, not least the one for the iron and steel industry which ultimately broke him. In his attempts to find the finance for them, however, faced with the implacable opposition of the Governor of the Bank of England, Montagu Norman, one of the few in the City able to resist the Hatry charm, 'he over-reached himself, abused the procedure of the Stock Exchange, and finally broke the law'.[13]

In September 1929 the Hatry group collapsed, with debts of some £14m. Money had been borrowed against forged certificates for loans that Hatry had promoted for a number of town councils – Gloucester, Swindon and Wakefield. At his trial in 1930 Hatry was found guilty of what Mr Justice Avory described as 'the most appalling frauds that have ever disfigured the commercial reputation of this country', a judgment many felt to be unnecessarily harsh; Hatry was sentenced to 14 years' imprisonment. John Crisp was one of the signatories to a small pamphlet produced in 1937 and intended to 'separate the fact from the legend' of Hatry and his affairs. It played a part; the signatories, who included A P Herbert (MP for Oxford University), George Lansbury MP, sometime leader of the Labour Party, and Harold Nicolson MP, as well as several accountants, believed in the Home Secretary's 'wise and humane decision' to reduce Hatry's sentence. Released from prison, Hatry went to the Continent to start life afresh. 'We understand,' his friends wrote, 'that Mr Hatry has no intention of returning to the City or of re-engaging in Finance.'[14] Unfortunately for the firm (see Chapter 8), the outbreak of the Second World War brought him back to Britain.

Hard on the heels of the Hatry collapse, it was discovered that the Royal Mail Group, which controlled some 15 per cent of British shipping, had unsecured liabilities totalling some £30m. The Group had been built up by John and Owen Philipps, now Lord St Davids and Lord Kylsant respectively, by the acquisition of a number of old-established shipping companies, many of them clients of Ashurst, Morris, Crisp & Co. William Morris had acted for the Philippses in 1910 when the Elder

The address prepared for presentation to Ernest 'Bill' Stallwood when he married was signed by most of his fellow-members of staff.

Dempster company was bought and subsequently in the purchase of the Lamport & Holt Line, the Nelson Line and the Union Castle Line. The debts had accumulated to such an extent, including some £4m in government loans under the Trade Facilities Act of 1921, and been successfully concealed, because the Group never produced consolidated accounts – nor was it obliged to do so at that time.[15]

Fearful of the effect on the economy of the collapse of Royal Mail, the Bank of England spearheaded a rescue which involved removing financial control from Kylsant and a long and complex reconstruction of the Group which lasted for most of the 1930s and involved many City solicitors. Edward Hora, the son of a Leicestershire schoolmaster, who had been articled to John Crisp and admitted a solicitor in 1926 was much concerned with devising schemes of arrangement to settle the claims of the debenture holders and other creditors of the Group.

Kylsant himself was prosecuted on a charge of issuing false documents under the Larceny Act in 1931. Tradition in the firm has it that Charles Crisp declined to act for Kylsant on the grounds that there might be a conflict of interest. Kylsant was found guilty and sent to Wormwood Scrubs for a year. While all this was going on, the country also entered a period of acute financial crisis in the wake of the collapse on the New York Stock Exchange in October 1929 which signalled the start of the worldwide depression of the 1930s.

The national economic crisis of 1931 led not only to the abandonment of the gold standard but also to a political crisis, a general election and the emergence of a coalition national government. The crisis also took its toll on the Stock Exchange and on domestic industry, and signs of this survive in the firm's records with the writing off in 1931 and 1932 of shares held by the partners. In December 1931 ordinary shares in the British Automatic Gramophone Company which had been taken in lieu of costs, were written off; the company had not paid any dividends and had been wound up, a note added. A year later, for the same reasons, 10,500 shares of a nominal value of two shillings each in Burnard's Dairy Equipment Company which had been taken in lieu of a fee when the company was formed in 1929, were written off.

Through the 1930s partners and staff – the latter now including four or five women – numbered in total about 60. The total amount paid out annually in wages and salaries was in 1929 and 1930, the only years for which records survive, some £16,000. In those years too the firm was paying just under £4,500 rent for its offices, still owned by John Morris's Trust. The firm's profits in those two years were £38,789 and £26,112 respectively. In February 1931 one member of the staff, Ernest William Stallwood, got married; 46 members of staff signed the illuminated address presented to Stallwood on this occasion.

The office was open from 9 a.m. until 6 p.m. on weekdays and 9 a.m. until 1 p.m. on Saturdays. The staff were allowed off one Saturday morning in four. The office routines were, by today's standards, cumbersome, time-consuming and very labour-intensive as the following account shows:

The mail would arrive at the office about 9 a.m. and would be opened and sorted in the cashier's office. The cashiers were responsible for indicating on each letter the partner or manager to whom the letter should be distributed and short details of the letters and their contents would be written on to prepared sheets of paper and eventually this information would be written into a book which would be numbered ... all outgoing letters would after signature be sent to the Post Room where a copy would be produced (by damping the original and putting it in a press) in a Letter Book which contained pages numbered 1 to 100. When each book had been filled the date of the first and the last letters would be placed on the outside of the book.

Laborious as it sounds, this meant that there was a complete record of all incoming and outgoing mail, the equivalent of the record provided in the nineteenth century waste books (see Chapter 2). It did not, however, end there:

Arthur Gilbert, West End clerk, worked for the firm for 70 years.

Ashurst Morris Crisp

Dinner for the partners and staff in 1938. 'Mac' Macaree (also pictured opposite) is seated in the foreground.

A further copy of the letter would be made on a separate sheet of paper using the same method to be sent to the department concerned to be placed on the file of the particular matter. It was the job of the Post Room to sort out all these copies every morning and send them out to the departments concerned.

There were two messenger boys in the Post Room and they would deliver by hand all letters which had addresses in the EC2 area. They would also deliver by hand any urgent letter to other parts of the City and West End.

Letters for posting would not normally be received by the Post Room until after 5 p.m. and even later, often the Post Room would work up to 7 p.m. and sometimes up to 8 p.m. and if there were letters to Scotland which were required to be delivered first delivery the next morning someone from the Post Room would take them to Euston Station or King's Cross Station to put them on the night mail train.

Just inside the entrance to Number 17 there was an 'Enquiry Lobby' or 'Box' as it was then generally referred to. It was normally manned by three employees, two being office boys … the third an ex-army man in charge of the Box.

In the Box there was a row of speaking tubes, each tube connected to a different room in the building. A whistle was inserted at each end of the tubes and if say a client arrived at the offices the person in the Box would blow up to the particular room concerned, a whistle would sound and the occupant of the room

The doldrums

would speak down the tube and the Box would in turn speak into the tube informing the person of the arrival of the client. The client would then be taken up to the partner or manager.

In the Box was a book in which all visitors were recorded, along with their time of arrival and the person whom they were visiting. The Box also kept another book recording the times of arrival and departure of all partners and staff and their whereabouts – lunch, the Courts, with a client – during office hours.

Also in the Box there was an instrument ... with a handle and when wound it would activate an indicator in the offices of the District Messenger Company. In a short time a messenger boy dressed in a uniform ... would arrive at the building ... All urgent messages to go abroad were sent by cable, the main cable companies being Western Union in Great Winchester Street, the Commercial Cable Company in Wormwood Street and Cable & Wireless in Moorgate.

The extensive record-keeping also extended to the telephone. In the 1930s the firm had a four-line, 20-extension switchboard.

All incoming and outgoing calls were recorded by the operator in a telephone message book and each morning the operator would fill in on a printed form the calls that each department had made and received the previous day.

Finally, all these detailed records were brought together.

Each department was required to complete daily entry forms which gave the name of the client and the subject matter and short details of all telephone calls, letters, appointments and interviews relating to that matter which had taken place during the day. Against each item a charge would be inserted, such as 3s 4d or 6s 8d [the then standard charges] for letters and phone calls and an appropriate amount for all meetings and interviews. These entry forms would then be passed to the Bill Office who would file them under the respective client's name and subject matters. When a matter had been completed the costs clerk would, from the entry forms and a perusal of the papers concerned, be able to arrive at a figure to bill the client. Subject to the partner or manager approving

S R Macaree, known in the firm as 'Mac', joined Ashursts in 1929. He was away on active service in the Navy during the Second World War and was then a managing clerk until he retired in 1970.

the figure the draft bill would go to the Bill Office to be typed and sent to the client.

In 1933 the senior partner, William Morris, retired from the partnership; he was now 78 years of age but he continued to work in his office in the building on an occasional basis until he died on 2 May 1934. His wife Emma had died the year before and he had inherited about half of his own estate, valued at £429,623, from her. After individual bequests to his domestic staff – the specific mentions of a coachman, gardener, butler, cook and chauffeur indicate a considerable establishment – much of it was left in trust to his three surviving children and to his grandchildren. He bequeathed £1,000 each to his partners John and Charles Crisp and left the furniture in his room at 17 Throgmorton Avenue and his law books to Roland Outen. Interestingly, Morris's will indicates that he had made loans to a number of the firm's staff to enable them to buy their homes. To his secretary and personal assistant at Ashurst, Morris, Crisp & Co., James Honess, 'in recognition of his life long and devoted service' he left £3,000 and shares in the Artizans', Labourers' and General Dwellings Company. Honess had been working for Morris at least since December 1887; at that time he was the most junior of Morris's staff, earning 17s 6d a week.

The obituary notices of William Morris were short; he had retired and, at 79, many of his own generation who might have thought he deserved a lengthier notice, were already gone. Throughout his professional life Morris had been overshadowed by his partners, first his uncle, John Morris and then by Sir Frank Crisp. An able lawyer – some put it higher than that – he had played, as this history has shown, a significant part in developing the firm's practice. He was, in his later years, much admired by the young men in the firm and by the staff.

John Crisp succeeded him as senior partner; it was not until the death of his elder brother, Frank, in 1938 that his father's baronetcy passed to him, for Frank had never married. Tall – he was over six feet – and handsome, John Crisp was to be the senior partner for 17 years and he was a popular figure with the staff. It was with his permission and encouragement that in 1936 the firm's staff club activities expanded. In March that year 41 members of staff signed up for table tennis and the Ashmor Table Tennis Club began to meet on Wednesdays and Fridays from 6.30 p.m. to 10 p.m.; the club was allowed the use of the firm's Library 'unless Mr John Crisp was staying late'. The Club flourished and in 1938 moved to playing every week night, subject to Crisp not staying late. Later that year a Darts section was established.

The early 1930s had been a grim time nationally with nearly 3m unemployed; as the immediate crisis passed, however, falling prices led to a reduction in the cost of living and those who had a job found, paradoxically, that they were better off. From the mid-1930s on the British economy began to pick up and the 1938 *Stock Exchange Year Book* evidences this with a number of new clients for the firm, many of them associated with the consumer products for which demand was growing. These included furniture manufacturers, businesses connected with motorcycle and motor-car manufacture and firms such as Davies of Slough, incorporated in 1936, manufacturers, *inter alia*, of radio cabinets; by the end of the 1930s three-quarters of families in Britain had radios. Many of the new leisure and entertainments industries which developed in the 1930s centred on the cinema; 20m people attended Britain's some 500 cinemas each week in 1937. The cinema was largely dominated by Hollywood productions but a British industry began, in which the firm had some clients.

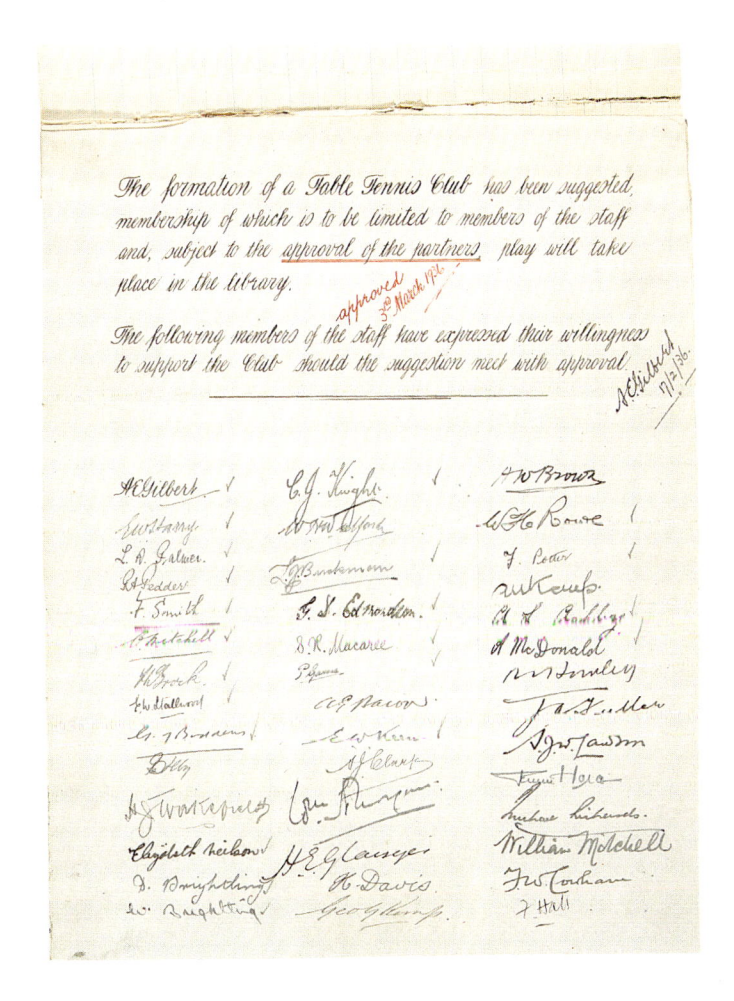

Among the young men who were attracted to the firm in the 1930s and became articled clerks with it were two of particular significance for the future. Michael Richards, born in 1915, was the son of a Leeds solicitor who served, as his father had done before him, as Clerk to the Justices. Educated at Leeds Grammar School, he was articled to John Crisp in 1932 and admitted a solicitor in 1937; he was awarded the

The firm's staff responded enthusiastically to a suggestion that the Ashmor Sports Club should establish a section to play table tennis regularly.

Broderip Prize, then the youngest man to achieve that accolade and, as Frank Crisp had done (see Chapter 3) he studied for an external degree (at Leeds University) during his clerkship.

Godfrey Charles D'Arcy Biss joined the firm in 1933, coming down from Worcester College, Oxford, with a first class degree in law. The son of a crime novel writer who died young, he had been educated at St Paul's School. He had first thought of becoming a stockbroker but was discouraged from doing so by the state of the economy. He was articled to Thomas Outen and was admitted a solicitor in 1936. According to one account of the firm's history, written in 1961, 'Rumour has it that about this time Biss won a moderate prize in a football pool and took himself off to Australia and New Zealand for the best part of twelve months.'

With the outbreak of war in 1939 Biss, like other young men on the staff went off to join the armed forces. The partners, the two Crisp brothers and the Outens, father and son, were too old for active service. In May 1941 Thomas Outen died. He had been with Ashurst, Morris, Crisp & Co. for 52 years and a partner for 23 of them. Although he was chiefly remembered by those who knew him as a dour man, who expected his clerks to work as hard as he did, his ability and hard work had won new clients for the firm at a difficult time as well as keeping clients like Courtaulds. Through the 1930s Outen had been particularly busy with litigation on behalf of Courtaulds.

Determined to protect its position as the leading manufacturer of rayon in the UK, Courtaulds had launched an action for patent infringement in 1925 against a firm called Kemil Ltd. The litigation dragged on without resolution until 1934. By then Courtaulds was more concerned with defending itself against its competitor, British Celanese, whose founder and managing director, Henry Dreyfus, a man of great pugnacity, had issued a writ in 1931 against Courtaulds for patent infringement. Judgment was given for Courtaulds in 1933 but Dreyfus went on to appeal. The Court of Appeal upheld the judgment as too, in 1935 did the House of Lords.

Between 1938 and 1940 there were lengthy negotiations on a merger proposal between the two companies, 'the British giants of rayon', but these were abandoned in June 1940 when it became clear that the wartime Excess Profits Tax would burden the merged company with heavy tax liability. As Courtaulds' historian has noted, two groups benefited from

The doldrums

the protracted struggle between Courtaulds and British Celanese: '… consumers, in the short-run whilst the price-war lasted … and lawyers'.[16]

Following Outen's death, Edward Hora (see page 148), who had for some years been manager of the litigation department and had also done company work, was made a partner, although two years later he too departed on active service in the RAF. At the same time as Hora was admitted to the partnership, Michael Richards also became a partner. A company lawyer, he had since his admission become interested in and developed a considerable expertise in a growing area of the law, taxation. Because he was unfit for active service – he was rejected by the Army – Richards remained with the firm during the war and was able to conduct the litigation, on behalf of clients, with the Inland Revenue.

In 1940 he acted for Borax Consolidated, a client of the firm, in a case brought against the company by the Inland Revenue. Not all the litigation during the war was concerned with taxation, although the introduction of Excess Profits Tax (at 60 per cent) intended to prevent profiteering, required complex calculations and negotiations as to what had been 'normal' profit in pre-war days and created a good deal of work. The five reported cases in 1941 concerned property, income tax, a will, a company dissolution and the prosecution, by the Ministry of Agriculture and Fisheries, of a farmer who had not complied with a directive under the emergency legislation to cultivate agricultural land. In 1945 the firm acted for the Lagonda Motor Company in a case the company brought for trademark infringement against the Bentley Motor Company.[17]

Ashurst, Morris, Crisp & Co. was fortunate during the war in that unlike many other businesses in the City, its offices were not destroyed by enemy bombing, although few records of the war years seem to have survived. New issues were, like most of the economy, subject to government control but

The firm's client, Courtaulds, grew in the interwar years; rayon was much in demand and Courtaulds' competitor, British Celanese, advertised extensively. It was not until after the war that the competition ended with Courtaulds' acquisition of British Celanese.

The extensive bomb damage in the City in the Second World War included the destruction of the Fore Street Warehouse, home of the firm's earliest client, the Morrison business. Its staff were given refuge at Throgmorton Avenue until they found new offices.

in any case, as we have seen, the firm had been doing less work in that area in the interwar years. Corporate, trust and taxation work at a reduced level no doubt kept the three partners and a reduced staff well employed at a time when civilian life was a struggle. Among its clients, the Fore Street Warehouse Company whose connection with the firm dated back to 1822, had its premises destroyed. It was, by this time a much smaller operation, with its capital reduced by writing down in 1910 and 1929.[18] Its staff, who turned to their solicitors as their natural protectors, were temporarily housed in the firm's library until other offices were found.

In 1946 Edward Hora and Godfrey D'Arcy Biss, along with a number of staff returned from war-time service. In that year too Charles Crisp died suddenly, of appendicitis. He had married late in life and had no children to follow him into the firm.

In 1947 D'Arcy Biss was admitted to the partnership. Thus five partners, John Crisp, Roland Outen, Michael Richards, Edward Hora and D'Arcy Biss faced the challenge of the post-war world.

CHAPTER 8

From crisis to success: the firm from 1947 until 1974

RECOVERY AND RECONSTRUCTION after the war lasted well into the 1950s with many of the war-time controls on manufacture for the domestic market, on raising finance, on building supplies and on food and clothing remaining. In the City many, if not most, institutions and businesses continued to be controlled until the mid- or late-1950s by the men of an earlier generation, cautious and risk-averse after their experience of the post-First World War slump and the depression of the 1930s. It was, however, soon evident in the immediate post-war years that business at home and overseas was changing rapidly.

When Edward Hora was discharged from the RAF and returned to the firm in 1946, he was plunged into the business of selling the British-owned Argentinian railways to the Argentine government. It was a transaction which illustrated the changing world economic and political order, marking the end of 'a chapter in the long and honourable financial association of both countries' and of a kind of British overseas investment with which the firm had been much concerned for a century or more.[1] The desire of Argentina to own its own railways reflected an upsurge in nationalism which was to spread worldwide. Nor was the transaction unwelcome to Britain which needed to realise its remaining overseas investments to pay off some of the enormous debts contracted during the war.

In all, 12 British-owned railway companies were involved, with Hora acting for two, the Buenos Ayres & Pacific Railway Company and the Entre Rios Railway Company, both clients of the firm since their establishment in 1882 and 1891 respectively. As a company lawyer, Hora had a reputation for being meticulous, a quality well-suited to the complexities of the schemes of arrangement which had to be drawn up for the shareholders and debenture holders in each company. All 12 schemes then had to be coordinated (there were five other firms of City solicitors involved), and submitted for the approval of the Court. This took place at a special sitting, held during the Long Vacation when the Court did not usually sit, in August 1947. Ownership of the Argentine railways passed into the hands of the government which paid £150m for them.

In Britain too there was increasing government or state ownership of industry and utilities as a result of the commitment of the Labour government, elected in 1945, to nationalisation of the 'commanding heights' of British industry. The Bank of England, cable and wireless, civil aviation, the coal industry, railways, the road haulage industry, electricity and gas were briskly nationalised in the years immediately following the end of the war. Next on the agenda was the iron and steel industry and, for one of the firm's clients, this posed a particular problem.

The Sheepbridge Coal and Iron Company had developed a large engineering business at Chesterfield which it did not want to see nationalised. Its chairman, Lord Aberconway, approached Michael Richards in 1948 shortly before the Iron and Steel Bill was introduced to Parliament. In the event the Bill proved to be so contentious that it was not passed until 1951. Richards prepared a 'hiving off' scheme, which provided a precedent for other companies, enabling Sheepbridge's engineering business to be separated from the company's iron and steel operations and therefore excluded from nationalisation. Hiving-off saved a number of businesses from becoming, as the iron and steel industry did, a political football: nationalised in 1951, denationalised when the Conservatives returned to power later that year, nationalised again in 1967 and finally privatised in 1988.

In 1950, at the age of 78, Sir John Crisp, the senior partner of Ashurst, Morris, Crisp & Co., died. He had been a partner for 44 years and although he was by no means as well-known in the City or the profession as his father, Sir Frank, he had, as senior partner, steered the firm through the difficult years of the war and its immediate aftermath. His death did not, however, mark the end of the Crisp family connection with the firm. Sir John's son, now Sir Peter, who had been educated at Westminster and then served with the Royal Navy during the war, had been articled to his father in 1948. He stayed with the firm and was admitted a solicitor in 1951. He became a partner in 1963 and although he was never, by his own admission, an enthusiastic lawyer, he took on much of the administrative burden of running the firm during the 12 years of his partnership. It was not until Sir Peter retired in 1975 that the three generations of the Crisp family connection with the firm, by then stretching over more than a century, ended.

Next in seniority to Sir John Crisp, Roland Outen succeeded Sir John as senior partner. Until the death of his father, Thomas, Roland Outen's practice had been mainly concerned with trust and general matters. He had, however, in 1941 inherited most of his father's major corporate clients, including Courtaulds, the International Harvester Company and the Royal Bank of Canada. Following the death of Charles Crisp in 1946, Outen also took on the work for the Fairey family and for the Fairey Aviation Company, of which he became chairman.

There had been a good deal of work for Fairey in the immediate post-war years. The company's airfield at Harmondsworth in Middlesex had been requisitioned by the government during the war and later used by the US Airforce. In 1944 the government had decided that it should never be returned to Faireys but instead should form part of a new civilian airport. The firm drew up the agreement between the Ministry of Civil Aviation and Faireys for the sale of the land and acted for the company when the matter came before the Lands Tribunal to determine the terms of compensation. These took so long to settle that the company issued a certificate to its shareholders for their share of whatever the value of the Great West Aerodrome was to be finally agreed. The first test flights left Heath Row (as the new airport was then known, now Heathrow), at that time a huge plain of earth populated only by a few tents, huts and telephone boxes, on 1 January 1946.

Four new partners were admitted in 1950; they were all treated as junior partners and guaranteed an annual income of £1,250 in the event of their small share of the profits falling below that amount. Alexander George Coulson was a friend of Roland Outen – they had been at Highgate

Roland Outen, a partner 1931–57 and senior partner 1950–57.

From crisis to success

161

School together – and before the war, when Coulson was a Chancery barrister, his advice had been regularly sought by the firm. Coulson had himself disbarred, joined the firm and was admitted as a solicitor in 1947. Also admitted in 1947 was Morton Morell Mackenzie who, like D'Arcy Biss, came from Worcester College, Oxford. The third new partner, Randolph Henry Albert Lerse, was a German-Jewish refugee who had served in the Pioneers during the war. A protégé of Michael Richards, he was articled and then admitted in 1946. Finally there was Philip Game. He had been with the firm in the 1930s, articled to Sir John Crisp and was admitted a solicitor in 1945. Coulson was a conveyancer while Game, Lerse and Mackenzie all worked on corporate and commercial matters.

It was Philip Game who inherited Clarence Hatry as a client from Sir John Crisp. Soon after Hatry's return to England in 1940 (see page 147) he had managed to borrow sufficient money to buy Hatchard's Bookshop. Hatry, his biographer says, 'launched his new enterprise with typical resolve and energy, turning substantial losses into substantial profits and

Heath Row airport in the early days. It was built on the site of the Fairey Aviation Company's airfield.

following the familiar path of merger, takeover and consolidation'. By 1950 Hatry, now 64 years old, was again a wealthy man, his business making profits of some £200,000 a year. However, he could not resist the ambitious and expensive schemes which, as in the 1920s, far outran his pocket.

Anxious to achieve a stable, vertically integrated structure for his bookselling, printing and publishing empire, Hatry sought to make the machines that stitched the books that his companies printed, published and sold. He bought the rights to one such machine and immediately became embroiled in successive rounds of teething problems, acrimonious litigation, boardroom disputes and substantial losses ... Virtually a broken man, Hatry retired to the country.[2]

Hatry was not, however, the only casualty of this affair.

In September 1950 Philip Game had been appointed, in place of Sir John Crisp, one of the trustees of William Morris's three Trust Funds, established for his three surviving children, Olive, Geoffrey and John; the firm then handled all the Morris family affairs. In October 1951, with the agreement of the two other trustees, Kenneth Dulake (a company director) and William Harris (a barrister), shares held by the three Morris Trusts were sold and the proceeds, some £71,000, were used to buy shares in James Upton Ltd, a printing business in Birmingham owned by Hatry's company, Hatchards Associated Interests Ltd. The transaction was clearly intended to help Hatry who agreed that he would repurchase the Upton shares in six months' time; when the time came, he could not do so and, late in June 1952 the agreement was repudiated by Hatchards.

Realising that the losses to the Morris Trusts could not be concealed, Game was obliged to make a clean breast of all the transactions connected with Hatry's affairs to his partners; they briskly terminated the partnership agreement and secured Game's immediate withdrawal from the firm. Further examination of Hatry's accounts with the firm led D'Arcy Biss to conclude and minute to his partners that 'we have been used on an infinite number of cases to provide temporary finance for Mr Hatry'. Meetings and investigations followed and a year later, in July 1953, litigation began. The Trustees of the Morris Trusts sued Hatchards, Hatry and his associates and, in turn, the beneficiaries of the Trusts, the children of William Morris, sued the Trustees. Ashurst, Morris, Crisp & Co. were third parties in this litigation but were also obliged to sue their own insurers; Freshfields acted for the firm.

Early in 1956 a settlement was reached before the litigation came to court. Under the terms of the settlement the Trustees were to pay some £95,000 to the three Morris Trust funds; Ashurst, Morris, Crisp & Co. guaranteed the payment and, in the event, had to fund it. Dulake and Harris, the Trustees, made some contribution through bank loans but Game had no funds and no security on which to borrow. Although £10,000 was recovered from the firm's insurers via the settlement, the partners had to find some £70,000 to pay to the Trusts. The payment was made, by raising loans and using contributions from the partners' capital. The partners endured a lean time for a few years, but the survival of the firm was secured with its reputation untarnished.

Philip Game was certainly not the first, and probably not the last, to be caught up in the schemes of the silver-tongued Hatry; but he paid a high price. He tried, unsuccessfully, to re-establish himself professionally and in business, but a few years later he committed suicide. A final note to this unfortunate affair concerns Hatry, a survivor if ever there was one. He was, by 1958, back in business, albeit, it is hardly necessary to say, this time without the firm acting for him. He became involved in the late 1950s in buying coffee bars in London's West End, then in the early 1960s, in industrial cleaning and finally, he took his talents to Scotland where, shortly before his death in 1965, he was seeking to merge a number of Scottish knitting firms.

Fears of a return of the economic depression of the interwar years faded as the economy began to grow in the 1950s. The quickening pace of change in the early years of that decade, much of it dominated by US corporations moving into the UK and Europe, offered new opportunities. Between 1957 and 1962 the value of US companies' investments in Europe more than doubled and between 1962 and 1967 they did so again. It was D'Arcy Biss who secured as a client one of the most significant of these, IBM, which announced the development of its first 'electronic brain' machine for business use in 1954. Biss acted on the establishment of IBM's UK subsidiary and thereafter there was a steady flow of work to the firm from Big Blue in the UK and in Europe. A measure of the significance of IBM as a client is the extent to which it came to dominate European markets in the 1960s. By 1969 IBM had more than 60 per cent of the market in France and Italy, and more than 50 per cent in Germany and the Benelux countries (see Chapter 9).[3]

In 1954 Michael Richards, whose expertise in company law and taxation had enhanced the firm's reputation and enriched its client list, left the partnership. He was, as his obituarist noted, 'an entrepreneur by instinct', and he wanted to exercise that instinct more widely than practice of the law allowed. He went to become chairman of a small merchant bank he had established with friends, Hart Son & Co., which soon gained a leading position in the areas of mergers, acquisitions, new issues and flotations. In 1960 Hart Son & Co. was acquired by Samuel Montagu & Co. of which Richards became an executive director until the early 1970s. At that time Samuel Montagu was acquired by the Midland Bank. Richards remained a non-executive director of Samuel Montagu but devoted most of his time and energy to building up the Wood Hall Trust, which he had founded in the 1950s. It had become, by the early 1970s, one of Britain's hundred largest companies, a conglomerate with interests in building, engineering and electricals; it was taken over in 1982 by Elders IXL. Michael Richards died in June 1994.[4]

It was in February 1957, on a Saturday visit on professional matters to the Fairey family that Roland Outen, who was only 56, unexpectedly collapsed and died. The Fairey Company had seen Outen at his best, as the company's notice of his death indicates: 'A man humane and gentle, he held steadfastly to his own high standards of behaviour and his utter integrity was perhaps the outstanding feature of his life, itself an example of Christianity in its best terms.' Within the firm, however, Outen was remote and distant, respected but not liked.

Outen had been a keen member of the City of London Solicitors' Company, founded in 1908 and granted its livery in 1944 and its charter in 1957. He had held office in the Company since 1945, progressing through its hierarchy first as steward and then warden in order to serve as the Company's Master in 1950.[5] Coulson, also an active Christian, carried on the firm's connection with the City of London Solicitors'

Michael Richards, a partner 1941–54.

Company, as too did Morell Mackenzie. The latter served as its clerk from 1952 to 1958 and later as Master (1968–9) and Treasurer (1970–4). During his time as Master, Mackenzie was largely responsible for the establishment of the professional Business Committee which later became the City of London Law Society.

Coulson was also more widely involved in the City's civic affairs, as a member of the Drapers' Company and a Freeman of the City. He served as a Councilman (as William Ashurst had done more than a century earlier), and then as an alderman. It was Coulson who ensured that the next generation in the firm would also play a part in the City's corporate life, by introducing Martin Bell (see below) to it and ensuring that he became a Freeman of the City.

By the strict rules of seniority, according to which most firms of solicitors then operated in appointing or choosing senior partners, Edward Hora was next in line to follow Outen. He was, however, unwell at the time and he 'retired' in 1961, although he continued for several years to act for some substantial clients. These included the Regis Property Company, which at that time owned Plantation House in Fenchurch Street, housing the London Commodity Exchange and the Rubber Exchange. Hora's approach to the law was academic rather than administrative; his attention to detail could and did infuriate his articled clerks and yet they remember him and his car number plate – AMC 100 – with affection. Michael Legge (see below) recalls that in 1960 Hora finally 'wound up a seven-year correspondence with the Stamp Duty people, winning the argument on all points; the amount of duty involved was five shillings'. In the same year he instructed Legge and Michael Zander, then an articled clerk with the firm, now Professor of Law at the LSE, to prepare an assignment of copyright for a charity client; Hora ignored a perfectly good version in the *Encyclopaedia of Forms and Precedents*, Legge recalls, adding that 'by the time [Hora] had done with us, some three months later, the result transcended perfection'.

It was, therefore, D'Arcy Biss, now in his late forties, who succeeded Outen as senior partner. A large man, in every sense of the word, known to his close friends by a schooldays' nickname as 'Bun', Biss had been instrumental in the resolution of the Game-Hatry affair and his concern for the firm's practice and good name was second to none. A traditionalist by nature, he liked new clients to arrive with a proper introduction;

**Ashurst
Morris
Crisp**
166

his partners still remember the occasion when two representatives of the US oil company, Amoco (formerly Standard Oil of Indiana), arrived to see him and explained that they had reviewed the major City law firms and decided that as Ashurst Morris Crisp was the only one without a major oil company client, they would appoint the firm their UK lawyers. Biss looked at them over the top of his small, gold-rimmed reading glasses and said: 'Well, gentlemen, that's all very fine, but we have not yet decided that we wish to accept Amoco as a client.'

The firm over which Biss began to preside in 1957 had only six partners, following the departure of Game and then of Richards and the death of Outen. In that year Miles Beevor, who had been admitted as a solicitor in 1925 but had spent some years of his life in business, joined the firm and became a partner; he did not practise but was head of finance and a financial consultant until 1962.

More significant for the firm's practice and its long-term development was the admission as a partner in 1957 of Martin Lampard, who had joined as a qualified solicitor in 1954. Born in 1926 and educated at Radley College and Christ Church, Oxford, Lampard had, through family connections (his father worked with Heilbut's brother on the London Rubber Exchange), been articled to Max Heilbut at Wilde, Collins & Crosse. Coincidentally, Heilbut had been connected with Ashurst, Morris, Crisp & Co. in the 1920s; he had been articled to Thomas Outen and admitted a solicitor in 1925. As a qualified solicitor, Heilbut had joined Wilde, Collins & Crosse, had left them for a time to work with a subsidiary of his wife's family bank, S Japhet & Co. and after war service in the War Office, had returned to Wilde Collins.

A year after Lampard became a partner, Heilbut too joined Ashursts as a partner, bringing with him his own practice of private wealthy clients on whose affairs he continued to advise as well as acting on trust matters. Although he was principally a family lawyer, Heilbut had acted in 1954 for his wife's family and other major shareholders in S Japhet & Co. in the negotiations which led to the sale of the bank to the Charterhouse Group.[6]

Tradition in the firm has it that it was Heilbut who, failing to find some documentation requested by another firm of solicitors, replied with what had become, by the late 1950s and the early 1960s, a rather well-worn excuse that the records must have been destroyed during enemy

FACING PAGE

G C D'Arcy Biss joined the firm in 1933; a partner 1947–74 and senior partner 1957–74.

Ashurst Morris Crisp

Ashurst commissioned the building of 6 Old Jewry in which the firm had its offices from 1847 until 1890. The internal walls were panelled with wood and, when the building was demolished in 1890, the panelling was used to make furniture for the new offices in Throgmorton Avenue. This chair has survived and is kept in the office of the senior partner of Ashurst Morris Crisp.

action. The reply came back swiftly, expressing surprise that bombs were still dropping on London in 1951, the date on the documents in question, by which time the writer had believed that all hostilities were well and truly ended! Heilbut was a keen player of real tennis and well known for his support and enthusiasm for the game at the Holyport Club. Within the firm Heilbut is remembered as a connoisseur of food, wine and people – 'He should have been an Edwardian – indeed, he behaved as one'. A very kindly and extremely sophisticated man, he was a member of the Carlton Club where, under his aegis for some years the firm held an annual dinner. Each partner asked one guest, usually a client, and the occasion was, for young partners, 'a strong evening'.

In 1959 Michael Gampell, who had joined the firm in 1955 as a qualified solicitor, became a partner. Gampell was the son of a City man, Sydney, who worked for Reuters, writing its weekly publication, *Economic X-Ray*, 'racy and amusing but risky' from 1935 until 1974.[7] Described by one of his clients as 'an ingenious, energetic and inventive solicitor', Gampell worked with Biss on IBM's affairs in his early years with the firm before he too developed, like Biss and Lampard, his own reputation as a corporate lawyer in the City.[8]

The recollections of those who joined the firm at that time and of the managing clerks (see below), evidence both the continuity with earlier times and the changes that were beginning to be made at Throgmorton Avenue in the late 1950s and early 1960s. Among those whose memories contribute to a picture of life in the office at the time is Martin Bell, who joined the firm in 1956 as an articled clerk, finding himself then to be the only articled clerk. Both his father and grandfather had been clients of the firm, his grandfather as managing director, from 1920 to 1935, of Courtaulds, then a client of the firm, and his father as a Lloyds underwriter. Educated at Charterhouse, Bell had thought of medicine as a career but after completing National Service, decided instead on law. At this time the firm took only one or two articled clerks a year, charging a premium of 300 guineas (the same sum as the founder had charged in the 1830s!) for doing so, a practice that ceased in the late 1950s. Bell, a prizewinner in the Law Society's examinations, was admitted a solicitor in 1961 and became a partner in 1963. Also made a partner in 1963 was Michael Legge, who joined the firm as a qualified solicitor in 1960; he had been admitted a solicitor in 1957, but had then to carry out his National Service, deferred while qualifying.

Life at Throgmorton Avenue is epitomised in the hackneyed but meaningful adjectives used to describe the offices and parts of the practice – Victorian and Dickensian. 'The furniture was reasonably pleasant'; some of it had been made for the firm, more than half a century earlier, from the wooden panelling taken out of the nineteenth-century offices at Old Jewry when Number 6 was demolished after the firm had moved to Throgmorton Avenue. Richard James, who was articled in 1958, coming from Worcester College, Oxford, recalls:

There was linoleum on the corridors and stairs and in the entrance there was what was known as the Box [see Chapter 7]. By the late 1950s most of the secretaries were female although there was still one male secretary and … he was paid overtime in the evening on the basis of the folios which he typed.

The one male secretary was Fred Smith who worked mainly for Randolph Lerse. Not an easy man to know, Lerse brought a considerable intellect to bear on the problems of his clients, which ranged from the insurance business empire created by Noble Lowndes to the consortium building the Mangla Dam in Pakistan. Fred Smith, who continued to work for the firm until he was well into his seventies, was 'a little mouse of a man … unfailingly accurate, and very fast' on the ancient manual typewriters which were the firm's main concession to the machine age. By 1960, however, there were four IBM electric typewriters in the office, two used by Biss's secretaries since they had been acquired when IBM objected to receiving letters from its solicitors typed on non-IBM machinery.

Payment by the folio had been the standard practice in the nineteenth century; a folio was 72 words and the going rate, in the 1950s, was 6s 8d for typing four folios. The firm's chief cost clerk still calculated the charge on documents according to the number of folios there were in them.

Articled clerks then, as they had for centuries and as their successors, trainee solicitors in the 1990s still do, sat with partners in each of the

IBM became a client of the firm in the 1950s and insisted that the firm should use its products.

firm's departments for a period of time. James remembers:

Alec Coulson was a conveyancing partner, but one who did not run the conveyancing department. Indeed no one ran the conveyancing department which was basically a collection of managing clerks. The senior one was Mr Macaree (known as Mac) [he had joined the firm as a boy in 1928] *and the others were Fred Brock, Jimmy Andrews and John Atkinson. Harry Johnson joined them later. The managing clerks all worked on their own responsibility and were very highly regarded and indeed considered the backbone of the firm.*

As well as the conveyancing managing clerks, there were also several others, including one who ran litigation matters, Ron Rumsey (there should have been two but one left and later Rumsey was joined by Alan Palmer and Joan Taylor), one trust and probate managing clerk, Gerry Lambert, and two company managing clerks, Arthur Heath and John Emitt, the latter working for D'Arcy Biss. It was explained to James that: 'articled clerks did not do anything except occasionally go to the cinema. When one left the office one had to say where one was going but "New Zealand" was accepted without the batting of an eyelid.' James continues:

I spent a year failing to understand conveyancing. There was a most extraordinary procedure whereby one made written enquiries before one allowed a client to enter into a contract to buy a property. The answers to these enquiries were normally unhelpful, for example 'the purchaser should make his own enquiries'. Occasionally, they were amusing as when an enquiry related to a building on Watling Street asked which authority was responsible and the answer came back, 'the mantle of the Caesars has fallen on Hertfordshire County Council'. Also some of the enquiries were splendidly irrelevant, for example enquiries about sea walls in regard to central London properties.

The rules of formal dress which had governed the City for more than a century were just beginning to weaken at the end of the 1950s. 'Shirts with detachable stiff or semi-stiff collars secured by front and back studs' were the norm, remembered by Richard James as very uncomfortable and by Martin Bell as very comfortable! Of greater moment was the question of the hat.

I stayed in a small hotel in Gower Street for the first few weeks of my articles and each day I walked down Tottenham Court Road to the tube station wearing a bowler hat. I had purchased this because a friend had persuaded me (perhaps maliciously but he might have believed it) that it was essential for the well-dressed articled clerk to wear a bowler hat. Furthermore he had taken me to Lock's in St James's to make sure I had the best. Despite the grandeur of Lock's and a strange technique of steam pressing or expanding the hat, it seemed to me to be too small and I felt that at any moment as I walked down Tottenham Court Road some right-thinking citizen would remove it with a well-aimed missile.

I was delighted, on entering the offices of the firm to see a very dignified person emerging in a bowler hat and I took him to be one of the senior partners until I discovered he was the West Clerk. This was not the most august of jobs as it

Martin Lampard (right) joined the firm in 1954, he was a partner 1957–86, and senior partner 1974–86. In this photograph, Lampard is seen with a friend John Goble (later senior partner of Herbert Smith) when they were both in the Navy, towards the end of the war.

mainly consisted of going to search company records at Bush House in the Aldwych but the possessor of the job certainly added lustre to it by his appearance. Some of the partners, including D'Arcy Biss and Max Heilbut, wore bowler hats but I don't think either of the other articled clerks did and I very soon and happily discarded it.

In 1963 Biss advised his new partners to get themselves hats but they never did.

There were no luncheon arrangements at the office for staff and articled clerks, as there are in the 1990s and, Richard James remembers:

Each lunch time I would have lunch with a friend from Slaughter and May at the Talbot in London Wall. This was a restaurant on several floors but the service seemed the same on all of them i.e. rather elderly waitresses who served brown Windsor soup and overdone beef whilst referring to each other as 'the girls'.

By 1960 the firm was growing, although by no means as fast as other City firms. At Slaughter and May ten new partners were created between 1955 and 1961; at Ashursts, discounting Miles Beevor, there were in the same period only three new partners, Lampard, Heilbut and Gampell. The firm's growth was sufficient, however, for it to find its offices overcrowded and cramped. Fortunately, the stockbrokers who had been occupying the first floor of Throgmorton Avenue decided to move and the firm was able to repossess its offices. While they were being refurbished and reintegrated (the first floor had been partitioned off from the rest of the building when it was let out), a modern electric lift was also installed.

The original lift, no doubt the acme of technology when the offices were built in 1889–90, worked hydraulically, through a system of pipes pressured from a pumping station located some way away in the City. It had been replaced with an electrically powered lift just after the war. By 1956 that had become, according to one account, 'temperamental' – Martin Bell goes further in describing it as having hiccups, jumping up and down – and the new lift, completed in 1961, proved to be a boon to those working on the third and fourth floors. In the early 1960s the firm acquired additional offices at 5 Throgmorton Avenue which also gave the partners scope to create their own lunching and dining facilities.

Through the 1960s, a decade of great change in the City (see below), the senior partner of Ashurst, Morris, Crisp & Co., D'Arcy Biss, was absent from the office more often than he was present. He was becoming more of a businessman than a lawyer as he took on an increasing number of directorships; he accumulated some 16 in all, many of them clients such as UK Optical and Aspro-Nicholas. In this way the commercial expansion of those years allowed Biss to achieve his early ambition to become a businessman, put aside during the pre-war depression. There were also his days at Newmarket, firmly marked off in his diary at the beginning of the year as 'Meetings', for he had, his partners recall, 'a passionate love of the Sport of Kings'. In the office he was an amazingly hard worker, even after entertaining clients with large meals. Always a *bon viveur*, it was characteristic of Biss that, when pressed by Lampard to hold regular partnership meetings, he organised them to take place over dinner at the Institute of Directors, then in Belgrave Square. Roland Outen had, through his business acquaintance with Sir Edward Louis Spears, been instrumental in the reconstitution of the Institute in 1949 and its acquisition of a Royal Charter. As a young partner attending these meetings, Martin Bell recalls that the wine was 'nectar for the gods'.

One company of which Biss became a director when it was first established in 1956 was Eastern International Property Investments, better known as Trafalgar House, the name it adopted shortly before it was floated on the Stock Exchange in 1963. Originally the vehicle of City financier, David Fremantle, for diversifying his Eastern International Investment Trust into property, Nigel (later Sir Nigel) Broackes invested in it and master-minded its rapid growth.[9] According to his own account Broackes decided that 'what I really wanted was a permanent stake in a real business' and he was able to persuade the Commercial Union to invest in Trafalgar House.[10] Trafalgar grew by takeover, firstly of several property companies, including in 1964 that of City and West End Properties, a transaction on which the firm was not able to act for Trafalgar because City and West End had been a client since the 1890s. Equally significant was the acquisition in 1964 of 49 per cent of Bridge Walker, a small building company owned and managed by Victor (later Lord) Matthews; Michael Legge acted on that transaction while much of the work for Trafalgar House was done by Michael Gampell.

It was not until 1967 that the rest of Bridge Walker was acquired and Victor Matthews became a close associate of Broackes in directing the affairs of what Broackes characterised as 'a growing concern'. Trafalgar House went on to acquire a number of building companies including the

Ideal Building Corporation in 1967, the old-established City builders, Trollope & Colls in 1968 and the Cementation Company in 1970. The acquisition of the shipping company, Cunard, in 1971 diversified the activities of Trafalgar House still further.

An interest in hotels led to Broackes's appointment to the Board of Trust Houses, also a client of the firm for which Charles Gane, who became a partner in 1965, did a good deal of the work. Sir Geoffrey (later Lord) Crowther, a chairman of Trust Houses, who had been on the Board of Trafalgar House for some time was appointed its chairman but in 1968 the relationship between the two companies went sour, resulting in the resignations of Crowther from Trafalgar and Broackes from Trust Houses. Biss's advice was, Broackes recorded, invaluable at this time. The firm acted on the subsequent merger of Trust Houses with Forte.[11]

Biss remained a director of Trafalgar House until 1980 and the firm continued to act for Trafalgar which, through the 1970s and the 1980s made the acquisitions which turned it into a conglomerate with interests in construction, engineering, shipping and hotels. Beyond the time scope of this chapter but appropriate to mention here is the fact that Sir Nigel Broackes also became involved with and acted as chairman of the London Docklands Development Corporation. It was established in 1980 as one of the first two urban development corporations, the chosen vehicles to fight urban decay. London Docklands Development Corporation became a significant client of the firm.

Biss had also succeeded Roland Outen as Chairman of the Fairey Company, a post that proved, through the 1960s, to be no sinecure; Fairey also continued to provide the firm with a good deal of work. In the post-war world the aircraft manufacturing industry became more concentrated, frequently pushed to do so by the government. Greater resources were required to produce more sophisticated aircraft capable of competing with the products of the much larger US industry. In 1961, in the wake of the formation in the previous year of the British Aircraft Corporation, Fairey sold its aircraft manufacturing interests to the Westland Aircraft Company.

This did not, however, prevent Westland from making, in partnership with the Bristol Aeroplane Company, a takeover bid for Fairey in December 1961. After Fairey's spirited – and expensive – defence, led by Biss, assisted by Martin Lampard, the bid was withdrawn in February

1962. Part of Fairey's defence was the hiving off of a recently acquired subsidiary, Siebe Gorman, and its flotation on the Stock Exchange; in the draft prospectus there was the usual statement that 'the Chairman has been employed by the Company for x years' and, when the number was filled in, it was 80 years. The Chairman was 92 and had first been employed as a boy of 12.

At that time Fairey had a large and successful engineering business, developed since the end of the war. The company had also, as early as 1946, become involved in building a nuclear reactor for the Atomic Energy Authority. Its expertise in this area took it into a partnership in 1957 with a consortium, Atomic Power Constructions (later the United Power Company), bidding to build the UK's first nuclear-powered electricity stations. The consortium, and therefore Fairey, was involved in building Trawsfynned but in 1964 the contract to build the next Magnox station, Wylfa, went to another consortium.

A year later the Fairey consortium was awarded the contract to build Dungeness B, one of the new Advanced Gas-cooled Reactors, believed – mistakenly as it turned out – to offer significant cost reductions on the Magnox design. Due for completion in 1970, Dungeness B overran all its deadlines on time and cost and was not commissioned until the 1980s. By that time Fairey was no longer involved; the complex negotiations to release Fairey and its consortium partner from the Dungeness B contract took up a good deal of Martin Bell's time in 1969 and 1970.

The 1960s was, as the discussion above of both Trafalgar House and Fairey has indicated, a decade of great takeover activity. A sign of the changes that were to come was the 'Aluminium War' of 1958. Two American companies, the Aluminum Company of America (Alcoa) and Reynolds Metals, the latter in partnership with the British company, Tube Investments, battled for ownership and control of the British Aluminium Company, a client of Ashurst, Morris, Crisp & Co. The Reynolds Metal-Tube Investments partnership, advised by a newcomer to the City, the merchant bank established in 1946 by Siegmund (later Sir Siegmund) Warburg, won the battle and the firm lost a client. Richard James recalls:

There was at that time (1959/60) no Take-over Code or Take-over Panel and the regulations governing companies quoted (now listed) on the Stock Exchange were very elementary compared with the massive (and heavy) tome which now governs these points. In the first take-over bid in which I was involved our clients won the day by paying one shareholder in the target company twice as much per share as was paid to everybody else because he had the holding which enabled our clients to obtain shares carrying just over 50% of the votes and thus to give them victory.

This was the Willet Company, founded by William Willet (1856–1915), better known as the man who invented British Summertime. Martin Lampard was acting in the transaction for a small but influential merchant bank, Rea Brothers, whose chairman was Walter (later Sir Walter) Salomon for whom Lampard did a good deal of work.

James continues:

There was, however, at the time (and this is contrary to views I have heard elsewhere) a healthy feeling that one did not indulge in insider trading. Also one did not breach section 54 of the Companies Act 1948 (now section 151 of the Companies Act 1985) which prohibited companies from financing, directly or indirectly, the acquisition of their own shares… Accordingly, we always checked relevant transactions against Section 54.

Between 1957 and 1961, Courtaulds, then a client of the firm, acquired eight companies, the largest of which was its longtime competitor, British Celanese. The acquisition, in 1957, put a value of £20m on Celanese. In January 1960 Courtaulds acquired, for some £16.5m, Pinchin Johnson but two years later Courtaulds itself became the target of an unwelcome takeover bid from ICI. Much to the annoyance of the senior partner, the firm was not instructed to act on the defence of Courtaulds.

The firm's company and commercial work was increasingly dominated by Martin Lampard and those who worked with him in the 1960s and the early 1970s have no hesitation in describing his abilities as 'tremendous'. To Lampard must go much of the credit, they say, for the development and the enhancement of the firm's reputation among clients and in the City. In this they decry their own contribution; perhaps inevitably the dramatic deals and the takeover battles snatch the headlines and remain most vividly in the minds of those who were there at the time. The firm's continuing success and growth in these years, however, depended also on the abilities and the performance of all of that generation of young partners and assistant solicitors working for it.

Lampard's ability and his intelligence won him respect as also did his extraordinary skill in getting himself out of what most people would have regarded as a quite indefensible position and into one where he could and did take the offensive. Moreover, working with him was enjoyable and fun, as not only his colleagues in the firm but also his clients and others outside the firm found. A man whose character and attitudes, although not his physique, were cast in the mould of Sir Frank Crisp, he has become something of a legend in the firm. Stories are legion of how Lampard would tell clients what to do; like Sir Frank, no whisper of the 'I am of the opinion that …' tainted his advice. After a year of articles Richard James moved to the company department and records:

The method of working with Martin Lampard was rather odd. I would spend the day trying to talk to clients about matters which I did not understand and it was only when we went off to the pub in the evening that Martin would explain to me who we were acting for and what it was all about. It was in a way rather stimulating.

Martin Lampard (left) being harangued by Robert Maxwell at a Pergamon Press Annual General Meeting. Lampard was acting for Rothschilds, financial advisers to Leasco which had made – and withdrawn – a takeover bid for Pergamon in 1969.

Martin Bell, who was one of Lampard's assistants in 1961 and 1962, has similar memories of amusing evenings in the pub, after which he gave Lampard a lift home to his house in Islington and was always taken in for a drink. James continues:

I well remember one particular meeting at Allen & Overy when Martin suddenly got up and announced that as it was 6 o'clock in the evening we were off to the pub. The other solicitors looked rather shaken and the client protested that we had not finished but was promptly told that he had repeated himself four times already and that we certainly had finished and that we were certainly going to the pub.

Martin's style was not based on the precept that the customer is always right and indeed he normally made it fairly clear where his clients were wrong and that what they should do was exactly what he told them.

A well-remembered and much relished story handed down in the firm is of a meeting in the office when Lampard told the client to shut up and the client angrily replied that he was not going to sit there and be gratuitously insulted. Lampard's response was: 'Insulted you may be, but I can assure you that it is not gratuitous. It is very expensive indeed.'

In the takeover boom of the 1960s and the takeover battles of the 1970s the merchant banks played a very powerful role. Lampard's abilities, and those of his group of young partners and assistant solicitors, were recognised by the merchant bankers of the City and this was an important factor in bringing more work to the firm. The combination of Richard James, with his highly inventive mind, and Lampard, with his worldly-wise sharp wits and aggression, made a formidable team whose imagination, determination and refusal to contemplate the possibility of failure all worked to the advantage of the client's cause.

Rarely was the firm not involved on one side or the other in a takeover and, in fact Lampard's reputation became such that merchant banks hastened to instruct him in a hostile takeover bid rather than leave him available for the other side to instruct. One reason for this was the way in which he had changed the traditional practice in a hostile takeover bid. It had become customary through the 1950s for the defence initially to portray itself as a successful company with strong and effective management which would continue, or be about, to deliver value to shareholders. In the second round the defence would attack the predator's business, its lack of success, its management failure and the incompatibility of its business. Only in the third round did 'mere vulgar abuse' become the order of the day. Lampard reversed the priorities and engaged in abuse at the earliest stage of combat! A non-traditionalist by nature, Lampard always questioned the established way of doing things.

D'Arcy Biss got on well with Siegmund Warburg, acting for Warburg personally in relation to his family's settlement and introducing Martin Bell to Warburg to advise him on tax questions. Lampard too became *persona grata* with Warburg, to the extent that he was offered, and turned down, a job at Warburgs. It was not the only offer he received from outside the firm and the fact that such offers were made to him indicates a wide perception of his abilities. Smith & Nephew, best known as manufacturers of Elastoplast, had been a client of the firm for many years and in the 1950s grew considerably by acquisition of its competitors. The company invited Lampard to become an executive director but he was not to be tempted away from Ashursts.[12]

Lampard's wide acquaintance among members of the Bar included a close personal friendship with Philip (later Sir Philip) Shelbourne, dating from their schooldays together at Radley. Shelbourne specialised in taxation matters at the Bar from 1951 until 1962 where he developed an extensive and distinguished practice. However, in 1962 he was invited to become a partner in and head of corporate finance at N M Rothschild & Sons, an invitation he accepted. Through this connection, work from Rothschilds came to the firm, regularly and in quantity; it was a significant and fruitful connection for Ashursts. One of the first big cases on which the firm acted for Rothschilds was the merger, in the early 1960s, of the Sun Alliance and London Assurance Groups. This was followed immediately by a major scheme of arrangement merging the life funds of Alliance Insurance and London Assurance, a scheme involving hundreds of millions of pounds, the like of which had not been undertaken since the 1920s. The firm acted for both Rothschilds and Sun Alliance on it and it occupied Martin Bell, he recalls, for a full year.

Rothschilds' work came to the firm not only through the Shelbourne connection. Lampard acted on bids and other matters for a number of Rothschilds' partners and directors as too did Martin Bell and Richard James, first as Lampard's assistants and later as partners in their own right. The significance of the connection lay not only in the Rothschilds' work *per se* but also in the work that came later from other merchant banks in the City to which those who had worked at Rothschilds moved. The result

Sir Philip Shelbourne (centre), an old friend of Martin Lampard, introduced Rothschilds and other merchant banking clients to the firm.

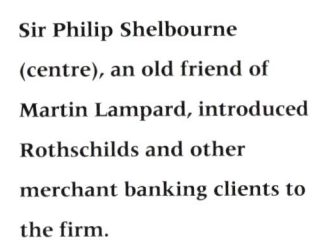

was that the firm developed an expertise in corporate finance work which made it one of the leading firms in the City in this work. The friendship between Philip Shelbourne and Martin Lampard was mutually beneficial. Lampard gave Shelbourne the benefit of the takeover know-how he had gained, particularly from Frank Smith of Warburgs, then regarded as the leading exponent of takeover tactics in the City. It was not long before Shelbourne's reputation in this field grew to rival even that of Smith.

It was Martin Lampard who introduced Philip Shelbourne to his clients, the Showering family, for whom both Lampard and Shelbourne did a great deal of work. The Showerings' small family-owned cider-making business grew phenomenally in the 1950s following the invention and national marketing of Babycham. A sparkling perry made from pear juice, the drink was invented by Francis Showering and, with skilful advertising, devised by Jack Wynne-Williams of the agency then known as Masius & Ferguson (a client of the firm), rapidly became a cult drink for women in pubs and clubs. 'The simple slogan "I'd love a Babycham" said it all, and they loved it enough to consume over 4 billion bottles in the next thirty years.'[13]

There developed a close relationship between solicitor and client during the years of expansion, echoing in the twentieth century the relationship of the founder with the Morrison family and its businesses in the nineteenth century. The Showering company was floated on the London Stock Exchange in 1959 and by then Babycham profits had already financed the acquisitions of other drinks companies, including Britvic, Vine Products, Gaymers and Whiteways; in 1965, after an acrimonious takeover battle in which both Lampard and Shelbourne were heavily engaged, Harveys of Bristol was acquired. In 1968 Allied Breweries made an agreed bid for Showerings and, later that year, the then largest merger ever was proposed between Allied Breweries, strengthened by its acquisition of Showerings, and Unilever, the Anglo-Dutch margarine, detergents and consumer products giant. The scheme was referred to the Monopolies Commission, set up in 1965 and, although it was given the go-ahead some six months later, by that time the stock market valuations of the two companies had changed so much that they were unable to come to satisfactory terms and the merger was abandoned.[14]

Allied Breweries, with Keith Showering (1930–82; he became Sir Keith in 1981), a nephew of Francis, in key positions, more particularly as Chairman and Chief Executive from 1975 to 1982, went on to acquire Teachers in 1976 and the Lyons food company in 1979.[15] Both Lampard and Shelbourne became directors of Allied Breweries; by then Shelbourne had left Rothschilds and become Chairman of Samuel Montagu & Co. and from this merchant bank also more work flowed to the firm.

The increasing number of mergers and acquisitions by takeover bids in the 1960s had led to a growing concern that such activity should be regulated. The City decided that it preferred to police its own affairs and in 1968 the City Panel on Take-overs and Mergers was established, to develop a code of conduct. In 1969 Antony Beevor, son of Miles (see page 167) who had been articled with the firm, admitted a solicitor in 1966 and made a partner in 1968, was recruited to the Panel. He worked

Special glasses helped to spread the 'I'd love a Babycham' cult.

Ashurst Morris Crisp

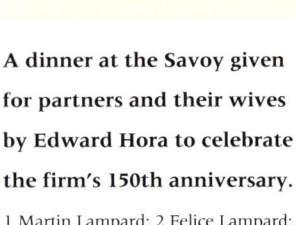

A dinner at the Savoy given for partners and their wives by Edward Hora to celebrate the firm's 150th anniversary.

1 Martin Lampard; 2 Felice Lampard; 3 Andrew Soundy; 4 Derakhshandeh Finburgh; 5 Jill Soundy; 6 Max Thum; 7 Michael Gampell; 8 Honor James; 9 Charles Gane; 10 Martin Bell; 11 D'Arcy Biss; 12 Sir Peter Crisp; 13 Richard James; 14 Rachel Gane; 15 Freda Thum; 16 Ethel Hora; 17 Max Heilbut; 18 Shirley Bell; 19 Cecilia Beevor; 20 Antony Beevor; 21 Mark Finburgh; 22 Eddie Hora; 23 Janet Bristow; 24 David Bristow; 25 Winnie Heilbut; 26 Dorothy Lerse; 27 Sheila Gampell; 28 Judy Crisp; 29 Randolph Lerse; 30 Jean Biss.

From crisis to success

for two years at the Panel as its Secretary, the first non-Bank of England employee to serve in that capacity. He returned to the firm for a short time before going in 1972 to Hambros where he became, in 1974, a Director. In 1987 he began a two-year term as Director-General of the Take-over Panel, subsequently returning to Hambros to take charge of the corporate finance department.

There had, however, been, from the mid-1960s on, considerable government support for mergers in the belief that British companies needed to be larger to compete effectively in the international market-place. In 1966 the Industrial Reorganisation Corporation (IRC) was established by the Labour government to foster structural change in industry by encouraging the formation of larger and stronger business units; or, as the Labour Prime Minister Harold Wilson described it, 'to drag Britain kicking and screaming into the twentieth century'. The firm acted on a large number of cases for the IRC.

Martin Bell remembers two main cases on which he acted for the IRC, one being on the major loans made by the government through the IRC to Rolls-Royce in 1970. Despite this infusion of funds, Rolls-Royce went bankrupt the following year. The other significant case with which Bell was concerned was the rescue of Cammell Laird which resulted in the formation of the Laird Group and Cammell Laird Shipbuilders, the latter half-owned by the government. Later the firm also acted for British Shipbuilders, a holding company for all the shipbuilding yards in England, Scotland and Wales, created in 1977 and subsequently headed by Graham (later Sir Graham) Day, who became a consultant to the firm in 1994. The firm acted on the sale of the constituent parts of British Shipbuilders when it was privatised in the mid-1980s.

By 1969 the Ashurst Morris Crisp partnership had grown to number 14 in all; 10 new partners had been admitted in the 1960s, two of them, Mark Finburgh and Max Thum in 1967 and two, Richard Hughes and Andrew Soundy in 1969. Three had retired, including Coulson in 1967 and Mackenzie in 1969. Michael Legge left the partnership in 1967 to work abroad. The removal of the limit of 20 on partnerships in the Companies Act of 1967 had little relevance to the firm although for other City firms like Slaughter and May and Linklaters & Paines who had been up against the limit, it provided relief. By 1969 Linklaters had 25 partners.

The buoyancy of the 1960s gave way to gloom in the early 1970s.

Superficially symbolic of the change was the break-up of the Beatles, who had dominated British pop music since 1962. Martin Lampard acted for Paul McCartney when he sued for the dissolution of the partnership in 1970. Unemployment and inflation rose sharply in 1970 and 1971 and were accompanied by slow growth and industrial unrest. A measure of domestic recovery in 1972 was not sustained and in 1973 inflation rose again, world commodity prices increased sharply and in October that year the outbreak of war between Israel and Egypt led to an oil embargo and a four-fold rise in the price of oil. With another miners' strike and a threatened go-slow on the railways, a state of emergency was declared in December, a mini-budget massively reducing public expenditure and increasing Minimum Lending Rate to 13 per cent was introduced and a three-day working week was to begin in January.[16]

In the City, too, there was a crisis, as restrictive measures were introduced. During the last 10 to 15 years new financial institutions, the secondary or fringe banks which had specialised in property and lending on second mortgages, had been established. They had flourished and grown, particularly since 1971 when the government's monetary policy had encouraged an increase in money supply and relaxed credit and control regulations. It was the plight of one of these institutions, Cedar Holdings, threatened with failure because of a large outflow of funds, which sparked off a City crisis on 17 December 1973. The Bank of England, fearing repercussions through the banking system as a whole from Cedar's failure, intervened to organise what became known as the Lifeboat, a support operation. The success of the Lifeboat operation prevented failures which, it was believed, might well have been on a scale not known since the nineteenth century.[17]

The property market – both commercial and private – slumped with falling prices and a much lower level of transactions. Ashursts had, as we have seen, a large conveyancing practice and inevitably this suffered in the mid-1970s. It was not, however, all gloom for the City's solicitors. New areas of practice were opening up. The introduction of corporation tax in 1964, combined with the increasing complexity of the fiscal system meant that more companies and individuals had to consider and take advice on the taxation implications of whatever they wanted to do. Companies were also becoming increasingly multi-national in their operations and the UK's entry to the European Common Market (EEC) in January 1973 gave a new significance for British industry and commerce to EEC directives and regulations. Most importantly, the development of the Eurodollar market in the 1960s had given back to the City much of the pre-eminence as a world banking and financial centre which it had enjoyed in the nineteenth century and then lost for a time.

In 1974 there were some major changes in the partnership. Edward Hora finally retired as also did Randolph Lerse and Max Heilbut. It was becoming increasingly clear that practising as a solicitor in the City was a stressful occupation and one more suited to younger men. The partners decided at this time to introduce a rule stipulating a retirement age of 60. Many City firms now operate such a policy and, with a few exceptions, City solicitors no longer continue to practise into their seventies and beyond or until they 'die in harness', the favourite phrase of the legal obituarist, as did most of the firm's earlier partners, including John Morris and Sir Frank Crisp.

D'Arcy Biss also retired as senior partner in 1974. He was the last of the pre-war generation to go. He had been with the firm since 1933, except while away on active service during the war and, during his 17 years as senior partner, had seen the firm emerge from the doldrums and crisis to take up, once again, a significant role in the City. He had played a major part himself in the creation of that role. Martin Lampard succeeded Biss as senior partner.

CHAPTER 9

'Truly modern' radicalism?

Ashurst Morris Crisp

THE CHANGES IN industry and commerce, in transport and communications, in legislation and in society that have taken place over the last two decades have had far-reaching effects on the City and the profession. The political framework in which these changes took place has been most transformed by the ending of the old hegemonies, recently that of the Soviet Union. The creation of networks of fast and reliable world transport and communication systems have contributed to rapid and increasing internationalisation of industry, banking and financial services. A further factor in this metamorphosis has been the electronic revolution, characterised by the *Financial Times* as a creator of 'waves of technological and economic change that are breaking up the established patterns of so many people's lives'.[1] And the waves have had a strong impact on solicitors, on their clients, on the nature of business and the ways in which it is conducted.

The first and most obvious change at Ashurst Morris Crisp, as with other firms of City solicitors, is that in the size of the firm. When Martin Lampard became senior partner in 1974 there were 15 partners; when he retired in 1986 the partnership had grown to 23 and the number of staff had increased correspondingly. Martin Bell succeeded Lampard as senior partner in 1986 and when Bell retired in 1992, there were 50 partners. Since Andrew Soundy became senior partner in 1992, the growth of the partnership has accelerated and in 1996 there were 74 partners and over 800 staff. There are now only 16 firms in the City larger than Ashursts: Slaughter and May and Linklaters & Paines reached the size that Ashurst Morris Crisp has now reached a decade ago and are still growing.

The firm's pattern of growth has been closely aligned to the economic ups and downs of the City. The years that followed the slump of the autumn of 1973 saw little growth in the domestic economy. The

Martin Bell, a partner 1963–92, senior partner 1986–92.

'Truly modern' radicalism?

Financial Times noted on 27 December 1973: 'The interlude of cheap oil – which lasted only a couple of decades – is now over … We face now a demanding decade or two of adjustment, of payments imbalance (like the old dollar famine) and of heavy investment – a prospect rather like that of 1945.'[2] This proved, in the event, to be an unduly pessimistic forecast, but the industrial discontent, high inflation and another rise in the price of oil in the late 1970s led into the recession of 1980; unemployment in the early 1980s rose to 3m. Recovery and profound change in the City's financial markets, which were liberalised and internationalised, created boom conditions in the 1980s although they, in turn led into the recession of the early 1990s.

The firm's growth has been sustained both by a policy of 'growing its own men' and by importing from other firms lawyers who were attracted by the style and the success of Ashursts. Among the latter, Christopher Crosthwaite, Ian Scott and Max Thum came from Sharpe Pritchard,

Correspondence between an aggrieved theatre-goer and senior partner, Martin Bell, the latter in whimsical mood.

The Senior Partner
Ashurst Morris Crisp & Co
7 Eldon Street
London EC2

23 April 1988

Dear Sir,

I spent yesterday evening most uncomfortably in seat C18 in the stalls of the Barbican Theatre, which is sponsored by your firm.

Unlike its neighbours, it fails to give adequate support because it has had the stuffing knocked out of it. Is it intended to symbolize the standard of service you offer, or has it been vandalized by a disgruntled client?

Yours faithfully,
Isobel Williams

ASHURST MORRIS CRISP

27th April 1988

ADDRESS CONFIDENTIAL

Dear Miss Williams

Thank you for your letter of 23rd April. I am sorry to learn of your discomfort.

There seems to be something of a curse on that seat. When our name first appeared on it a complaint was made to the Law Society that we were thereby breaking its rules against advertising, as it might attract clients' custom. My predecessor replied that if that had been the intention the ploy had proved singularly unsuccessful, but offered to have the plaque and, indeed, the seat removed entirely. Unfortunately his offer was not taken up but the Law Society warned (and I do not jest) that if the seat did effect the introduction of a client then the rules would have been broken.

It was, therefore, at first of some comfort to me, though I appreciate of none to you, that the seat was unlikely to have that effect; but on reflection one does not wish one's reputation to be at the mercy of an unstuffed seat and I will therefore write to the Manager of the Barbican.

Yours sincerely,

M. G. H. BELL

Ashurst Morris Crisp

Laurence Rutman and Barry Walker from Paisner & Co., Jack Amos from Clifford-Turner, David Macfarlane from Stephenson Harwood and Michael Johns from Withers.

Christopher Crosthwaite, who acted for the first Names association when the disputes between the Names and Lloyd's began, now runs the Paris office (see below). Ian Scott looked after Trafalgar House for many years and has been instrumental in developing the major infrastructure project practice; Max Thum built up a successful litigation department (now headed by Edward Sparrow), acting for Allied Breweries in landmark actions concerning the definition of 'sherry' and 'champagne'; while Jack Amos built up the tax department (now led by Stephen Machin). Barry Walker became a highly regarded corporate lawyer. Laurence Rutman, who had, after achieving a first-class degree, taken a postgraduate degree at Yale, has, with the help of David Albert, David Perks, Ian Nisse and others, transformed the conveyancing department into today's commercial property department. What had been solely a service for corporate clients is now a free standing department, servicing not just the property needs of existing corporate clients but also attracting major property work directly to itself. Most recently, the banking department was started, effectively from scratch, by Stephen Mostyn-Williams and Clifford Atkins, who both joined Ashursts from Barlow, Lyde & Gilbert and became partners in 1991.

David Macfarlane and Michael Johns – the latter playing a major role in the creation of the firm's energy practice – joined the company department, working with, amongst others, Andrew Soundy, Alastair Macpherson, John May and Geoffrey Green, all of whom had done their articles at Ashursts. Andrew Soundy acted for both IBM and Allied-Lyons (now Allied Domecq). Alastair Macpherson not only acted for Smith & Nephew but has also for some years been a director of the company. John May, a non-graduate five-year articled clerk, made his name initially in the firm by, after failing the Part I examination twice, changing gear radically and achieving first-class honours and the top position in the Finals examination and thereby scooping the majority of the available prizes. He now specialises in infrastructure project finance and has made a major contribution to the firm's development of that area of the practice. Geoffrey Green, now head of the company department, is a leading corporate finance practitioner, particularly in the field of management buy-outs.

Five of the firm's partners were members of a seven-man syndicate owning two race horses, *Corrupt Committee* **(top) and** *Crooked Counsel.*

It has been the mingling of home-bred lawyers and those coming in from other firms which has created the firm of Ashurst Morris Crisp in the 1990s; its culture is one of respecting and cultivating the traditions of the firm but not to the exclusion of innovatory ideas and practices. It was a principle first articulated by D'Arcy Biss and instilled in those who followed him that one must never fear talent in the next generation; indeed partners should actively seek to recruit people they believed to be better than themselves. As a policy it was implemented by Biss's successors, Martin Lampard and Martin Bell, and the legacy to the firm is a population of high-quality lawyers who form the partnership in the 1990s, more genuinely, and deliberately so, a partnership, than the firm had ever been before.

Ashursts' slightly smaller size has not prevented it from competing on equal terms with its rivals among the top City law firms, and winning. *The Legal 500* has consistently described it, in recent years, as 'one of the most well-regarded and admired partnerships … the commercial law firm that other lawyers most admire'. In 1995 Ashursts was top of the list of 20 legal advisers on UK private takeovers, and in 1996 the firm ranked third in terms of the largest number of stockmarket clients. *The Lawyer*, reviewing the work of solicitors in 1994 and 1995 wrote of Ashursts that the firm 'can now match some of the biggest in terms of PLC clients managed and flotations and new issues handled'. In 1995 it was considered to be the best firm of City lawyers in the area of management buy-out practice.[3] In the years 1993 through 1996 Ashursts was the country's leading legal advisor to companies seeking a flotation; a happy 'full cycle' to its position a hundred years ago![4]

By the early 1980s the firm's expansion was such that it could no longer be comfortably accommodated at 17 Throgmorton Avenue, despite the additional offices acquired close by. In 1981, after nearly a century there, it moved into new offices in Eldon Street. Continued growth after the move meant that more space was soon needed and further and adjoining premises in Finsbury Pavement were found. It was a temporary but far from satisfactory solution and eight years after the move to Eldon Street, there was another move, this time to Broadwalk House, part of the City's new and very successful Broadgate development. In 1989 the firm occupied two floors and had room to spare in Broadwalk House; in 1996 it takes up three and a half floors, 140,000 sq. ft in all.

Ashurst Morris Crisp

192

A partners' dinner at the Ritz on 8 June 1993, to mark Martin Bell's retirement.

1 John Watson; 2 Jeff Sultoon;
3 Bill Innes; 4 Mark Wippell;
5 Roger Walsom; 6 Ian Nisse;
7 John Evans; 8 Michael Johns;
9 Adrian Knight; 10 Roger Finbow;
11 Stephen Machin; 12 David Albert;
13 Laurence Rutman;
14 David Kershaw; 15 David Perks;
16 Bill Drummond; 17 Adrian Dear;
18 Michael Cunliffe; 19 Ian Scott;
20 John May; 21 Simon Cookson;
22 Edward Sparrow; 23 Chris Vigrass;
24 Richard James; 25 Graham Webb;
26 Jeremy Sheldon; 27 Ian Johnson;
28 Guy Wheatcroft; 29 Jack Amos;
30 Andrew Soundy; 31 Jeremy Hill;
32 John Yolland; 33 James Nimmo;
34 Charles Leach;
35 Charles Crosthwaite;
36 Elizabeth Morris; 37 Martin Bell;
38 Susan Roy.

'Truly modern' radicalism?

Ashurst Morris Crisp

Broadwalk House in Broadgate, designed by architects Skidmore, Owings and Merrill, into which the firm moved in 1989. The building is faced with terra-cotta and, in the words of the Prince of Wales in *A Vision of Britain*, **'it provides quite a neat solution to the problem of designing a building at the apex of a triangular site. The tower resembles the spine of a half-opened book.'**

The growth of the City's law firms has taken place as a response to the increased business, both domestic and international, in the City as well as to the increasing volume and complexity of legislation. The expansion of business in the City was fuelled first by the development of the Eurocurrency and then the Eurobond markets which began in the late 1950s. The development of these Euromarkets and the evolution of other new financial instruments was further stimulated by the huge surpluses from oil sales in the late 1970s resulting from the large price rises imposed by the Organisation of Petroleum Exporting Countries (OPEC). In the 1980s the government's privatisation programme and deregulation of the UK's financial services industry created new opportunities for solicitors and attracted new business to the City. Despite the recession of the early 1990s, the last few years have seen high takeover and merger activity. More recently, telecommunications and computer technology have linked the world's financial centres into a global trading system which allows almost round-the-clock trading to take place.

More work for the practice meant that more lawyers were needed and not only in London. The firm's clients have become increasingly international in the scope and scale of their operations. In the last two or three decades of the nineteenth century, the firm was closely involved in international work, for example the structuring and financing of energy, transport, utilities and other infrastructure projects in South America and in the Indian subcontinent. This has been replicated and enhanced with the work the firm does on international infrastructure projects in the late twentieth century. As work became more international, Ashursts built up close connections with major law firms throughout the world but the demand for its legal services also came to require the establishment of offices in the world's major financial centres.

In the early 1970s the firm opened an office in Paris. When Paris became the centre from which the firm's client, IBM, defended itself against proceedings taken by the European Commission – under Articles 85 and 86 of the Treaty of Rome – alleging abuse by IBM of a dominant market position, Andrew Soundy moved there to manage the office and the IBM defence. It was a landmark case, generating such activity in the firm's Paris office that in August 1981 there were twice as many lawyers and support staff engaged on the case in Paris as there were employed in the firm's office in London! After the IBM case was settled in 1984, with little other work in prospect, the Paris office was closed down. It was re-opened in 1990, since when it has flourished under the leadership of Christopher Crosthwaite with UK referral as well as locally generated work.

Ashurst Morris Crisp opened an office in Brussels in October 1989 and early in the following year it went much further afield in a joint venture with the US law firm, Sidley & Austin, opening an office in Tokyo. The joint venture lasted until early 1993 since when Ashurst Morris Crisp has operated on its own in Tokyo. In 1994 the firm opened an office in New Delhi; Ashursts was the first, and to date the only, UK firm to be licensed to operate a liaison office in India. Most recently, in October 1996, the firm opened an office in Singapore, committing two partners and three assistants to its South East Asia regional headquarters.

Seven of the firm's partners are in the foreign offices while the distribution of the rest between departments reflects the balance of the practice. There are 34 partners in the company and commercial department, 11 in property, ten in litigation, seven in banking and international finance, four in tax and one (Paul Randall, head of the department) in the most recently created department, that of employment law. Ashursts' departmental boundaries, however, have always been fluid, allowing partners and staff to overlap.

Increasingly, cross-departmental teams work on transactions which require an input of expertise from different areas of the law. In December 1995 the firm was instructed by Cinven, one of the UK's foremost private equity investors and a regular client of Ashursts, to act on a management buy-out. 'Project Driver', as the transaction was known, concerned the management buy-out of the Dunlop Slazenger Sports Group from the conglomerate, BTR plc. Dunlop Slazenger is a leading international sports equipment group, manufacturing and distributing golf, tennis, squash, badminton and other sports products carrying a number of well-known brand names; it is also the sole distributor in the UK of Puma sports wear and equipment.

The principals concerned in the buy-out – Cinven and the company established to make the acquisition which raised more than £370m to finance the deal – required specialist advice in a large number of areas. These included not only due diligence, acquisitions and finance but also intellectual property rights and brand protection, property, pensions, tax and licensing matters. More than 50 of Ashursts' solicitors were involved at various stages and, additionally, lawyers from more than 15 jurisdictions, including the firm's Paris and Tokyo offices, were called upon to advise. 'Project Driver' was coordinated from the firm's London office and completed in just over three months.

There are also identified areas of practice which cross departmental boundaries and for which the firm has established groups, drawing on partners and staff from several departments. These include matters falling into such areas as energy, environmental, intellectual property, competition, construction and engineering, the media and communications and the establishment, financing and management of major projects. Among the latter, the firm acted for the consortium, led by Trafalgar House, which built the third crossing of the Thames at Dartford, the Queen Elizabeth II Bridge, opened in 1991. It was a trail-blazing project, the first in this century in which the private sector was involved in the financing, design, construction and management of a major public infrastructure project. As the law has become more complicated and specialised, transactions that could, in the 1950s and the 1960s, be dealt with by one or two solicitors, for example the purchase or sale of a private company, now require in addition property, pension, taxation and employment law specialists to advise.

The reputation of individual partners in the City has been a significant factor in attracting clients. Martin Bell was one of the outstanding City lawyers of his generation, his expertise in company and commercial law and tax matters widely recognised. Like others of his generation, Martin Lampard and Richard James, for example, he made the transition from training as a generalist to practising in an age of increasing specialisation. From the mid-1970s through to the early 1990s, Barry Walker was regarded as one of the top ten City corporate finance law practitioners; he also served as Chairman of the Company Law Committee of the City of London Solicitors' Company. Laurence Rutman is generally considered to be one of the country's leading commercial property lawyers and his clients include British Telecom, British Gas and the Church Commissioners.

In contrast to the 1950s, life in the office in the 1990s is physically much more comfortable. Carpeted offices and corridors, dining rooms and lunch facilities contribute to this. More than 5,000 sandwiches a month are sold in the cafeteria known as the Writs; today's solicitor working through the day can find better sustenance in the office than Sir Frank Crisp's bar of chocolate and tea and toast! As Richard James notes:

The reception is large and open and has three charming women as receptionists – a far cry from the old Victorian mahogany box with its sergeant.

The electronic revolution has permeated the offices and the practice. Secretaries have personal computers rather than manual typewriters

The Queen Elizabeth II Bridge, the third crossing of the Thames at Dartford, opened in 1991. The firm acted for the consortium, led by Trafalgar House, that built the bridge.

(over the years there was a progression from manual typewriters to electric typewriters and now to personal computers). Copying has been revolutionised by the Rank Xerox copier and the telex (which was only usable in capital letters and often hard to read) has been overtaken by the fax and 'electronic mail' which puts further pressure on lawyers to react instantaneously.

The extent of the communications revolution can be clearly seen in the amount of cabling the modern office requires; in 1996 the firm's voice and data cabling ran to about 200 miles. Use of this network is heavy; in one day the firm's incoming and outgoing external telephone calls total approximately 12,000 and there are some 10,000 internal calls made. This is very different from the days when John Morris was instrumental in establishing a company to exploit the new device of the telephone and the firm was the first of the City solicitors to install a telephone; it had one line. It is fortunate that there are now more sophisticated methods of logging the calls than the handwritten entering of them in books used in the interwar years (see Chapter 7). In early 1996 the firm received more than 10,000 faxes a month and sent out more than 15,000 messages a month by this medium. There are, however, no signs that the technological revolution has reduced the amount of paper in circulation. Ashursts has had a paper recycling programme for some years and the average amount recycled every three months is the equivalent of 350 trees.

Instant communication and the need to carry out international transactions very quickly have put increasing pressures on solicitors to work longer hours and at weekends. While City solicitors – particularly those who achieved the kind of eminence and position of Sir Frank Crisp – have always tended to work long hours, evening and weekend work until the 1960s was more likely to be the solitary perusal of papers. In the 1990s work out of normal office hours is just as likely to involve client meetings and working out deals.

The need for speed in accomplishing transactions without loss of quality is a characteristic of work in the 1980s and the 1990s. Large companies today would not accept the stately pace of litigation which was the norm a century ago. When Amerada Hess wanted to dispose of an interest (which was held jointly with four other co-owners) in a North Sea oilfield, the firm acted for it in the commercial litigation, achieving

Linda Bailey (now Walker) was the firm's first female partner; she was a partner from 1985 until 1994.

'Truly modern' radicalism?

The Christmas lights at Canary Wharf in 1995, sponsored by Ashursts, were not only a landmark but also a symbol of the regeneration and development of the docklands by the London Docklands Development Corporation, a client of the firm.

a successful outcome in less than two months in the Court of Appeal, despite an earlier defeat in the Commercial Court.

In buy-out transactions, where the firm has become one of the leading practitioners since it acted for the National Freight Consortium in its employee buy-out in the early 1980s, much often has to be accomplished in a short time. Late in 1992 Ashursts acted for a Legal & General consortium supporting a management buy-out of the consumer products division of BP Nutrition. In three weeks the legal work and the documentation had to be completed and this was achieved early in 1993. Funding of more than £270m made this the largest such transaction in

Europe in that year; the new company formed was named McBride plc, with Lord Sheppard, then chairman of Grand Metropolitan, as its chairman. More recently, the management buy-in has become the preferred format and in the summer of 1995 the firm's client, Allied Domecq, divested itself of its tea business, Lyons-Tetley, in this way; £100m of the £190m cost was supplied by Prudential Ventures and Schroder Ventures to finance the buy-in.[5] In 1991 the firm acted on the leveraged buy-out of Brunner Mond, one of the original companies united in 1926 (see page 142) to create ICI, which owns Lake Magadi. The lake is a natural source of soda from which soda ash is produced. Brunner Mond was refloated in 1996.

The changes in the speed and complexity of legal transactions have been accompanied by other changes in the way life is lived in the City in the 1990s. As a partner in the 1960s recalls:

Many more people smoked and the expression 'a smoke-filled room' often had a real meaning. We had cigarettes delivered in yellow boxes holding 100 each, untipped of course, from John Brumfits, a chain of tobacconists now, so far as I know, completely vanished from the City.

Lake Magadi in Kenya is a source of natural soda, exploited since 1911.

The changes in the practice of law have of course also extended to articled clerks, now known, by Law Society decree, as trainee solicitors. A recently retired partner reflects:

Instead of about three articled clerks per year the firm now recruits some 35-40 trainees… In spite of this large increase in the number of trainees it appears to be much more difficult for a young person to get a traineeship in a City firm than it was to get articles 37 years ago. A large proportion of trainees are now women (40 per cent in our case) whereas when I started my articles there were no female articled clerks and never had been any and indeed there were none until Linda Watson (now Humphreys-Evans) joined in 1964. It was not until 1985 that Ashursts admitted its first female partner, Linda Bailey (now Walker). In 1996 there are five female partners. One reason why there are more applicants than traineeships available is that the number of graduates has increased massively over the period. Indeed … one did not need a degree 37 years ago but even so the number of applicants for law greatly exceeds the positions available.

One of the reasons why traineeship is so popular is that trainees are now given a living wage whereas we received nothing. In the recent years of the recession this has meant that the law has been very attractive for young people because they have received a reasonable wage at the same time as obtaining a qualification which has been much better than trying to get a job elsewhere without a professional qualification.

Within the firm the trainees are encouraged to join its thriving sporting and social life, the latter varying from rock and karaoke evenings to tennis, barbecues and cocktail parties. Where once there were one or two football and cricket matches per season, there are now full fixture lists with other City firms, merchant banks, accountants and clients for the firm's football, rugby, cricket and hockey teams. Organised sport keeps the partner of the present day fit, whereas it was for John Morris a system of Swedish exercises and before that for Ashurst himself, a gentle game of bowls on his Muswell Hill lawn. Other sports, individual and team are also played and for the less actively inclined there are competitive quiz challenges. Some of these events are combined with money-raising activities for charities that the firm supports, ranging from Guide Dogs for the Blind to Cancer Research.

Despite the similarities which superficially make City law firms much of a muchness, they do differ and not only in their size and the services they offer to clients. There are significant cultural differences between

Linda Watson (now Humphreys-Evans), the firm's first female articled clerk shown here in 1967 with fellow articled clerk, John May.

Annie Keener, who was presented with an award at the 1995 VE Day 50th anniversary celebrations in recognition of her service during the War, has been serving tea in the firm for 22 years.

Ashurst Morris Crisp

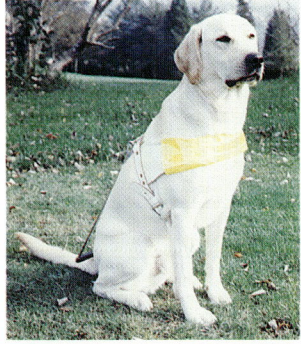

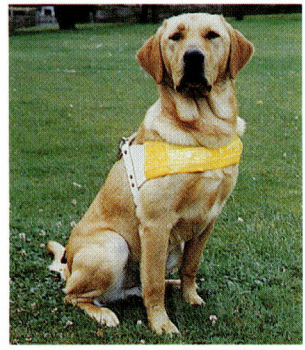

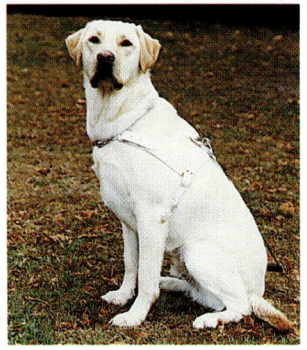

The firm's charitable activities include support for local communities adjacent to the City and the sponsorship of three guide dogs for the blind, aptly named *Ashurst*, *Morris* and *Crisp*.

them, but these are much more difficult to pinpoint and to describe accurately. Ashursts' own identification of the way in which it differs from other firms, derived from what clients say, rests on four key features characterising the way the firm works; commercialism, radical lateral thinking, good transaction management and client involvement. Examples of all of them, redefined in terms less specific to the 1990s, can be found in earlier times of the firm's history.

A firm's history provides more clues to its culture, for we look to the past for a sense of identity and continuity and an understanding of the past gives meaning to the present. The partners of the past, particularly those who became so pre-eminent in the profession, have left their stamp on the firm.

The radicalism of the firm's founder, William Ashurst, and that of his son dominated the practice directly for the first 40 years of its existence and indirectly, through John Morris for another half-century. It is from this tradition that the sense that Ashursts inclines to be a radical rather than an establishment firm derives. From Sir Frank Crisp's approach to the law in the nineteenth century, re-echoed in that of Martin Lampard in the twentieth century, comes a robust dedication to finding a way for the client to do what he or she wants to do within the law and with integrity and honesty. The formality and pomposity which characterise the public image of the profession are absent from the Ashursts' tradition. Partners have not been reluctant to break the shibboleths of the profession, even concerning dress, as a recent exchange between Judge and Counsel evidences. Following the appearance of an Ashursts' partner in the witness box in a suit not of the traditional navy or grey hue:

QC: Do you remember — in the rather nice suit?
Judge: With the tie.
QC: And the rather snazzy tie…
Judge: A truly modern solicitor.

Another clue to the culture of the firm comes from the recollections of a recently retired partner:

I look back on my 37 years in the law with great pleasure. It has been fun, intellectually stimulating and I have made some good friends (both partners and clients) and a reasonable amount of money. What more can one ask from a career?

Fun and friendship, like informality and unstuffiness are not the qualities that spring most to mind as characterising the practice of law in the

City. But there is a strong sense of fun that comes through in the firm's house newsletter and which contributed to the five-star satisfaction rating given to the firm as a place to work by Ashursts' staff. This accolade was accorded by *Legal Business* in 1992.

A history of the firm that is now Ashurst Morris Crisp yields more than a perspective on a particular professional culture. 'We look to the past '... for evidence of the human spirit made manifest in a variety of ways ... for the sources of achievement and failure ... for the joys or sufferings of groups, nations, or social classes; and for the unconscious working-out of the great themes of survival or decay'.[6]

Through the 175-year history of Ashurst Morris Crisp we have seen glimpses – and sometimes more – of 'the great themes': from the early-nineteenth-century radical causes supported by the founder and his son to the development of the City and its businesses in the early days of incorporation. Most significantly, however, the history of the firm has shown its role at the heart of the growth of corporate business from the small – as they now seem to us – incorporations in the mid-nineteenth century to the large global corporations of the 1990s.

Partners' list: 1822–1997

Partner's Name	Became a partner	Ceased to be a partner	Period of partnership
ASHURST William Henry	1822	1855	33
GREEN William Henry	1823	1828	5
GAINSFORD Edward Barnevelt Elliott	1835	1840	5
ASHURST William Henry (Jr)	1843	1863	20
MORRIS John	1854	1905	51
WALLER William	1854	1854	
KNIGHT Finlay	1863	1865	2
HARVEY Thomas Morton	1865	1874	9
DAVIS George	1869	1874	5
CRISP Sir Frank	1871	1919	48
MORRIS William	1883	1933	50
MORRIS Edward Ashurst	1888	1890	3
STEVENSON John	1898	1911	13
CRISP Sir John Wilson	1906	1950	44
CRISP Charles Oak	1906	1946	40
OUTEN Thomas	1918	1941	23
WELLS Arthur Manfred Wintle	1920	1920	
ADAMS Appelbe Chisholm	1926	1927	1
OUTEN Roland Thomas	1931	1957	26
HORA Edward Etzel James Whinfield	1941	1961	20
RICHARDS Michael	1941	1954	13
BISS Godfrey Charles D'Arcy	1947	1974	27
GAME Philip	1950	1952	2
COULSON Alexander George	1950	1967	17
LERSE Randolph Henry Albert	1950	1974	24
MACKENZIE Morton Morell	1950	1969	19
LAMPARD Martin Robert	1957	1986	29
BEEVOR Miles	1957	1962	5
HEILBUT Max Herbert	1958	1974	16
GAMPELL Michael Simon	1959	1973	14
BELL Martin George Henry	1963	1992	29
CRISP Sir (John) Peter	1963	1975	12
LEGGE Michael Harry	1963	1967	4
JAMES Richard Baker	1964	1995	31
GANE Charles Aldis	1965	1985	20
FINBURGH Mark	1967	1975	8
THUM Maximilien John Alexandre	1967	1993	26
BEEVOR Antony Romer	1968	1972	4
HUGHES Richard Lionel Creswell	1969	1970	1

Ashurst Morris Crisp

Partner's Name	Became a partner	Ceased to be a partner	Period of partnership
SOUNDY Andrew John	1969		
BRISTOW David William	1971	1976	5
CROSTHWAITE Christopher David	1972		
SCOTT Ian Russell	1972		
MACPHERSON Michael Alastair Fox	1974		
MAY John Nicholas	1974		
RUTMAN Laurence David	1974		
WALKER Barry Matthew	1974	1994	20
YOLLAND John	1975	1994	19
McINTYRE Ian William Robert	1976	1979	3
ALBERT David Edward Peter	1978		
PICKERILL Geoffrey Martin	1978	1983	5
SMYTH James Spence Sealey	1978	1984	6
GREEN Geoffrey Stephen	1979		
AMOS Christopher John	1980	1995	15
PERKS David Rowland	1980		
CROSTHWAITE Charles Michael	1981	1994	13
SPARROW Edward Charles Awdeley	1981		
HARRISON Michael Storm	1983	1986	3
BAILEY Linda Ann	1985	1994	9
FINBOW Roger John	1985		
HARWOOD-SMART Philip Mervyn Harwood	1985	1990	5
ASHWORTH Christopher John	1986		
KERSHAW David Robert	1986		
KITCHIN Alan William Norman	1986		
MACFARLANE David John	1986		
SULTOON Jeffrey Alan	1986		
CUNLIFFE Michael David	1987		
JOHNS Michael Charles	1987		
MACHIN Stephen James	1987		
NISSE Ian Bertram	1987		
SHELDON Jeremy Nigel	1987		
EVANS John Ceredig	1988		
INNES William	1988	1995	7
NIMMO James Alexander	1988		
VIGRASS Christopher	1988		
WALSOM Roger Benham	1988		
GUBBINS Richard Simon	1989		
LEACH Charles John Edward	1989		
WATSON John George	1989		
WHEATCROFT Guy Stuart	1989		
CLARK Adrian Spencer	1990		
DEAR Adrian Arthur Hounslea	1990		

Partners' list

Partner's Name	Became a partner	Ceased to be a partner	Period of partnership
ELLISON Julian James	1990		
WIPPELL Mark Alexander	1990		
COOKSON Simon Timothy	1991		
GEFFEN Charles Slade Henry	1991		
MORRIS Elizabeth Anne	1991		
WEBB Ian John	1991		
ATKINS Clifford	1991		
MOSTYN-WILLIAMS Stephen Robert Pyers	1991		
HILL Jeremy Grahame	1992		
KNIGHT Adrian Geoffrey	1992		
ROY Susan Elisabeth	1992		
WARD Nigel Timothy	1992		
JOHNSON Ian	1992	1997	5
FORSCHBACH Thomas	1993		
STARR Ian Crichton	1993		
WEBB Graham Phillip	1993		
CRAWFORD Susan Lavender	1994		
ELSEY Mark Philip	1994		
ELVY Mark Charles	1994		
HURST Philip Alan Desmond	1994		
KENDALL Richard	1994		
KING Ronald Compton	1994		
PARR Alan Nigel	1994		
PICTON-TURBERVILL Geoffrey	1994		
ROBINS Michael George	1994		
SANDERS Janis	1994		
WHITE Stewart Dale	1994		
GHEE Anthony William	1994		
BRODSKY, Scott	1995		
EVANS David John	1995		
MADDEN Michael	1995		
RANDALL Paul Nicholas	1995		
SLATER Mark Andrew	1995		
GRIFFIN Paul	1995		
CLOUGH Mark Gerard	1996		
CURNOW Anthony Geoffrey Tremearne	1996		
HANTON Bruce John	1996		
JOHNSON Ian Leslie	1996		
LUBBOCK Mark Adrian	1996		
REID Timothy Michael Charles	1996		
SHARROCK Judith	1996		
WARD Anthony John	1996		
SPENDLOVE Justin	1996		

Appendix 1
Ashurst, Morris, Crisp & Co. Profits and Costs, 1883–1927

Year	Costs debited[1] £	Net profit[2] £	Undebited costs[3] £
1883	18,159	17,882	22,083
1884	35,947	21,589	26,479
1885	39,852	23,508	26,595
1886	33,103	20,270	45,998
1887	49,801	26,041	54,936
1888	54,434	27,746	68,160
1889[4]	49,986	14,900	68,474
1890[5]	149,508	71,052	42,538
1891	58,277	46,799	50,743
1892	47,282	29,404	64,133
1893	46,032	26,269	83,919
1894	45,851	24,813	110,432
1895	90,825	46,159	103,047
1896	81,732	56,595	126,361
1897	81,625	49,582	143,392
1898	85,324	47,040	151,665
1899	70,894	44,814	179,326
1900	98,418	39,671	185,317
1901	80,019	40,705	196,658
1902	83,943	38,811	204,083
1903	88,889	33,711	189,202
1904[6]	–	–	–
1905[7]	93,960	44,640	199,102
1905[8]	17,155	16,028	194,752
1906	49,390	29,921	167,262
1907	59,129	36,823	148,399
1908	79,931	39,619	143,633
1909	84,261	42,033	125,478
1910	100,037	57,561	123,795
1911	86,841	44,255	128,921

Appendix 1

Year	Costs debited £	Net profit £	Undebited costs £
1912	100,591	50,260	126,062
1913	87,962	42,209	128,854
1914	82,915	29,683	108,937
1915	73,227	20,612	106,548
1916	89,274	25,421	104,572
1917	63,850	24,976	93,130
1918	65,535	28,691	90,124
1919[9]	29,318	16,481	122,643
1920[10]	69,716	34,409	50,737
1921[11]	56,688	21,642	56,688
1922	89,442	32,199	36,625
1923	62,732	19,998	34,652
1924	66,718	21,500	43,869
1925	77,031	20,305	40,171
1926	70,067	23,211	39,894
1927	72,710	21,101	45,412

1   i.e. bills charged, the equivalent of turnover.

2   After the deduction of rent, rates, taxes, salaries, heat and lighting, postage and other office expenses and, the largest item in most years, fees paid to counsel. The latter would have already been charged to clients as appropriate in their bills, that is in costs debited.

3   This was, in effect, work in progress which would be billed later.

4   Nine months only.

5   15 months.

6   For some unknown reason no balance sheet and profit and loss seems to have been drawn up in 1904, but two were drawn up in 1905.

7   March; John Morris died in March and the books of the old partnership were closed. These may well be 15 months' totals but it is not explicitly stated.

8   December, i.e. 9 months.

9   Sir Frank Crisp died in April this year; the effect was immediate on the accounts department which did not, apparently, get its bills out. A new partnership was formed and the decrease in the volume of business from 1920 is noticeable. Particularly marked is the drop in work in progress (undebited costs), and by comparison with earlier years its real value would be even smaller if wartime inflation were taken into account.

10 Undivided profits, £200,000 in 1883, grew steadily until 1912 when they reached £1m. They were counted as an asset of the firm, increasing its capital base, although partners only had a claim on them to the extent that they had had an interest in the partnership producing them. After 1912 they gradually declined.

11 Of the office expenses, rent was, after salaries, the largest single sum. In 1883 when the firm was still at 6 Old Jewry, the annual rent was £900. After the firm moved to its new offices in 1890 the annual rent was £1,750 until 1897, when it went up to £2,000. It stayed at that figure until 1919 but then rose sharply, in 1921 to c. £7,000. In that year, perhaps partly because of that high figure, the firm reduced the amount of office space it used and for the next six years it was paying c. £4,000 a year.

Appendix 2
Cost of living comparison table

1886

Ashurst, Morris, Crisp & Co.
Profit
£20,270

Frank Crisp's share
20%
£4,067

THE COST OF FOOD		INCOME TAX
Bread	5½d a loaf	8d in the £ over £150 p.a.
Tea	4s a lb	
Sugar	2d a lb	Basic wage 30s a week
Cheese	7¼d a lb	
Butter	1s 3d a lb	
Beer	1½d – 6d a pint	

1909

Ashurst, Morris, Crisp & Co.
Profit
£42,033

Frank Crisp's share
50%
£21,016

THE COST OF FOOD
Much the same as in 1886

INCOME TAX
Supertax imposed on incomes over £5,000 p.a.
Old age pension introduced at 5s a week

1925

Ashurst, Morris, Crisp & Co.
Profit
£20,305

William Morris's share
25%
£5,076

THE COST OF FOOD		INCOME TAX
Lyons Swiss roll	1s	4s in the £
Shredded Wheat	8d a packet	
Beer	10d – 1s 2d	
Bottle of whisky	12s 6d	

Appendix 2

TRANSPORT
A horse and carriage:
purchase price c. £260
annual running cost c. £165
Train
London to John O'Groats (third class)
£2 19s 4d
A barrel of three dozen oysters
delivered postage paid for 10s

MEN'S CLOTHING
Trousers 8s 11d – 12s 6d
Jacket   15s 6d – 29s 6d
(morning coat 2s 6d extra)

TRANSPORT
8 h.p. Humber car £150 – £200
45 h.p. Mercedes £900
Introduction of the road fund licence
at 6 guineas
Petrol in London cost 1s 2d a gallon
plus 3d tax

HOUSEHOLD
Cook   £80 a year
Butler   £100 a year

Electricity 2d a unit

Remington standard typewriter
£21 17s 0d

TRANSPORT
11.9 h.p. Morris Cowley two-seater
£175 inc. a year's insurance
annual running cost c. £16
14/28 h.p. Morris Oxford
from £260
Air travel: London – Paris single
15 guineas (British Imperial Airways)

HOUSEHOLD
Electricity 2d a unit

Remington standard typewriter
£26 10s 0d

Sources and bibliography

Unpublished sources

The archives of Ashurst Morris Crisp, consisting of ledgers, boxes of correspondence and papers and records of family partners and staff have been a rich resource.

The Stansfeld family papers threw more light on the Ashurst family. Also consulted were Ashurst family papers and the Asquith Papers at the Bodleian Library, Oxford, the Courtaulds papers in Essex County Record Office, various papers in the Oxfordshire and Buckinghamshire County Archives, the British Telecom Archive, The Stock Exchange papers and the IGI Index at the Guildhall Library.

Published sources

Abel, R L, *The Legal Profession in England and Wales*, Blackwell 1988

Adburgam, A, *A Radical Aristocrat*, Padstow 1990

Adler, D R, *British Investment in American Railways*, University Press of Virginia 1970

Ashurst, W H, *Facts and Reasons in Support of Mr Rowland Hill's Plan for a Universal Penny Postage*, 2nd edition, London 1838

Barker, T C & Robbins, M, *A History of London Transport*, 2 Vols, Allen & Unwin 1963 & 1974

Barty-King, H, *A Short History of the River Plate & General Investment Trust plc*, London 1988

Baylen, J O & Gossman, N J, eds, *Biographical Dictionary of Modern British Radicals*, Harvester Press 1984

Bell, E A, *These Meddlesome Attorneys*, London 1939

Bennett, J D, *Leicestershire Portraits*, Leicester 1988

Birks, M, *Gentlemen of the Law*, Stevens & Sons 1960

Bowers, B, *A History of Electric Light and Power*, Peter Peregrinus Ltd. 1982

Branson, N & Heinemann, M, *Britain in the 1930s*, Panther Books 1973

Broackes, N, *A Growing Concern*, Weidenfeld & Nicolson 1979

Brock, M & E, eds, *H H Asquith Letters to Venetia Stanley*, OUP 1982

Chapman, S, *The Rise of Merchant Banking*, Allen & Unwin 1984

Checkland, S, *The Mines of Tharsis*, Allen & Unwin 1967

Clapham, J, *The Bank of England*, 2 Vols, CUP 1944, reprinted 1970

Cockerell, H A L & Green, E, *The British Insurance Business 1547–1970*, Heinemann 1976

Sources and bibliography

Cole, G D H, *Life of Robert Owen*, London 1930
Cole, H, *50 Years of Public Work*, 2 Vols, London 1884
Coleman, D C, *Courtaulds: An Economic and Social History*, 3 Vols, OUP 1969 & 1980
Coleman, D C, *History and the Economic Past*, OUP 1987
Collett, C D, *History of the Taxes on Knowledge*, 2 Vols, London 1899
Colman, H C, *Jeremiah James Colman: A Memoir*, privately printed at the Chiswick Press 1905
Crathorne, N, *Tennant's Stalk*, Macmillan 1973
Daunton, M, *Royal Mail*, Athlone Press 1995
Davis, W, *Merger Mania*, Constable 1970
Dennett, L, *The Charterhouse Group 1925–1979*, Gentry Books 1979
Dennett, L, *Slaughter and May: A Century in the City*, Granta Editions 1989
Donaldson, F, *The Marconi Scandal*, London 1962
Evans, D M, *The Commercial Crisis 1847–48*, London 1849
Ferrier, R W, *The History of The British Petroleum Company*, Vol. 1, CUP 1982
Foreman-Peck, J, *Smith & Nephew in the Health Care Industry*, Edward Elgar 1995
Foss, E, *The Judges of England with Sketches of their Lives*, 9 Vols, Longman, John Murray 1848–64.
Fowler, M, *Below the Peacock Fan*, Penguin 1988
Gattrell, V A C, *The Hanging Tree*, OUP 1994
Gatty, R, *Portrait of a Merchant Prince: James Morrison 1789–1857*, Northallerton 1977
Glendinning, V, *Trollope*, Pimlico 1992
Gourvish, T R & Wilson, R G, *The British Brewing Industry*, CUP 1994
Gower, L C B, *Gower's Principles of Modern Company Law*, 4th edition, London 1849
Graham-Yooll, A, *The Forgotten Colony*, Hutchinson 1981
Green, E & Moss, M, *A Business of National Importance*, Methuen 1982
Hammond, J L & B, *James Stansfeld*, Longman 1932
Hannah, L, *Electricity Before Nationalisation*, Macmillan 1979
Harte, N & North, J, *The World of University College 1828–1978*, UCL 1978
Hill, Sir R & G B, *Life of Sir Rowland Hill and History of Penny Postage*, London 1880
Hinde, K S G, *History of the City of London Solicitors' Company*, London 1994
Holyoake, G J, *Sixty Years of an Agitator's Life*, 2 Vols, Unwin 1892
Jenkins, R, *Asquith*, Collins 1964
Jeremy, D, ed., *Dictionary of Business Biography*, 5 Vols, Butterworth 1984–6
Keane, J, *Tom Paine: A Political Life*, Bloomsbury 1995
Kirk, H, *Portrait of a Profession*, Oyez 1976
Kynaston, D, *The City of London*, 2 Vols, Chatto & Windus 1994 & 1995
Kynaston, D, *Cazenove & Co: A History*, Batsford 1991
Kynaston, D, *The Financial Times: A Centenary History*, Viking 1988

Lamoine, G, ed, *Charges to the Grand Jury 1689–1803*, Camden Fourth Series, Vol. 43, Royal Historical Society 1992

Lewis, J R, *The Victorian Bar*, Robert Hale 1982

Linton, W J, *Memories*, 1894, reprinted New York 1970

Lipscomb, G, *History and Antiquities of the County of Buckingham*, 1847

Maccoby, S, *English Radicalism 1832–52*, Allen & Unwin 1935

Maccoby, S, *English Radicalism 1853–86*, Allen & Unwin 1938

Mario, J W, *The Birth of Modern Italy*, London 1909

Marriott, O, *The Property Boom*, London 1967

Matthias, P, *Retailing Revolution*, Longman 1967

McCalman, I, *Radical Underworld*, CUP 1988

Merrill, W M & Ruchames, L, eds, *The Letters of William Lloyd Garrison*, 6 Vols, Camb., Mass. 1971

Mineka, F, *The Dissidence of Dissent*, University of Carolina Press 1944

Morgan, E V & Thomas, W A, *The Stock Exchange*, Elek 1969

Morris, R B, *The Morris Family*, privately printed 1908

Newbury, C, *The Diamond Ring*, OUP 1989

Nowell-Smith, S, *The House of Cassell 1848–1958*, London 1958

O'Hagan, H O, *Leaves from My Life*, 2 Vols, London 1929

Orme, T, *University College School Register 1831–1891*, London 1892

Pemberton, T E, *Ellen Terry and her Sisters*, London 1902

Platt, D C M, *Latin America and British Trade 1806–1914*, A & C Black 1972

Porter, A, *Victorian Shipping, Business and Imperial Policy*, The Boydell Press 1986

Porter, R, *London: A Social History*, Hamish Hamilton 1994

Read, D, *The Power of the News*, OUP 1992

Reader, W J, *A House in the City*, Batsford 1979

Reader, W J, *Imperial Chemical Industries: A History*, Vol. 1, OUP 1970

Reid, M, *The Secondary Banking Crisis 1973–5*, Macmillan 1982

Richards, E F, *Mazzini's Letters to an English Family*, 3 Vols, Bodley Head 1920

Richmond, L & Stockford, B, *Company Archives*, Gower 1985

Richmond, L & Turton, A, eds, *The Brewing Industry*, Manchester University Press 1990

Ritchie, J E, *British Senators*, London 1869

Scott, J, *Legibus*, King, Thorne & Stace 1980

Sheppard, F, *London 1808–1870: The Infernal Wen*, Secker & Warburg 1971

Simpson, A W B, *Biographical Dictionary of the Common Law*, Butterworth 1984

Slinn, J A, *Freshfields: A History*, privately printed 1984

Slinn, J A, *Linklaters & Paines: The First 150 Years*, Longman 1987

Slinn, J A, *Clifford Chance: Its Origins and Development*, Granta Editions 1993

Smith, D M, *Mazzini*, Yale University Press 1994

Sources and bibliography

Steen, M, *A Pride of Terrys*, Longman 1962
Sugarman, D, *A Brief History of the Law Society*, The Law Society 1995
Swan, E J, ed., *The Development of the Law of Financial Services*, Cavendish 1993
Taylor, H A, *Fairey Aircraft since 1915*, Naval Institute Press 1974, reprinted 1988
Terry, E, *The Story of My Life*, Longman 1908
Thompson, E P, *The Making of the English Working Class*, Penguin 1968
Thornbury, W, *Old and New London*, London 1881
Tugendhat, C, *The Multinationals*, Eyre & Spottiswood 1971
Venn, J, *Alumni Cantabrigienses*, Part 2, 6 Vols, CUP 1959
Venturi, E A, *William Henry Ashurst: A Brief Record of his Life*, privately printed n.d.
Wainwright, D, *Henderson*, Quiller Press 1985
Weinreb, B & Hibbert, C, eds, *The London Encyclopaedia*, Macmillan 1983
Wilsher, P, *The Pound in Your Pocket 1870–1970*, Cassell & Co. 1970
Wilson, C, *The History of Unilever*, Cassell & Co. 1954
Woodhead, J R, *The Rulers of London 1660–1689*, London 1965
Young, P, *Person to Person*, Granta Editions 1991

Newspapers and periodicals

British Almanac & Companion
Burdett's Stock Exchange Intelligencer
Business History
Financial Times
Law Journal
Law List
Solicitors' Journal
Stock Exchange Year Book
The Times
Who Was Who

Notes and references

Unreferenced information comes from the archives of Ashurst Morris Crisp.

CHAPTER 1

1. International Genealogical Index (IGI); parish register of St Giles, Cripplegate, 18 July 1785, Guildhall Library. For Sir William and the Ashurst family (sometimes also spelled as Ashhurst) see *Dictionary of National Biography (DNB)*, Vol.ii, p.182.
2. Information about the Brazil family from Buckinghamshire County Archives, Aylesbury; wills, parish registers, IGI, the Buckinghamshire *Posse Comitatus*, 1798 and G Lipscomb, *History and Antiquities of the County of Buckingham*, 1847. Information about Sir William Henry Ashurst from *DNB*, Foss, *Lives of the Judges*, Vol. VIII, pp234–6, A W B Simpson, *Biographical Dictionary of the Common Law*, Butterworth 1984, pp16–17.
3. Emilie Ashurst Venturi, *William Henry Ashurst: A Brief Record of his Life*, privately printed n.d.
4. Elizabeth Ashurst Biggs to her cousin Joe Stansfeld. Letter undated but pre-1901. Stansfeld family papers.
5. Ashurst on aristocracy from Venturi, op. cit.; ed. G Lamoine, *Charges to the Grand Jury 1689–1803*, Camden Fourth Series, Vol.43, Royal Historical Society 1992, pp447–50.
6. *DNB*, Vol.ii. See also J R Woodhead, *The Rulers of London 1660–1689*, p.19.
7. PRO CP5/172/16. Affidavit of 25 January 1822, swearing that duty (£120) had been paid on articles of clerkship between William Henry Ashurst and John Preston made on 28 November 1816. J A Slinn, *Freshfields: A History*, privately printed 1984, p.41.
8. Clients listed in the *Law Lists*. For information on the Corn Exchange and Sion College, see ed. B Weinreb & C Hibbert, *The London Encyclopaedia*, Macmillan 1983.
9. IGI; parish register of St Mary Magdalene, GLC Archives; Stansfeld family papers.
10. For the Freethinking Christians see F Mineka, *The Dissidence of Dissent*, University of Carolina Press 1944, pp82–3, and I McCalman, *Radical Underworld*, CUP 1988, pp73–4. For Ashurst's membership see Venturi, op. cit. and R Gatty, *Portrait of a Merchant Prince: James Morrison 1789–1857*, Northallerton 1977.
11. First two quotations from J Keane, *Tom Paine: A Political Life*, Bloomsbury 1995, p.x., second two from E P Thompson, *The Making of the English Working Class*, Penguin 1968, pp99–105.
12. *DNB*, Vol.lviii, p.440.
13. D Kynaston, *The City of London*, Vol.1, Chatto & Windus 1994, p.29.
14. *Law Lists*.
15. Figures from R L Abel, *The Legal Profession in England and Wales*, Blackwell 1988, pp412–13. Quotation from McCalman, op. cit., p.83.
16. Morrison to Sir John Bowring, quoted in Gatty, op. cit., p.23.
17. Quoted in F Sheppard, *London 1808–1870: The Infernal Wen*, Secker & Warburg 1971, p.51.
18. Gatty, op. cit., chapter 5.

Notes and references

19 Kynaston, op. cit., p.30, Sheppard, op. cit., pp56, 160; R Porter, *London: A Social History*, Hamish Hamilton 1994, p.185.
20 PRO CP5/161/23.
21 W J Reader, *A House in the City*, Batsford 1979, p.17.
22 Gatty, op. cit., p.68.
23 For Bank of England mortgages see J Clapham, *The Bank of England*, Vol.2, CUP 1944, reprinted 1970, pp81–4. For Morrison see Gatty, op. cit., chapter 10.
24 The description of Sambrook Court comes from a novel written by Ashurst's youngest daughter, Emilie, and published under the title *The Owl's Nest in the City*, under the name Edward Lovell; it is quoted in E F Richards, *Mazzini's Letters to an English Family*, Bodley Head 1920, Vol.3, p.88. For Green, *Law Lists*.
25 Weinreb and Hibbert, op. cit., p.269. V A C Gattrell, *The Hanging Tree*, OUP 1994, p.671.
26 Gatty, op. cit., pp133–44.
27 S Chapman, *The Rise of Merchant Banking*, Allen & Unwin 1984, p.41.
28 A Adburgam, *A Radical Aristocrat*, Padstow 1990, p.1. See also *DNB*, Vol.xxxviii, p.123.
29 Guildhall Library. HO/107/722 Book 20 Folio 11–13. For Freshfields see Slinn, op. cit., p.68.
30 Richards, op. cit., Vol.1, p.23.
31 PRO KB 107/9/1626.
32 *DNB*, Vol.xxvi, pp416, 425.

CHAPTER 2

1 For Hill and the penny post, see *DNB*, and M Daunton, *Royal Mail*, Athlone Press 1985. Quotation from H Cole, *50 Years of Public Work*, London 1884, 2 Vols, Vol.1, chapter 2.
2 Sir Rowland Hill and G Birkbeck Hill, *Life of Sir Rowland Hill and History of Penny Postage*, London 1880, p.295.
3 W H Ashurst, *Facts and Reasons in Support of Mr Rowland Hill's Plan for a Universal Penny Postage*, 2nd edition, London 1838.
4 Ed. W M Merrill and L Ruchames, *The Letters of William Lloyd Garrison*, Camb., Mass., 6 Vols, 1971, Vol.3, p.368, Letter to M W Chapman, July 10, 1840.
5 E L Rasor on W H Ashurst in ed. J O Baylen and N J Gossman, *Biographical Dictionary of Modern British Radicals*, Vol.2, Harvester Press 1984. Quotation from Merrill and Ruchames, op. cit., Vol.2, p.659.
6 E F Richards, *Mazzini's Letters to an English Family*, Bodley Head 1920, Vol.1, pp23 and 40.
7 *Ibid*.
8 Quotation from *Law Journal*, Vol.35 in H Kirk, *Portrait of a Profession*, Oyez 1976, p.51. House of Commons Select Committee on Education Report, 1846, in D Sugarman, *A Brief History of the Law Society*, The Law Society 1995, p.8.
9 Kirk, op. cit., p.55. See also J A Slinn, *Linklaters & Paines: The First 150 Years*, Longman 1987, pp21–2; R L Abel, *The Legal Profession in England and Wales*, Blackwell 1988, p.402.
10 Temple Orme, *University College School Register 1831–1891*, London 1892.
11 N Harte and J North, *The World of University College 1828–1978*, UCL 1978.
12 Shaen obituary, *Solicitors' Journal*, 12 March 1887, p.320; see also J Ewing Ritchie, *British Senators*, London 1869, p.68, Richards, op. cit., Vol.1, p.20, and Shaen in Baylen and Gossman, op. cit.
13 J L and Barbara Hammond, *James Stansfeld*, Longman 1932.

14. Merrill and Ruchames, op. cit., Vol.3, p.568; Emilie Ashurst Venturi, *William Henry Ashurst: A Brief Record of his Life*, privately printed n.d.
15. G D H Cole, *Life of Robert Owen*, London 1930, pp306–7; Hammonds, op. cit., p.17.
16. W Thornbury, *Old and New London*, London 1881, Vol.3, Part 1, p.573.
17. J D Bennett, *Leicestershire Portraits*, Leicester Library and Information Service 1988. I am grateful to Mrs J M Jenkins, Assistant Keeper of Leicester Archives for this information.
18. Denis Mack Smith, *Mazzini*, Yale University Press 1994, pp45–6.
19. Quoted in Hammonds, op. cit., p.19.
20. J W Mario, *The Birth of Modern Italy*, London 1909, p.107; W J Linton, *Memories*, 1894, reprinted New York 1970, pp99–100.
21. Merrill and Ruchames, op. cit., Vol.3, p.394. For Fox see *DNB*, Vol.xx, p.137. For South Place Chapel, Thornbury, op. cit., Vol.2, Part 1, p.206. For links with Taylors and Courtaulds, D C Coleman, *Courtaulds: An Economic and Social History*, Vol.1, OUP 1969, pp206–7.
22. Coleman, op. cit., pp218–21. This account of the Braintree rate case is based on Coleman, as well as various reports in *The Times* between 1837 and 1850, an article in *Justice of the Peace*, 12 January 1839 and the obituary of Samuel Courtauld, *The Times*, 24 March 1881.
23. Ed. B Weinreb and C Hibbert, *The London Encyclopaedia*, Macmillan 1983, p.560.
24. L C B Gower, *Gower's Principles of Modern Company Law*, 4th edition, 1979.
25. Guildhall Prospectuses, fiche 99.
26. Quotation from D M Evans, *The Commercial Crisis 1847–48*, London 1849, pp33–5; Guildhall Prospectuses, fiche 120.
27. A Adburgam, *A Radical Aristocrat*, Padstow 1990, pp32–4.
28. Weinreb and Hibbert, op. cit., p.584.
29. Hammonds, op. cit., p.29; Richards, op. cit., Vol.2, p.111.
30. R Burnet Morris, *The Morris Family*, privately printed 1908, p.36.
31. Ashurst's diary, Stansfeld family papers.
32. Merrill and Ruchames, op. cit., Vol.4, p.248.
33. Richards, op. cit., Vol.3, p.26.
34. Guildhall Prospectuses, fiche 34.
35. Richards, op. cit., Vol.3.
36. Obituaries in the *Solicitors' Journal* and *The Daily News*, July 1879.

CHAPTER 3

1. E V Morgan and W A Thomas, *The Stock Exchange*, Elek 1969, p.131.
2. *Law Lists* show Knight as a partner in 1863 and 1864. Guildhall Prospectuses.
3. C Jones, *Charles Morrison*, in ed. D Jeremy, *Dictionary of Business Biography (DBB)*, 5 Vols, Butterworth 1984–6, Vol.4, pp341–5.
4. D Kynaston, *Cazenove & Co: A History*, Batsford 1991, pp38–9. T R Gourvish, *Sir Edward William Watkin*, in *DBB*, Vol.5, pp682–5.
5. D R Adler, *British Investment in American Railways*, University Press of Virginia 1970, pp165–7.
6. T C Barker and M Robbins, *A History of London Transport*, Vol.1, Allen & Unwin 1963.
7. *British Almanac & Companion*, 1867, p.26.
8. *Ibid*. J Clapham, *The Bank of England*, Vol.2, CUP 1970, pp263–7.
9. Adler, op. cit., p.108; *British Almanac & Companion*, 1867, p.28.
10. Counsel for the prosecution's speech at the trial of Overend's directors, accused of publishing a false prospectus, quoted in D Kynaston, *The City of London*, Vol.1, Chatto & Windus 1994, pp238–9.
11. Census 1871, RG 11/96. 31–33.

12 S Nowell-Smith, *The House of Cassell 1848–1958*, London 1958, p.36; C D Collett, *History of the Taxes on Knowledge*, London 1899, Vol.2, pp176–7, 212.
13 Nowell-Smith, op. cit., pp117–21.
14 *The Times*, various dates August–November 1869; H A L Cockerell and G Green, *The British Insurance Business 1547–1970*, London 1976, p.37.
15 Kynaston, 1994, op. cit., pp258–9.
16 Obituary of Sir Frank Crisp by Dr B D Jackson in *The Linnaean Society Proceedings, 1918–19*.
17 School bills from Crisp family papers; Linnaean Society Obit., op. cit.
18 Article on Crisp, additional to obituary, *The Times*, 1919.
19 Barker and Robbins, op. cit., Vol.1, pp183–4.
20 Guildhall Prospectuses; fiche 42.
21 Ed. B Weinreb and C Hibbert, *The London Encyclopaedia*, Macmillan 1983, p.15.
22 Guildhall Prospectuses.
23 Letter from John Morris to Frank Crisp, 3 April 1876; Crisp family papers.

CHAPTER 4

1 W H Ashurst, *Facts and Reasons in Support of Mr Rowland Hill's Plan for a Universal Penny Postage*, London 1880.
2 P Young, *Person to Person*, Granta Editions 1991; L Richmond and B Stockford, *Company Archives*, Gower 1986, p.36.
3 Young, op. cit., p.19.
4 D Kynaston, *The City of London*, Vol.2, Chatto & Windus 1994, pp26–7: Guildhall Library Prospectuses, fiche 465 and 466.
5 Kynaston, 1994, op. cit., Vol.2, p.17.
6 L Hannah, *Electricity Before Nationalisation*, Macmillan 1979, p.3
7 Hannah, op. cit., p.4.; B Bowers, *A History of Electric Light & Power*, Peter Peregrinus Ltd 1982, pp115–16; Guildhall Prospectuses; *Burdett's Stock Exchange Intelligencer*, 1890 and 1900.
8 Hannah, op. cit. and Bowers, op. cit.
9 Bowers, op. cit., pp144–50. Guildhall Prospectuses.
10 M Steen, *A Pride of Terrys*, Longman 1962, p.152. Subsequent unreferenced quotations from this source
11 Ellen Terry, *The Story of My Life*, Longman 1908, p 112; Ed. B Weinreb and C Hibbert, *The London Encyclopaedia*, Macmillan 1983, pp27, 527.
12 T E Pemberton, *Ellen Terry and her Sisters*, London 1902, p.205.
13 *Burdett's Stock Exchange Intelligencer*, 1900 lists the Lyceum as a client.
14 C Jones, *British Financial Institutions in Argentina 1860–1914*, unpublished Cambridge PhD, 1973.
15 D C M Platt, *Latin America and British Trade 1806–1914*, A & C Black 1972, pp65, 68; A Graham-Yooll, *The Forgotten Colony*, Hutchinson 1981, p.227.
16 Guildhall Prospectuses, fiche 343; C Jones, *Charles Morrison* in *DBB*, Vol.4, pp341–5; Graham-Yooll, op. cit., p.228.
17 Jones, op. cit., pp292, 302; H Barty-King, *A Short History of The River Plate & General Investment Trust plc*, London 1988.
18 Richmond and Stockford, op. cit., pp66–8; Guildhall Prospectuses, fiche 414.
19 All E.R [1881–5] Ch D 1135–38; *DNB*, Vol.xxxiv, p.380; M Fowler, *Below the Peacock Fan*, Penguin 1988, pp169–235.
20 J R Lewis, *The Victorian Bar*, Robert Hale 1982, pp121–3. For Edward Ashurst Morris's involvement see R Burnet Morris, *The Morris Family*, privately printed 1908, pp26–7.

21 Letter in Crisp family papers.
22 Morris, op. cit.; J Venn, *Alumni Cantabrigienses*, Part II, Vol.4, CUP 1959.
23 Letter J Morris to F Crisp, 3 April 1876; Crisp family papers.
24 L Dennett, *Slaughter and May: A Century in the City*, Granta Editions 1989, p.63.
25 J A Slinn, *Linklaters & Paines: The First 150 Years*, Longman 1987, p.41.
26 *The City Press*, 6 July 1889; *The Citizen*, 6 July 1889.
27 *Financial Times*, 20 December 1890.

CHAPTER 5

1 Census of 1891, D Kynaston, *The City of London*, Vol.2, Chatto & Windus 1994, p.21; *The Financial News*, 2 November 1887.
2 H O O'Hagan, *Leaves from My Life*, London 1929, Vol.2, p.460. *Vanity Fair*, 31 May 1890.
3 E V Morgan and W A Thomas, *The Stock Exchange*, Elek 1969, p.131.
4 Guildhall Prospectuses, fiche 503.
5 E A Bell, *These Meddlesome Attorneys*, London 1939, p.189.
6 Guildhall Prospectuses, fiche 492; W J Reader, *Imperial Chemical Industries: A History*, Vol.1, OUP 1970, chapters 5, 7 and 9.
7 Reader, op. cit., p.104; Guildhall Prospectuses, fiche 561.
8 H O O'Hagan, op. cit.; D Kynaston and R Davenport-Hines, *H O O'Hagan*, in *DBB*, Vol.4, pp479–83.
9 Kynaston, 1994, op. cit., Vol.2, pp179–82, 186.
10 Kynaston and Davenport-Hines, op. cit.
11 O'Hagan, op. cit., Vol.2, p.461; *The Times*, 1919; *Vanity Fair*, op. cit.; *Proceedings of the Linnaean Society of London*, 1918–19, obituary of Crisp; Bell, op. cit., p.189.
12 Guildhall Prospectuses, fiche 11; O'Hagan, op. cit., Vol.1, chapter 16.
13 C Wilson, *The History of Unilever*, Cassell & Co. 1954, paperback edn, 3 Vols, 1970, Vol.2, pp67, 80–81; *Financial Times*, 1 May 1919; D Oddy, *Thomas Lipton* in *DBB*, Vol.3, pp799–802.
14 P Mathias, *Retailing Revolution*, Longman 1967, chapter 1; L Dennett, *Slaughter and May: A Century in the City*, Granta Editions 1989, chapter 3.
15 O'Hagan, op. cit., Vol.1, pp397–400. For Kearley see also J G Stark in *DBB*, Vol.3, pp561–3.
16 T R Gourvish and R G Wilson, *The British Brewing Industry*, CUP 1994, p.250; Guildhall Prospectuses, fiche 471; ed. L Richmond and A Turton, *The Brewing Industry*, Manchester University Press 1990, p.267.
17 Guildhall Prospectuses, fiche 576; O'Hagan, op. cit., Vol.1, chapter 15; *Burdett's Stock Exchange Intelligencer*, 1890 and the *Stock Exchange Year Book*, 1900. For the latter I am indebted to Meta Zimmock's analysis of AMC clients, compiled for the history of Slaughter and May.
18 Cecil Braithwaite's memoirs, quoted in W J Reader, *A House in the City*, Batsford 1979, pp98–9.
19 S Checkland, *The Mines of Tharsis*, Allen & Unwin 1967, p.100; Guildhall Prospectuses; N Crathorne, *Tennant's Stalk*, Macmillan 1973, pp138–41.
20 A Porter, *Victorian Shipping, Business and Imperial Policy*, The Boydell Press 1986, chapter 4.
21 Kynaston, 1994, op. cit., Vol.2, pp105, 110–11.
22 For West Australian Companies, Guildhall Prospectuses and the *Stock Exchange Year Book*, 1900. For Queensland see A L Lougheed *British Company Formation and the Queensland Mining Industry 1886–1890*, in *Business History*, Vol.XXV, 1983, pp76–82.

/ **Notes and references**

221

23 H C Colman, *Jeremiah James Colman: A Memoir*, privately printed at the Chiswick Press 1905; V Glendinning, *Trollope*, Pimlico 1992, p.483.
24 O'Hagan, op. cit., Vol.1, p.534.
25 Bell, op. cit., pp188–9.
26 *Financial Times*, 1 May 1919.
27 J A Slinn, *Linklaters & Paines: The First 150 Years*, Longman 1987, p.52; J A Slinn, *Freshfields: A History*, privately printed 1984, p.132.
28 Letter to Frank Crisp, 3 December 1888, Crisp family papers.
29 O'Hagan, op. cit., Vol.2, pp460–1.

CHAPTER 6

1 T C Barker & M Robbins, *A History of London Transport*, Vol.2, Allen & Unwin 1963, chapter 3, p.38.
2 *Ibid*, p.47.
3 *Ibid*, pp25–6.
4 Ed. B Weinreb and C Hibbert, *The London Encyclopaedia*, Macmillan 1983, p.659.
5 *Stock Exchange Year Book*, 1900.
6 *Solicitors' Journal*, 25 March 1905, Vol.49, p.357.
7 D Kynaston, *The City of London*, Vol.2, Chatto & Windus 1994, pp33, 243–4.
8 *Henley Standard*, 4 June 1978.
9 *Ibid*.
10 *Timpson's English Eccentrics*, p.175. This account is based on that and on an article in *The Sunday Express*, 22 January 1995 and on information in the *Henley Standard*, June 1978.
11 C Newbury, *The Diamond Ring*, OUP 1989, p.179.
12 Quote from Edward Manson in *Law Quarterly Review*, 1900. See also J A Slinn, *Solicitors and Business Regulation*, in ed. E J Swan, *The Development of the Law of Financial Services*, Cavendish 1993.
13 *Stock Exchange Year Book*, 1900.
14 R W Ferrier, *The History of the British Petroleum Company*, CUP 1982, Vol.1, pp199, 290.
15 M Birks, *Gentlemen of the Law*, Stevens & Sons, London 1960, pp248–9.
16 For the Marconi scandal, see F Donaldson, *The Marconi Scandal*, 1962.
17 R Jenkins, *Asquith*, Collins 1964, pp228, 541; ed. M and E Brock, *H H Asquith Letters to Venetia Stanley*, OUP 1982, p.28.
18 W J Reader, *Imperial Chemical Industries: A History*, Vol.1, OUP 1970, chapters 14 and 17.
19 For Courtaulds, see D C Coleman, *Courtaulds: An Economic and Social History*, Vol.2, OUP 1969, chapter 6.

CHAPTER 7

1 Description from his godson, Sir John Gielgud, in letter to the author, 1995.
2 R L Abel, *The Legal Profession in England and Wales*, Blackwell 1988, p.165.
3 Will of Sir Frank Crisp, *The Legal Journal*, 2 August 1919.
4 Crisp's granddaughter in the *Henley Standard*, June 1978.
5 D Kynaston, *The Financial Times: A Centenary History*, Viking 1988, p.82.
6 Quoted in W J Reader, *A House in the City*, Batsford 1979, p.140.
7 L Dennett, *Slaughter and May: A Century in the City*, Granta Editions 1989, pp152–3; J A Slinn, *Linklaters & Paines: The First 150 Years*, Longman 1987, pp122–3; J Scott, *Legibus*, King, Thorne & Stace 1980, p.58.
8 *Stock Exchange Year Book*, 1928 and 1938.

9 N Branson and M Heinemann, *Britain in the 1930s*, Panther Books 1973, p.261; *Stock Exchange Year Book*, 1928. By 1938 the firm had ceased to act for Morris Motors. For Morris see R J Overy, *William Richard Morris*, in *DBB*, Vol.4, pp334–41.
10 H A Taylor, *Fairey Aircraft since 1915*, Naval Institute Press 1974, reprinted 1988.
11 *Law Lists*. Information from Stephenson Harwood.
12 D Wainwright, *Henderson*, Quiller Press 1985, p.65
13 The following account is based on D Fanning, *Hatry* in *DBB*, Vol.3, pp110–14 and W J Reader, 1979, op. cit., pp146–56. According to the latter, Cecil Braithwaite told the Governor of the Bank of England in 1929 that Hatry's business had first come to Foster & Braithwaite via *inter alia* Sir Frank Crisp and the firm.
14 *The Hatry Case: Eight Current Misconceptions*, reprinted 1938.
15 For the Royal Mail Group see E Green and M Moss, *A Business of National Importance*, 1982.
16 D C Coleman, *Courtaulds: An Economic and Social History*, Vol.2, OUP 1969, chapter 10. See also Coleman, *Dreyfus*, in *DBB*, Vol.2.
17 AELR 1940, 412–19; AELR 1941; AELR 1945.
18 *Stock Exchange Year Book*, 1938.

CHAPTER 8

1 A Graham-Yooll, *The Forgotten Colony*, Hutchinson 1981, p.15.
2 D Fanning, *Hatry* in *DBB*, Vol.3.
3 C Tugendhat, *The Multinationals*, Eyre & Spottiswood 1971, p.28 and chapter 9.
4 Obituary, *The Times*, June 1994.
5 Obituary of Outen, *The Law Journal*, 22 February 1957. For the City of London Solicitors' Company see K S G Hinde, *History of the City of London Solicitors' Company*, 1994, Appendix 1.
6 L Dennett, *The Charterhouse Group*, 1979, p.83.
7 D Read, *The Power of the News*, OUP 1992, p.160.
8 N Broackes, *A Growing Concern*, Weidenfeld & Nicolson 1979, p.139.
9 O Marriott, *The Property Boom*, London 1967, pp.174–8.
10 Broackes, op. cit., p.65.
11 *Ibid*, p.160. For Crowther see also C Shaw in *DBB*, Vol.1, pp854–9.
12 For Smith & Nephew see J Foreman-Peck, *Smith & Nephew in the Health Care Industry*, Edward Elgar 1995, chapter 8.
13 Obituary of Francis Showering by D Holden-Brown, *The Independent*, 9 September 95.
14 W Davis, *Merger Mania*, Constable, London 1970.
15 *DNB* 1981–85, OUP 1990, pp374–5.
16 OECD Reports, *The UK economy, 1970, 71, 73, 75*.
17 M Reid, *The Secondary Banking Crisis 1973–5*, Macmillan 1982.

CHAPTER 9

1 24 December 1984. Quoted in D Kynaston, *The Financial Times: A Centenary History*, Viking 1988, p.494.
2 27 December 73, quoted in Kynaston, op. cit., p.400.
3 Chambers & Partners' Directory: *A Guide to the Legal Profession*, London 1996, pp134–5.
4 League table produced by KPMG 1996.
5 *Financial Times*, 17 May 1996.
6 D C Coleman, *History and the Economic Past*, OUP 1987, p.146.

Index

223

Page numbers in bold refer to illustrations and their captions

Abbotscliff, Kent 56
Abingdon Street office 67
Adams, A C 144-5, 146
agency arrangements 86
Agra & Mastermans Bank 55
aircraft industry 144, 174-5
Albert, D 190, **192**
Albert Life Assurance Co. 57, 59
Alexandra Palace Co. 66
Allen & Overy 178
Allied Breweries 181, 190
Allied Domecq 190, 200
Aluminium War 175
Amerada Hess 198
American railways 51, 52, 67
Amoco 167
Amos, J 190, **192**
Andrews, J 170
Angel Court 13
Anglo-Argentine Tramways Co. 120
Anglo-Persian Oil Co. 126-7, **128**, **129**, 142
Anti-Corn Law League 32
arbitration 140
Argentina, trade with 80-1
Argentine railways 158-9
Armstrong, Sir W G 110
articled clerks 4, 7, 27-8, 38, 60, 61, 65-6, 124-5, 137, 170, 200-1
Artizans', Labourer's & General Dwellings Co. 82, 121
Arts Club 76
Ashmor Football Club 145
Ashmor Musical Society 129-30
Ashmor Sports Club 145, 152-3, **153**
Ashmor Table Tennis Club 152, **153**
Ash(h)urst family 2-4, **5**
Ashurst
   Brazil 2-3, **5**
   Caroline **5**, 7, 26, **27**, 30, 42, 46
   Eliza **5**, 7, 26, 27, 30, 40
   Elizabeth Ann (née Brown) **5**, 7, **8**, 15, 40, 41
   Elizabeth (née Ogle) **5**, 36, 42, 45
   Emilie 3, **5**, **6**, 7, 13, 24, **26**, 42, 45, 46, 76
   Matilda **5**, 7, 26, 30, 45
   William, Sir 4, 40
   William Henry, Sir 2, **3**, 4, **5**, 122
William Henry
   early life 2-9, **5**, **6**
   family & marriage 10, 21, 26-31
   legal career 10-15, 17-22, 28, 32-3, 35-40
   penny post 24-5
   publications 17, 24-5, 26, 32-3
   radical causes 15-17, 25-7, 32-3
   visits USA 40-1
   death 42
   passim 48, 57, 70, **74**, 86, 90, 122, 165, 201, 202
Ashurst & Gainsford 19, 21
Ashurst & Green 12, 13, 14, 15
Ashurst & Morris 44-5, 50
Ashurst & Son 28, 33, 35, 36, 40
Ashurst, Morris & Co. 54
Ashurst Morris Crisp 188-203
Ashurst, Morris, Crisp & Co. 68, 71, 79, 85-6, 88, **92-3**, 96, 98, 106, 108, 111, 115, 132, 150, 155-6
Ashurst Morris Crisp dogs **202**
Ashurst, Morris & Knight 50
Ashurst, Son & Morris 50, 54
Asquith, H H 107, 130, **131**
Association for Promoting the Repeal of Taxes on Knowledge 57
Atkins, C 190
Atkinson, J 170
Atomic Energy Authority 175
Australian mining clients 108-9

Babycham 180, **181**
Bacon, Sir J 83
Bank Charter Act 55
Bank of England 4, 14, 71, 148, 159
Bank of London 55
Bank Rate 55, 185
Bank Station **119**, 119
banking department 190
Baptists 8
Barings 18, 24
Barlow, Lyde & Gilbert 190
Barrett's Brewing & Bottling Co. 105
Barry, Sir C 36
Bartholomay Brewing Co. 105, 142
Bates, J 24
Baxter, Rose, Norton & Co. 64, 66
Beatles, the 184-5
Beevor, A 181, **182**, 184
Beevor, M 167, 181
Bell, Alexander Graham 70-1
Bell, M 168, 170, 172, 173, 175, 177-8, 179, **182**, 184, **188**, **189**, 191, **192**, 196
Belle Sauvage 57, **58**
Belt v Lawes 83
Bentham, J 21, 28
Bentley Motor Company 155
Biggs, J & family **5**, 30, 45
bills of exchange 11-12, 18
Biss, G C D'Arcy 154, 156, 162, 163, 165, **166**, **167**, 169, 170 172-3, 174, **182**, 186, 191

Bleak House 44
Boodle, Hatfield & Co. 118
Borax Consolidated 155
Bottomley, H 100
bowls 41, 201
BP Nutrition 199
Bradbury & Greatorex 18
Braintree Rate case 32-3
Braithwaite, C 106
Bramwell, Baron 63
brewing industry 37, 104-5
Bridge Walker 173-4
Bridgnorth 19
Bristol Aeroplane Co. 174
Bristowe, D **182**
British Aircraft Corporation 174
British Aluminium Co. **137**, 175
British & Foreign Tramways Co. 64-5
British & Foreign Water & Gas Works Co. 66
British Automatic Gramophone Co. 149
British Celanese Ltd 154, **155**, 176
British Museum 73
British Shipbuilders 184
Broackes, Sir N 173-4
Broadwalk House 191, **194**
Brock, F 170
Broderip Prize 154
Brooke, H D 91
Brown Shipley & Co. 18
Brunner Mond 142, 200
Brussels office 195
BTR 195-6
Bubble Act 13-14
Buenos Aires 80-1
Burdett-Coutts, Lady 91
Burmah Oil Co. 127
Burnard's Dairy Equipment Co. 149
Burton Ale Brewers 18
Bush House, Aldwych 172

Cable & Wireless Co. 151
cables 151
Calcutta Tramways Co. 79
Caldicott & Co. 18
Cammell Laird 184
Canary Wharf **199**
capital punishment 15, 26
Capper & Co. 18
Carlyle, Jane 31
Cassel, Sir E 118
Cassell & Co. 56-7, **58**, 109
Cedar Holdings 185
Cementation Co. 174
Central Hill House School 62, **63**
Central London Railway Co. 118-19, **119**
Central Railway Co. of Venezuela 50

Chancery, Court of 12
Chantrey, Sir Francis **11**
Chapel Royal, Whitehall 90
Chapman & Hall 109
charitable activities **202**
Charterhouse Group 167
Charterhouse School 84, 86
Cheapside **16**, **20**, **50**
Chester & Crewe Railway Co. 19
Childs, C 62
Childs, J 32, 62
Church rates 19, 32-3, 133
cinemas 153
Cinven 195-6
City & South London Railway Co. 118
City & West End Properties 121, 173
City business 12-13, 59, 72, 194
City clerks **101**
City of London Solicitors' Co. 164-5
City Panel on Take-overs and Mergers 181
City Safe Deposit Co. 91-4
City Under-Sheriff 15
Clay & Bock & Co. 102-3
Clerks 20, 43-4, **60**, 67, 84, **88**, 90-1, **110**, 111, 127, 129, 140-1, 170
Clifford-Turner 142, 190
Coleman St 4, 10
Colls & Son **92**
Colman, J & J 36, 109
Commercial Cable Co. 151
Commercial Credit Mutual Assurance Society 38
Commercial Union 173
common law department 66
Common Pleas, Court of 10
communications revolution 197-8
company department 190
company law 13-14, 35, 50, 59, 126
  (see also incorporation, joint stock companies act & limited liability)
company promotion 100-5
company work 36, 51, 66, 82, 96-7, 109
computers 197
Consolidated Bank 55, 56
Contagious Diseases Act 46
conveyancing 170
Cookson, S **192**
copying 7, 8, 27
Cordingley & Co. 18
corporate finance work 179-80, 190
Corrupt Committee **190**
County of London Tramways Syndicate 120
Court of Aldermen 15, 17
Court of Common Council 15, 165
Courtauld, S 32, 33, 132
Courtaulds 132, **133**, 136, 154-5, 160, 176
Coulson A G 160-1, 165, 184
Cowham, F W 140-1

Crawford, Earl of 74
Crisp family 124, 138, 152
Crisp, Charles 124, 136, 137, 143-4, 146, 148, 152, 156, 160
Crisp, Sir Frank
  early life 61-3, **63**, 67-8,
  legal career 68, 74, 83-4, 89-90, **91**, 94, 96, 98, **99**, 100-11, **107**, 130-2
  family 63, 124-5
  Friar Park 111, **112-13**, **114**, **125**
  politics **114**, 130
  death 133-4, 136, 138
  passim 152, 159, 177, 198, 202
Crisp, Sir John 124, **124**, 136, 137, 146-7, 152, 153, 159, 160, 161
Crisp, Sir Peter 159-60, **182**
Crooked Counsel **190**
Crosthwaite, Charles **192**
Crosthwaite, Christopher 189, 190, 195
Crown & Anchor Tavern 31
Crowther, Lord 174
Cullinan Diamond **126**
Cunard Steamship Co. 174
Cunliffe, M **192**
Currie, D 108

Danckwerts, Q.C. 110
Dartmouth, Lord 33, **34**
Davies (of Slough) 153
Davis & Emmanuel **92**
Davis, G 61, 67, 85, 89
Day Dawn Co. 109
Day, Sir Graham 184
Dear, A **192**
Delhi office 195
de Ferranti, S 74
departments 190
de Zoete, W 71
Dickens, C 30, 44, 109
Dillon, J 10, 24, 35, 42, 44
Direct London & Manchester Railway Co. 35
Disraeli, B 7, 121
District Line 52, **53**
District Messenger Co. 151
Drummond, B **192**
Dulake, K 162-3
Dungeness B power station 175
Dunlop Co. 100
Dunlop Slazenger 196-7
Du Pont Co. 99
Durban-Roodeport Gold Mining Co. 107

East Cornwall 20
East India Tramways Co. 79
Ebury, Lord 102, 103-4
Echo, The 57
Edinburgh Tramways Co. 64
Edison, T 73

Edison & Swan United Electric Light Co. 73
Egypt 56
Elder Dempster Co. 148
Eldon St 194
electric light patent 42, **74-5**
electric lighting **42**, 72-3, 74, **75**
Electric Lighting Acts 73, 74
electricity undertakings 72-4, 96, 120-1
El Nacional 81
Emitt, J 170
English & Russian Bank 50
English Joint Stock Bank 55
engrossing 7, 8, 27
Equitable Labour Exchange **29**
Erie Railway 52, 67
Eton 85, 124
European Economic Community (EEC) 185-6
Evans, J **192**
Excess Profits Tax 131, 154, 155
Exploration Co. 118, 120
Explosives Trades Ltd 134, 142

facsimile machine 198
Fairey Aviation Co. 143-4, 160, **161**, 164, 174-5
Faraday, M 72
Faringdon, Lord 146
Farrar, Porter & Co. 144
Fauntleroy, H 15
film industry 153
Financial Union Bank 36
Finburgh, M **182**, 184
Finsbury Pavement 191
Fleming, R 52, 118
folio 169
Fore St 2, 9
Fore Street Warehouse Co. Ltd 50, **156**
  (see also Morrison, Dillon & Co.)
Forest Hill 41
Foster & Braithwaite 106
Fox, W J 32
France, war with 7, 12
Free-thinking Christian Magazine 8
Free-thinking Christians 8, 9, 10
French Revolution 4, 9
Freshfields 20, 115, 163
Friar Park 111, **112-13**, 125-6, **125**, 129, 138

Gainsford, E B E 19, 20, 21
Game, P 161, 162-3, 167
Gampell, M 168, 173, **182**
Gane, C **182**
Garden House **91**, **92-3**
Garibaldi Fund **51**
Garrison, W L 25-6, 29, 32, 41
Gielgud, Sir J **139**
Gilbert, A **149**
Glasgow Tramway & Omnibus Co. 64

Index

Globe & Phoenix Assurance Co. 124
Goble, J **171**
Gold Fields of Mysore 106, 107
Gordon, H Panmure 103
Gould, J 52
Grand Jury of Middlesex 4
Grand Metropolitan 199
Grand Trunk Railway of Canada 51-2
Great Eastern Hotel 129
Great Eastern Railway 53, **54**
Green, G 190
Green, W H 13, 15
Greenland Co. 44
Grosvenor Gallery Co. 74
Guinness Trust 121
Gutta Percha Co. 42, 70

Halsbury, Lord 83
Hambros 184
Harris, D 43
Harris, W 162-3
Hart Son & Co. 164
Harvey, T M 53-4, 61, 67, 89
Hatchards Associated Interests 162
Hatry, C C 146-7, 161-3
Havana Cigar & Tobacco Co. 103
Hawkes, S **5**, 30, 31, 37, 40
Heath, A 170
Heathrow 144, 160, **161**
Heilbut, E 145, 152
Heilbut, M 167-8, **182**, 186
Henley Regatta 124, 125
Herbert, A P 147
Highgate Cemetery 40, 42, 94, 123
Hill family school 21-2
Hill, J **192**
Hill, R 21, 24
Holborn Restaurant 90
Holyoake, G J 44
Holyport Tennis Club 168
Honess, J 129, 152
Hooley, E 100
Hora, E 148, 155, 156, 158, 165, **182**, 186
hotel companies 50
Hotel Metropole 121, 122
Houlden Line 109
House of Commons 14, 17, 18, 20, 24, 30, 73
Hove House School 28
Huelva & San Juan Copper Co. 106
Hughes, R 184
Humphreys-Evans, L **201**

IBM 163-4, 168, **169**, 190, 195
ICI 99, 131, 142, 176, 200
illegitimacy 3
Imperial Mercantile Co. 85

incorporation 13-14, 35, 50, 66-7, 97
 (*see also* company law, joint stock companies act & limited liability)
industry in London 13
infrastructure projects 190, 194
Inner Temple 2, **3**, 85
Innes, B **192**
Institute of Directors 173
International Harvester Co. 142, 160
International Tea Co. 104
IRC 184
Irving, H 76, 79
Isaacs, G 130
Isaacs, R (Lord Reading) 130

James, R B 169, 170, 175-6, 177-8, **182**, **192**, 196, 197
Jameson Raid 108
Japanese Navy **109**
Japanese ship contract 109-10
Japhet, S & Co. 167
Johns, M 190, **192**
Johnson, H 170
Johnson, I **192**
Joint Stock Companies Act 35
 (*see also* company law, incorporation & limited liability)
Joint Stock Companies Arrangement Act 1870 59
Judicature Acts 83

Kaffir boom 108
Kearley & Tongue 104
Kearley, H 104
Keener, A **201**
Kemit Ltd 154
Kennard & Court 103
Kershaw, D **192**
King's Bench, Court of 2, **3**, 10
King's College School, London 65
Knight, F 50, 53
Kyffhauser Mining & Smelting Co. 50
Kylsant, Lord 147, 148

Lagonda Motor Co. 155
Lake Magadi Co. **200**
Lambert, G 170
Lampard, M 167, 168, **171**, 174, 176-7, 178, 180, **182**, 185, 186, 191, 196
Lamport & Holt Line 148
Lansbury, G 147
Larceny Act 148
Law Courts 83
Law Debenture Corporation 94
Law List 21, 68
Law Society 27, 200
Leach, C **192**
Lead Company 7

Leahy, J & Mrs 21
Legge, M 165, 169, 173, 184
Leicester 30
Lerse, R H A 161, 169, **182**, 186
Lewis, A J 76, 79
Lewis & Allenby 76, 79
Lewis, Sir G 78
Leyland & Co. 109
Liberal Party 130
Liberator, The 25, 26
lifeboat operation 185
limited liability 35, 96
 (*see also* company law, incorporation & joint stock companies act)
Lindsay, Sir C 74
Ling's exercises 56, 201
Linklaters & Paines 88, 106, 115, 132, 141, 142, 184, 188
Lipton, Sir T 103, 104
litigation 82, 123-4, 154, 155, 162-3
litigation, uncertainty of **127**
Liverpool St Station 53, **54**
Lloyd George, D 130, 138
Lloyd's 190
Lombard St 55
London & Colonial Bank 44
London Assurance merger 179
London Corn Exchange 7
London County Council 120, 121
London Docklands Development Corporation 174, 199
London Electricity Supply Corporation 74
London Review 20
London Street Tramways Co. 120
London Warehouse Co. 67
Long-Wellesley, W 15
Lorimers' Co. 15
Lowndes, Noble 169
Lowtonian Society 136
Lyceum Theatre 76, 78, 79
Lyons-Tetley 200
Lytton family litigation 82-3

Macaree, S R **150**, **151**
MacArthur-Forrest process 107
Macfarlane, D 190
Machin, S 190, **192**
Mackenzie, M M 161, 165, 184
Macpherson, A 190
management buy-outs 190, 191, 199-200
managing clerks 10, 38, 84, 111, 140-1, 168-9
Manchester Hydraulic Power Co. 67
Manchester, Sheffield & Lincs Railway Co. 51
Mangla Dam, Pakistan 169
Mansion House 73
Mappin & Webb 45
Marconi scandal 130
Marlow election 14

225

Martineau, H 30
Masius & Ferguson 180
Matthews, V (Lord) 173-4
Maxwell, R **177**
May, J 190, **192**, **201**
May, W 86
Mazzini, G **27**, 30-1, **31**, 42, **51**
McBride plc 199
McCartney, P 185
McCulloch & Co. 90
McGowan, Lord 99, 131
Mercantile Committee 24
Mesmer, F A 30
Metropolitan Line 52
Metropolitan Street Tramways Co. 64
Middle Class Dwellings Co. 121
Midland Bank 164
Minimum Lending Rate 185
mining companies 105-6
Moffat, G 24
Molesworth, Sir W **19**, 20, 36
Monopolies Commission 181
Montagu, S & Co. 164
Moray Lodge 76, 78, 79
Morgan Grenfell 142
Morning Chronicle 19, 30, 36
Morris & Harvey 54, 60
Morris family 56, **64**, **91**, **122**
Morris family trusts 162-3
Morris, E **192**
Morris, E A **64**, 83, **84**, 90-1, 94
Morris, F (née Terry) 74, **77**
Morris, Harvey & Davis 61
Morris, Harvey, Davis & Crisp 61
Morris, J
  background & personality 43-4, 48-9, **49**, **50**, **122**
  marriage & family 56-7, 84-5, 94, 121-2, 122-3
  legal career 45, 48-9, 50-3, 67-8, 70-2, 74, 79, 80-1, 86, 89-90
  death 123
  passim 104, 115, 198, 201, 202
Morris Motors Ltd 143
Morris, W
  background & early life 63, **64**, 65-6
  marriage & family 74, 75-6, 78-9, **91**, 96, 132, 145-6, 162
  legal career 65-6, **67**, 72-4, 82, 89-90, 118-19, 120, 121, 123, 136, **138**, **139**, 146, 147-8
  death 152
Morris, W (of Hove) 63, **64**, 66
Morris, W R 143
Morrison, C 42, 51, 80, 123
Morrison, Cryder & Co. 18
Morrison, Dillon & Co. 11, 45, 50
Morrison family 50, 79, 80-1, 89, 180

Morrison, J 9-10, **11**, 12, 14-15, 17-18, 22, 24, 42, 51, 79
Morrison, W 11, 12, 48
Mortgage Co. of the River Plate 81
Mostyn-Williams, S 190
Muswell Hill 21, 29-30, **31**, 32, 41, 202
Muswell Hill Brigade 26

Namaqua United Copper Co. 108
National Freight Consortium 199
National Telephone Co. 72
nationalisation 159
Neilson, G E 78
Nelson Line 109, 148
Nelson Square 62
New Bridge St 20, 21
New Lanark Mills **29**
Newgate prison 15
Newgate St 15
Nicolson, H 147
Nimmo, J **192**
Nisse, I 190, **192**
Nobel, A 98
Nobel-Dynamite Trust Co. 98-9, **99**, 106, 131, 142
Nobel's Explosives Co. 98, 131
Noel Park Estate 82
Nonconformism 4, 8, 28, 29, 32-3
Norman, M 147
North Wales & Chester & Birkenhead Railway Co. 67
nuclear industry 175

office expenses 20
office rents 20, 21, **92-3**, 149
office routine 61, 149-52
O'Hagan, H H 90, 100-1, 102-5, 110
oil companies 126-7
Old Bailey 15
Old Jewry 6, 33, **34**, 35, 42, 44, 48, 49, 60-1, 65, 71, 89-90, **168**, 169
Oppenheim, H 118
Outen, R 146, 154, **160**, 164-5, 167, 173, 174
Outen, T 110-11, 132, 136-7, **137**, 138, 140-1, 142-3, 154, 160, 167
Overend, Gurney & Co. 54-5, 57
Owen, R **29**, 29-30

Paine, T 8-9
Paisner & Co. 190
Palmer, A 170
Park St 56, 67
Park Village West 36
parliamentary practice 67, 79, 96
parliamentary reform 17, 20
Paris Land Co. 44
Paris office 190, 194-5, 196
Parr's Bank 55

partnership agreements 39-40, 49-50, 54, 61, 67-8, 79, 137, 144-5, 146
partnership arrangements 19, 74, 83-4, 124, 137, 140, 160
Pearce, G 38
Penny Black **25**
penny post 24-5
People's International League 31
Perks, D 190, **192**
Petter & Galpin 45, 57, **58**
Philipps, J & O 147
Pimlico, Peckham & Greenwich Street Tramways Co. 64
Portman Estate Mansions Co. 121
Post Office 45, 123
practising certificates 10
premiums 4, 7, 86
Preston, J 4, 10
Prince of Wales 118
Prohibition 142
property department 190
property work 121, 185
Prudential Ventures 200
public executions 15
Puleston, Sir J H 90, 122

Queen Elizabeth II Bridge 196, **197**
Queen Victoria 71

radicalism 8
radios 153
railway mania 36
Randall, P 195
Rank Xerox 197
Rea Brothers 176
Reform Club 36, **37**, 44
Regis Property Co. 165
Reid, P 91
Rhodesia Goldfields 123-4
Rialto 110
Ribblesdale, Lord 107
Richards, M 153-4, 155, 159, 161, 164, **164**, 167
River Plate & General Investment Trust Co. 81
River Plate Trust, Loan & Agency Co. 80, 90
Rolls-Royce Co. 184
Rothschilds **177**, 179-80, **180**
Routledge, G & Sons 109
Rowe, W **141**
Rowton Houses 121
Rowton, Lord 121
Roy, S **192**
Royal Academy 73
Royal Bank of Canada 142, 160
Royal Mail Group 147
Royal Microscopical Society 102

Index

Rumsey, R 170
Rush, R 9-10
Rutman, L 190, **192**, 197
Rutter, W 38

St Giles Church, Cripplegate 2
St Ives election 14-15
St Luke's Church, Old Street 2
St Mary Magdalene Church 7, **8**
St Rollox Chemical Works 106
Salomon, Sir W 176
Salt Union 99-100
Sambrook Court 10, 12, 15
Samuel, Sir H 130
Saratov Water Works Co. 67
Savoy Theatre 73
Schroder Ventures 200
Scott, I 189, **192**
Select Committee on Legal Education 27
Shaen, W 28-9, 30, 31, 36, 86
Shaw, G B 71
Sheepbridge Coal & Iron Co. 159
Shelbourne, Sir P 179, **180**, 181
Sheldon, J **192**
Sheppard, Lord 199
ship-building 109-10
shipping clients 109
Showering family 180-1
Showering, F 180
Showering, Sir K 181
Siebe Gorman Co. 175
Singapore office 195
Sion College 7
Skidmore, Owings & Merrill **191**
Slaughter and May 86, 106, **110**, 141, 142, 172, 184, 188
Slaughter, W C 84-6, **87**, 96
Smallman, G A T 147
Smith & Nephew 179, 190
Smith & Osman 18
Smith, Herbert 171
Solomon, A F 111
Soundy, A **182**, 184, 188, 190, **192**
South African mining 107-8
South American business 121, 142
South Kensington 52
South Molton 38
South of England Telephone Co. 71
South Sea Co. 14
Sparrow, E 190, **192**
Spears, Sir E L 173
staff sports 201
Stallwood, E W **148**, 149
stamp duty 7
Stanley, V 130
Stansfeld, J **5**, **27**, 29, 30, 31, 37, 40, 42, 46

Stansfeld, J J **5**, **27**, 46, 122
Stephenson, Harwood & Co. 144, 190
Stevenson, J 84, 115-16, 123-4
Stock Exchange, The 50, 59, 66, 73, 97, 100, 105, 106, 108-9, 119, 140, 149, 175
Stone, F, RA 27
Sudlow & Sons & Torr 35
Sullivan, A 76
Sultoon, J **192**
Sun Alliance merger 179
Sunningdale 145
Swain, Stevens, Maples, Pearce & Hunt 7
Swan Brewery 37, 40
Swan, J 72-3

takeovers 175-6, 178-80
takeover tactics 180
tax department 190
taxation work 156, 179
Taylor, J 170
Taylor, P 32, 42, 44
telegrams 59
Telephone Co., the 71-2, **72**
Telephone Co. of Austria 72
telephone, development of 70-1, **72**
telephone (office) 151, 198
Tennant, Sir C 105, 106-7, **107**, **131**
Terry family 76, 78-9
Terry, E 76, **77**
Terry, F *see* Morris, F
Terry, Fred 78-9
Terry, M 76, 78
Thackeray, W 76
Thames Iron Works 66
Thompson, S 8
Throgmorton Avenue 99, **91**, **93** 3, 100, 116, 141, 146, 149, 156, 169, 172, 191-2
Thum, M **182**, 184, 188, 190
Tilson, T 4, 7, 10
Todd, Messrs & Co. 9-12
Tokyo office 195, 196
Trade Facilities Act 148
Trafalgar House Ltd. 173-4, 190, 196, **197**
trainee solicitors 200-1
  (*see also articled clerks*)
tram companies 63-4, **65**, 67, 79, 96, 100, 119-20
Trinity Hall 84, 85
Trollope, A 76, 109
Trollope & Colls 174
Trust Houses 174
typewriters 169, 197

Unilever 181
Union Castle Mail Steamship Co. 108, 148
Unitarianism 8, 29, 30

United Telephone Co. 72
University College, London 28-9, 30
University College School 28, 62
Upper Rosoman St 43
US breweries 105, 142

Van den Bergh Co. 97, 103-4
Venturi, C **5**, 45, 46
Vernon, J 85
Vigrass, C **192**
Vizard, W 20

wages books **39**, **43**
Waitham, R 9
Walker, B 190, 196-7
Walker, L (née Bailey) **198**
Waller, W 17, 38-9, 43
Wantage, Lord 74
Warburg, Sir S 175, 179
Ward Lock 45, 62
Waterstock, Oxon 2, 3, 4
Watkin, Sir E W 51-2
Watson, J **192**
Watson, R **192**
Webb, G **192**
Wells, A M W 137
Wernher, Beit & Co. 120
Western Union Cable Co. 151
Westland Aircraft Co. 174
Westminster Journal **19**, 20
Wharncliffe Dwellings Co. 121
Wheatcroft, G **192**
White & Greenwells 18
Whittington Club 44
Wickens, Pease & Co. Ltd 97-8
Wilde, Collins & Crosse 187
Wilkinson & Drew 84
Willett, W 176
Williams-Wynn, Lady 91
Wippell, M **192**
Withers & Co. 190
Wood Hall Trust 164
Wood Street Warehouse 67
Wood, W P (Lord Hatherley) 55
World Anti-Slavery Convention 25-6
World War I 131-2, 137
World War II 155-6, **156**
Wragg, A 118
writs 197
Wynne-Williams, J 180

Yarmouth 18
Yolland, J **192**

Zander, M 195

227